HISTORY OF
THE UNITED STATES

VOLUME VI

General Douglas MacArthur

THE MARCH OF
DEMOCRACY

A

HISTORY OF THE UNITED STATES

By

James Truslow Adams

Volume VI

SECOND PART OF ANNUAL CHRONICLE

NEW YORK

CHARLES SCRIBNER'S SONS

VOLUME VI

SECOND PART OF ANNUAL CHRONICLE

CONTENTS

CONTENTS

ILLUSTRATIONS

ILLUSTRATIONS

ILLUSTRATIONS

ILLUSTRATIONS

END OF VOLUME

FRUITS OF AMERICAN INDUSTRIES

CHAPTER I

THE RECORD OF 1942

THE year 1942 started as one of the most sombre in the history of the United States, certainly the most sombre in the lives of living Americans. As a nation we have had little experience of war. Only in the American Revolution, ended about a hundred and sixty years ago, and the Civil War ended about eighty years ago, had the national existence been at stake or a large part of the people involved. The Mexican and Spanish Wars were "side shows" and menaced neither the nation as a whole nor any great number of its citizens. Even the first World War was fought far from our shores and the total number of lives lost in action or as a result of wounds was less than 50,000, whereas 40,000 were killed in automobile accidents in our own country in 1941. This war is different, and for the first time in the memory of most of us it is being brought home to every household in one way or another.

It began with the sickening disaster to our forces and our pride in the dastardly attack by the Japanese on Pearl Harbor on that December "Day of Infamy," as the President called it, which we mentioned at the end of the review of 1941. It soon became obvious that the blow had been heavy, though just how heavy the people were not to learn until a year later. However, Mr. Knox, Secretary of the Navy, flew to Hawaii at once, and on December 18, 1941, the President despatched a commission of enquiry headed by Associate Justice Owen J. Roberts of the Supreme Court to make a report, which was given to the public on January 25, 1942. According to Knox the battleship *Arizona* and the target ship *Utah* had been sunk, the battleship *Oklahoma* capsized, a mine layer and three destroyers sunk, and heavy damage inflicted on our air fleet. In February the President broadcast the casualties as 2340 killed and 946 wounded.

The Roberts Report may be summed up in the words of an editorial in the *New York Times* which said that it was evident that "Prior to the attack almost every military mistake possible seems to have been made by those immediately in charge of the defense of Hawaii, while the evils of unlucky chance added to those of incompetence." The Report amply confirmed this estimate of the situation, as have later papers issued by the Government. Those responsible on the spot had received ample warning from Washington far in advance but had not taken the necessary precautions. Japan had spun out the negotiations ostensibly looking toward a peaceful solution but meanwhile had for weeks been making every military preparation for the attack. Washington was not unaware of what was going on and both the Secretaries of State and

War had informed the local commanders. The likelihood of an attack on the harbor had been foreseen by the government at least as early as the preceding January. Yet even in December the fleet was concentrated in its narrow waters and everyone locally was wholly unprepared.

The trouble, however, had been more than local. It stemmed in part from the old-time antagonism and jealousy between the two departments of the forces, military and naval, both in Washington and in the field. Even in spite of urgent cables from Washington, the two leaders at Hawaii, Major General Walter C. Short and Rear Admiral Husband E. Kimmel had not conferred together or taken any concerted steps to protect Hawaii from November 27 on, though the attack did not come until ten days later, December 7. The full truth was not revealed until the anniversary of the disaster, in December 1942, and we may note the final revelations here, well out of their chronological order, so as to complete the tale of what was perhaps the greatest blow ever struck against us owing to our own inefficiency. Knox's first report, a year earlier, had been quite inadequate. Even the Roberts Report did not tell the whole story. We did not know the whole truth until the Navy Department revealed the facts just a year later. A certain reticence at first was obviously necessary for military reasons, but the Japanese government had known what had happened many months before the American people learned it.

In brief the statement was that (although we had no

two-ocean navy), the backbone of our whole fleet, eighty-six of our larger vessels, had been concentrated in Pearl Harbor. The revised figures informed us that eight battleships, seven cruisers, twenty-eight destroyers and five submarines were gathered there. Of these, five battleships, three destroyers, a mine layer and target ship, and the large floating dry dock were sunk or damaged so severely as to be useless for a long time. Three other battleships, three cruisers, and other vessels were heavily injured. Of the 202 naval airplanes at the island base, 150 had been disabled at once by the Japanese; and of the 273 army planes, "very few were able to take off" when the attack occurred. The catastrophe was colossal. Our men had fought and suffered with the utmost courage and, as always, there had been conspicuous examples of gallantry, but none could stand before the treachery of the enemy and the inefficiency of our own command. In February the government accepted the requests of General Short and Admiral Kimmel to be retired, but it did so "without condonation of any offense or prejudice to any future disciplinary action," and with the additional notice that the officers would be court-martialled but not "until such time as the public interest and safety would permit." No action known to the public has as yet been taken.

The year was to be so crowded with military movements and events all over the globe that it will be impossible for us to treat them with anything like the same detail we have given in speaking of Pearl Harbor. We may note that the mere chronology of the events of the war, in its first twelve months, occupies fifty-four pages, double column, and very fine print, in the *World Almanac*. Even to mention all these, apart from discussing them and speaking of other factors in our history for the year, is impossible within the limits of a single chapter. Let us hope that there will never again in our annals be a Pearl Harbor. That attack was for us the beginning of the war, and so calls, perhaps, for more space than we can give to the innumerable engagements which were to follow.

As we noted at the end of the last chapter, Winston Churchill, the British Prime Minister, with a party of eighty-five high members of government and experts in various lines, had come to Washington, for a fortnight, just before Christmas. For the time being that city was the center of planning for the global war, and far-reaching decisions of the utmost importance had to be taken by the Premier and the President. There were two temptations for us as Americans yet untouched by war on our own continent. One was to wait until we felt every preparation had been made,—the "perfectionist theory"—and the other was to concentrate on licking Japan for what she had done to us. In a war, however, involving fields of operation and dangers in every quarter of the earth, high strategy involved problems never faced before by any belligerents.

It is reported that when Woodrow Wilson was leaving his home in Princeton to take up his duties as President in the White House, he remarked to a friend that "it would be the irony of fate if during his term he should have to transfer his attention from national to international affairs." Roosevelt, on the other hand, has shown great ability in the handling of international matters and understanding of the present world crisis. What decisions may have been arrived at by the President and Mr. Churchill cannot be known, but in his speech to Congress on the state of the nation on January 6, the President said that during the coming year our operations would have to be both defensive and offensive, and that American land, air and sea forces would be found in the Pacific, in the British Isles, "which constitute an essential fortress in this world struggle," and in bases elsewhere, in protecting this hemisphere.

By the end of the month a large contingent of our new "A.E.F." had landed in North Ireland, the first of an ever-increasing stream to go overseas. De Valera, on behalf of Eire, protested that this was an infringement of Irish neutrality, though it is difficult to understand why, and the protest had no effect on later events.

Meanwhile, on January 1, a Declaration by the United Nations had been signed in Washington, accepting the Atlantic Charter on behalf of all of them. Each government pledged itself to use its full strength against those members of the Tri-partite Pact with which it might be at war, and to make no separate armistice or peace with the enemy. The nations signing were the United States, the United Kingdom of Great Britain and Northern Ireland, the Union of Soviet Republics, China, Australia, Belgium, Canada, Costa Rica, Cuba, Czecho-Slovakia, the Dominican Republic, El Salvador, Greece, Guatemala, Haiti, Honduras, India, Luxembourg, the Netherlands, New Zealand, Nicaragua, Norway, Panama, Poland, South Africa and Yugoslavia. They all stated that they were "convinced that complete victory over their enemies is essential to defend life, liberty, independence and religious freedom, and to preserve human rights and justice in their own lands as well as in other lands, and that they are now engaged in a common struggle against savage and brutal forces seeking to subjugate the world." This was the New Year's greeting of the liberty-loving nations to the Germans, Italians and Japanese.

We may note the names of the South American Republics included in the list. During January an inter-American conference had been held at Rio Janeiro which ended on the 28th after adopting resolutions for the severance of diplomatic, commercial and financial relations with the Axis Powers by all the participants. Brazil immediately did so, and in the course of the year all the other South American nations did likewise, with the exception of Argentina.

In the Pacific the Japanese continued to push the initial advantage they had gained. Our forces were distributed in Hawaii, the Philippines and in smaller islands, such as Guam and Wake, which latter were unprepared for attack because Congress had never been willing to appropriate the necessary money. Moreover, all our troops were widely scattered over the great stretches of the Pacific Ocean and with our navy, on which we had counted heavily, temporarily out of commission, our situation seemed desperate. The enemy had been bombing the more than three-century-old city of Manila and on December 26 General MacArthur had not only declared it to be an open town but withdrew both his troops and the anti-aircraft installations so as to save the defenseless inhabitants from wanton slaughter. The Japanese, however, had no regard for international law and the following day blasted the city from the air, destroying among other buildings the ancient cathedral and the long demilitarized historic fort of Santiago built in 1591. Secretary Hull denounced this complete disregard of all long-accepted military law as "fiendish inhumanity." On January 2 the city fell and the American forces which had been located outside of it retreated to the Bataan Peninsula, finally withdrawing to Corregidor, one of the strongest armed fortresses in the Pacific area, located on a steep rock about four miles long and situated two miles south of Bataan in Manila Bay. The epic of Bataan-Corregidor had begun.

While the Japanese command was living in the luxurious Manila Hotel and using the former residence of the United States High Commissioner as their headquarters, General MacArthur and his men—and we must not forget the women army nurses—were carrying on a terrific struggle against the conquerors, among the peaks, ravines, jungle swamps and "fox-holes" of the strange landscape of Bataan.

Although it will carry us somewhat out of our chronological order we may here finish the story of this aspect of the war. Glorious as the defense of the peninsula was, it was to be hopeless in the absence of reinforcements or additional supplies. Meanwhile, the Japanese, as will be noted later, had been extending their conquests elsewhere in the Pacific. Australia feared that its own hour had struck, and had asked for General MacArthur to help in its defense. Nothing was known to the public of this, but three weeks later the world was electrified to learn by a laconic cable that MacArthur had escaped from Bataan by motor boat and plane and was in Australia as "supreme commander in that region, including the Philippine Islands." The men in Bataan and Corregidor continued to fight but Bataan fell to the enemy in mid-April and Corregidor on May 6.

We shall return to the Pacific theater of war presently but will consider first the civilians on the home front.

On January 7 the President presented to Congress the budget for the current year which amounted to over $59,-000,000,000, which was $25,000,0000,000 more than was spent on the whole of the First World War. The deficit, even after an increase in taxation of $9,000,000,000, was estimated to be probably over $35,000,000,000, and the President asked to have the debt limit raised to $110,000,-000,000. Such figures are as far beyond our realization as are astronomical distances but they have to be recorded, and were to be greatly increased later. What the ordinary citizen could understand was that his taxes would be enormously enlarged, his future work mortgaged, and that prices and the cost of living would undoubtedly rise. Ominous from another angle of war's possible impacts, and more easily understood by the man in the street than the astronomical figures of finance, were the gradual disappearance of treasures from libraries and museums. The first week of January the Constitution of the United States, the Declaration of Independence, the Gutenberg Bible on vellum, and the British Magna Carta all disappeared from the Library of Congress, sent to an unknown hiding place for safe-keeping; and such disappearances became common.

On New Year's Day something else disappeared from American life with a startling suddenness—new cars. The government issued a decree that all retail sales of passenger cars or trucks would be absolutely prohibited until the 15th, when it would ration the 650,000 then on hand, or to be made during the month, as it saw fit. The motor industry, employing directly and indirectly nearly 7,000,-000 Americans, came to a halt as abruptly as though one of its own cars had run into a stone wall. As the year went on, the manufacturing part of the industry was to be completely transformed into the greatest mass production plant for instruments of war the world has ever seen. In 1942 General Motors alone produced $1,900,000,000 of

Harper in The Birmingham Age-Herald

THE HIGHWAY WILL BE PATROLLED: MR. HOARDER MEETS
GENERAL RATIONING

war matériel. But if the industry was set on its feet so also were most Americans. The bicycle business boomed, until bicycles also were prohibited and practically unobtainable. Later, on account of the rubber and gas shortages, came the rationing of gas and driving. The U-boats were beginning to sink our tankers (*e.g.,* the *Rochester* off the Virginia coast and many others in January), and we had built no pipe-lines from the oil fields of the West and Southwest to the great industrial areas of New England and the Middle States. Then we found that, with our sources of raw rubber cut off, we had no means of making any. Next we woke up to the fact that about one third of our sugar came from the Philippines, which were lost to us, and from Hawaii, where the crop would be cut in half, and that half of the whole came from Porto Rico and Cuba, involving the problem of shipping again. So sugar rationing came, and even chewing gum became scarce. Mr. and Mrs. Ordinary Citizen were beginning to feel the pinch and by February had started a vast hoarding spree, which helped to force rationing all along the line later. Another item which brought home to all a change in daily life was the adoption of nation-wide, year-round daylight saving, which was to be called "War Time" and not "Daylight Saving Time."

Meanwhile the country was becoming somewhat alarmed by the failure of the Civilian Defense program. This had been in the hands of Mrs. Roosevelt and Mayor LaGuardia but both were busy with other matters. Yet the possible safety of the entire population was at stake, and even by January investigation was still going on to devise some means of turning off the 31,000 street lights in New York City other than by hand in the case of each individual light, which required the service of 93,000 air

Hungerford in *The Pittsburgh Post-Gazette*

THE COUNTRY WAS BEING STIRRED TO NEW EFFORTS IN
THE CIVILIAN DEFENSE PROGRAM

wardens or substitutes. Finally the President appointed Dean James M. Landis of the Harvard Law School as

Executive Officer of the department, with LaGuardia still as nominal head and Mrs. Roosevelt as Assistant Director, although both the latter resigned later. The sinkings of ships along our coast were increasing but we may now turn again briefly to affairs in the Pacific so far as they directly concerned ourselves. In a sense, of course, every event of the world struggle has concerned us, whoever has been involved and wherever, so that the comparatively few events which are all that can be mentioned cannot possibly be made to offer a complete picture.

Following Pearl Harbor the Japanese appeared off Alaska in the Aleutian Islands and have not as yet been dislodged. It is unpleasant to have them on American soil, and in a later phase of the war, when Germany has been defeated and the death blow to Japan may be in view as the *finale* of the drama, these islands may take on a new importance. Meanwhile one of the results of their occupation has been the building of the great highway to Alaska from our own northern boundary across Canadian territory, a military road about 1600 miles long and completed toward the end of the year several months ahead of schedule in spite of the great difficulties encountered. Aside from the strategic importance in the present war of this long road through the wilderness, it may eventually prove of great value in the development of Alaska and of our friendly relations with our neighbor on the north, with whom we share almost the whole of the North American continent. Looking ahead to a post-war world it is a satisfaction to realize that this common struggle in which we have been engaged has immensely improved our relations with every other nation in the New World, with the possible exception as yet of the Argentine. Moreover, although we are—also "as yet"—the most powerful of them all, it is well to recall that we are only the third in size, Canada and Brazil both being larger than the United States, even though one is thought of as largely Arctic waste and the other as tropical jungle. Nevertheless, with new raw material discoveries or needs, altered trade routes, and so on, things change. When in 1763 England had to decide whether to take Canada from France, or the "rich sugar islands" of Guadelope and Martinique, the government was severely criticized for choosing Canada. Who today would swap that great Dominion for the two West India islands? In any case, and without travelling too far into the realm of the future, one of the encouraging things about the war has been the new relations and more friendly understandings it has fostered among the nations of the New World.

In the four months following the attack on Pearl Harbor the enemy scored a series of successes throughout the entire South Pacific area which would have been considered unbelievable when the war began. Roughly, the area formed a triangle each side of which was about two thousand miles long, and within it were sections of Asiatic mainland and innumerable islands, some of very large extent and some mere dots in the watery waste but of marked strategic importance. The distances were enormous, such as the three thousand miles from Yokohama to Singapore and the two thousand from Singapore to Port Darwin in Australia. Control of the air was to prove a deciding factor in the Japanese advance, which was amazing in its speed and completeness. We speak of speed but in each case the enemy advanced step by step and it is hard to set particular dates for their conquest of any particular spot, even naval battles sometimes lasting for a week or more.

In brief, during January the British Crown Colony of Hong Kong had been taken, and the Japs were in Borneo, the Celebes and New Guinea; also heading toward Singapore; advancing against the British through Malaya; and attacking the Dutch East Indies. In February they were fighting in Java and Burma, bombing Rangoon, threatening India and raiding the Indian Ocean with their submarines. On the 15th, to give a precise date, they received from the British local command the unconditional surrender of the supposedly "impregnable" naval base and fortress of Singapore, the strongest and most important point possessed by the Allies in the Far East. The blow not only to British prestige in the whole East but to the Allied cause was a terrific one. Churchill in London next day made no effort to minimize it. "Tonight," he said in Parliament, "the Japanese are triumphant. They shout their exultation 'round the world. We suffer. We are taken aback," but there was no yielding by either the Prime Minister or the British people, only a grimmer determination to win. Nor was there any weakening in America. In a radio broadcast February 23 President Roosevelt admitted that we had suffered serious reverses and would meet more but affirmed that we were wholly committed to the destruction of the power of the Axis aggressors and that we were gaining steadily in strength.

With the loss of the citadel the British also lost thirty-two warships and transports, and also at sea the only two capital ships the Allies had, H.M.S. *Repulse* and H.M.S. *Prince of Wales*. Another great disaster was soon to follow. In the Battle of the Java Sea, February 27–March 1, the United Nations lost most of their ships in that section, including British, American, Dutch and Australian, twelve warships being sunk against Japanese losses of only seven. In a report Admiral Hart admitted that our Asiatic fleet had lost a campaign.

During March the Japanese continued their successful advance. On the 7th the Netherlands Government in London received a laconic cable from Java which said, "We are shutting down. Good-bye till better days. Long live the Queen." Java had fallen; Timor was occupied; Australia attacked; and India threatened. Then came the fall of Sumatra, and the Japanese landing on the Solomons. Japanese occupation of Burma had cut off the Burma Road along which alone supplies had been able to reach the hard-pressed Chinese, who had put up a magnificent fight for over four years. At the beginning of April American planes began flying supplies to Chiang

Kai-shek from bases in India. That country, however, was in the throes of an imperial crisis, and the mission of Sir Stafford Cripps, which had offered every possible concession to the Nationalists under the circumstances of the time, had failed. The American Government also sent a mission to India the end of March but without result.

The Japs had also seized the Moluccas and the Marshall Islands, the latter being among those for which they had been given a mandate under the Versailles Treaty and the League of Nations. When Japan had withdrawn from the League she had refused to give up the mandated islands, in accordance with the terms under which they had been entrusted to her. Not only that, but in absolute violation of her pledge she had fortified them, and they had been useful as stepping stones in her march of conquest. We had declined to join the League ourselves, partly because we did not wish to assume responsibility for policing the world. We were now being forced to "police it" to an extent we had never dreamed of! The American Navy had taken more than one sound thrashing, and American troops had been captured in the Philippines, and were now being poured into remote places in the South Pacific of which most Americans had never before heard. American flyers were not only transporting supplies to China but—for the most part at this time volunteers—were fighting the Japanese from the Chinese lines.

On April 9 occurred the naval Battle of the Indian Ocean in which the Japanese sank two British heavy cruisers. It is, as I have said, simply impossible to note all the sinkings and engagements even in the Pacific area (where we were chiefly engaged in the early part of the year), much less what was happening to our Allies and enemies all over the globe, all of which was of either direct or indirect importance to us. Not merely are the facts too numerous and complex for a brief account but many of them were not made public until months later and many are even yet military secrets.

For example, good news at last came from the Pacific war area on April 18 when Americans read that American flyers had bombed Tokio and other Japanese cities. Official confirmation of any sort was slow in coming. A few days later, one U. S. bomber was reported as having been grounded in Siberia and its crew interned by the Russians. Where our planes had started from has always remained a mystery. When asked, Mr. Roosevelt merely smiled and said from "Shangri-la," obviously a false name. Some of the story was disclosed a month later when the leader of the raid, Brigadier General James H. Doolittle, was decorated in Washington. No mention was made of any loss until six months afterwards when it was announced that four of our planes had failed to return. At the time, the raid made a great impression both in Japan and America, but the mystery in which it was always shrouded has continued, and it was never repeated. This indicates some of the difficulties in trying to write in detail of military events so near to us and which for obvious reasons cannot as yet be authentically described. This is perhaps especially true of the numbers, types of forces, and locations of our troops in all theaters.

On April 25 our government announced that we had taken possession of the French island of New Caledonia in the Southwest Pacific with the consent of the local French authorities. This brings us to a fresh point regarding the Japanese conquests and threats. The small island, aside from its purely strategic importance, has always been a considerable producer of nickel and chrome, and the Japanese advance had already played havoc with the sources of many of the basic materials essential to both our peace and war economy. For example, all of the burlap we have used has come from India, and 99 per cent of that from the provinces most closely threatened by the Japs. We need about 500,000,000 pounds a year of it to pack and handle our farm produce and other products. Nothing else can take its place. Hemp for ropes and other purposes had largely been lost to us when the Philippines went. We are the greatest makers of steel in the world but almost wholly dependent for manganese, a most important factor in the industry, on imports from India and Soviet Russia. The war had stopped practically all imports from the latter. Mica does not sound important to the average man but it is essential as an insulator in almost all electrical apparatus. It is in your radios, your telephone, your motor engine, in almost everything connected with electricity. Eighty per cent of it comes from India. We

Harris-Ewing Photographic News Service

TROOPS OF U. S. ARMY TASK FORCE MARCH THROUGH HILLS OF THE FRENCH ISLAND
OF NEW CALEDONIA

Harris-Ewing Photographic News Service

DEFENSE PLANT EMPLOYEES MAKING POSTERS STRESSING THE NEED
OF SAVING RUBBER

have already spoken of the loss of rubber and sugar, and could continue the list—with the loss of tea from Java and Sumatra, oil from that island and Burma, shellac, and other things—but have already pointed to enough to indicate the seriousness of the damage which Japan was inflicting on us.

It must also be recalled that what we were losing for *our* war effort Japan was gaining for *hers*. Moreover, shipping was becoming scarce. The demands on it for transport of troops and supplies, for imports from wherever we could get them, all made the submarine the increasing peril which it was to remain increasingly to the end of the year. The British were also badly off in that regard. They, too, had heavy needs and had suffered heavy losses, and in addition, owing to the closing to them of the Mediterranean and the Suez route, all their ships to the Near and Far East had to ply the many thousands of miles extra involved in going round the Cape of Good Hope. All this added poignancy to the cry of chagrin and rage which went up when on February 9 the *Normandie* was burned at her dock in New York. This great ship, one of the finest, largest and latest afloat, which had been taken over by the government from the French and rechristened the *Lafayette,* was being refitted when fire broke out and almost completely destroyed her. rendering her useless for the duration of the war even if she may ever be salvaged. The giant ship was almost 80,000 tons, over 1000 feet long, and had originally cost $59,000.000

to build. Several courts of enquiry decided that there had been no sabotage but that there had been gross carelessness.

Before continuing with the story of military operations we may note other happenings at home during these months.

More and more America was turning to war as its sole interest. Industries were continually being shifted from the mass production of civilian goods at mass prices to the making of war supplies. As an instance, we may mention the $200,000,000 radio industry which was ordered on February 13 to convert its whole facilities to the production of arms. It may be noted here that although American industry was to make a wonderful showing and enormously increase its output, its earnings, contrary to the case in the previous war, were not to increase. In fact in many cases they were to be sharply curtailed, owing to taxation. There were no "war babies" in the stock market this time, and the great increase in national income was almost wholly given to labor and not to the owners of industries. It may also be noted at this point that not only was labor more careful, perhaps, of its spending than in the earlier war boom, but as goods grew scarcer and in many cases were strictly rationed or taken off the market entirely, labor had less on which to spend. The changes in all phases of our life related to automobiles were notable in this regard as were also new restrictions on instalment buying. One result was that, as the year advanced, the savings of the lower income classes increased by leaps and

Shoemaker in The Chicago Daily Sun

THE RACE FOR LIFE: THE FIGHT AGAINST THE SUBMARINE

bounds, in the form of savings bank and other deposits, government bonds and stamps, life insurance and paid-off mortgages. War for the first time in America had assumed a wholly new aspect, which may prove to be of great importance when peace comes and savings are released coincident with a return to civilian production.

Meanwhile we may note the growing war effort in other ways. Whereas in January the estimate that there would be 3,600,000 men eventually in the army was considered "huge" by some leading newspapers, by May Under-Secretary of War Patterson announced that the army goal had been raised to 8,000,000, and as it had been previously announced that the goals for the Air Force and Navy were 2,000,000 and 1,000,000 respectively, this meant a future possible stepping-up to a total in the armed forces of 11,000,000, or about three times the number then in service. A slight but interesting sidelight on what this meant in the way of providing for them was given in a Reuter despatch from aboard a large transport "in the Pacific" in April, which stated that 10,000 eggs were eaten for breakfast every morning, requiring the all-night service of four men to crack the shells. No soldiers in history have ever had such ample supplies of the best quality of food and clothing as have our troops in this war, whenever it was possible to get them to them. We may contrast the 10,000 eggs daily for breakfast on the transport with the one a week which is the ration of the British Prime Minister!

Without entering too deeply on the maze of government finance bills, we may glimpse another step-up in the war effort by one or two examples. On February 2 the Senate made a record in time and figures by passing the largest single appropriation made in our history, a $26,500,000,000 Navy Supply Bill, after only two hours of debate. A week later the President asked Congress for an additional $5,430,000,000 for the Lease-Lend program, which would bring our total for that purpose to almost $30,000,000,000. On the other hand, it was estimated that overtime pay was adding some $4,000,000,000 to the cost of naval contracts, and throughout the year there was much discussion of the unfairness of a forty-hour week for labor at home when our soldiers, sailors, marines and fly-ers were risking their lives in an "all round the clock" all over the world. March 17 the limit for the national debt was raised to $130,000,000,000, and estimates were made that before the end of the war it might reach $300,000,-000,000.

Apart from Lease-Lend operations we were far from limiting our activities to the Pacific, though that was the area in which the most spectacular news items were being made. In addition to what we already mentioned there were sinkings on both sides, Japanese warships by Ameri-can submarines, even in the China Sea, and more attacks on ourselves, which would make only a bare catalogue of names and dates in the telling, and can be found else-where. For a moment we may turn to the Old World.

Throughout the year we were to have our difficulties in steering a tortuous course with the French government at Vichy, and the Free French, now called the Fighting

French, under the leadership of General de Gaulle with headquarters in London. The details of this diplomacy are too complex for this brief survey of the year, but we may note that on April 7 the Vichy government protested against our recognition of the Free French in Equatorial Africa and the Cameroons. The same day word was received of the arrival in London of General George C. Marshall, Chief of Staff of the U. S. Army, and of Mr. Harry Hopkins, Chief of the British-American Munitions Assignment Board. In view of future events the coincidence was interesting. It was evident that another and important step had been taken in joint planning of major strategy.

Meanwhile the traitor Laval had returned to power and influence at Vichy and was trying to provide "full collaboration" of France with the Nazis. What that meant was clear. The sinister SS-man, Prince Waldeck-Pyrmont, arrived in Paris, to be followed by Richard Heydrich, head of the dreaded Gestapo, known even to Germans as "the Hangman." Then came Göring and Hitler himself. Laval was also conferring with the Japanese Ambassador to Berlin, who had come from thence with Admiral Nomura, head of the Japanese Mixed Axis Commission in Germany and Admiral Abe who held a similar post at Rome. Far-reaching plans were being laid, but of immediate concern to the Allies was the fate of the great island of Madagascar, which was to be occupied by the Japanese, and would be a base from which the Axis could attack British shipping to the Near East and India even when it took the long route around the Cape. The immediate answer was the beginning of the seizure of the island by the British, completed after a few weeks, and the announcement by the United States that it was firmly behind the British in their move. We had learned that the Vichy government had surrendered Indo-China, with all the important results of that move, to the Japs, and this time we were not to be caught napping. It is an added illustration, however, of how the foreign policy of the United States, backed by our forces, was gradually circling the entire globe.

At home, events were also moving fast, and we may note here the beginning of the organizing of women in the war effort. They were not, as some in Russia, to take up arms and form a "battalion of death" but were to perform most useful service, as well as to add to the alphabetical complexities of government departments and organizations. First there were the WAACS. Starting with 25,000 women, the Act authorizing this women's auxiliary army permitted an ultimate enrollment of 150,000. Women between 21 and 45, married or unmarried, provided they did not have children under fourteen years of age, were eligible if they passed certain required tests. It was an army organization and its members served as typists, clerks, operators of office machines and telephone switchboards, drivers and repairers of cars, aircraft warners, dieticians, cooks, pharmacist's assistants, and in many other capacities, freeing men for the fighting line. They could go wherever the army went and were liable to overseas service.

The WAVES formed a branch of the Naval Reserve and their work was usually highly technical, including knowledge of such subjects as mathematics, aeronautical engineering, astronomy, accounts and business statistics, foreign languages, radio operating, and many others. Starting with only 10,000 the service proved so efficient that it was much enlarged.

Next came the WAFS. This was an auxiliary aviation unit made up of pilots with the necessary administrative members. Among other duties they flew planes from the point of manufacture to that of service, including trans-Atlantic flying.

Women in these organized services were, however, but a small proportion of the total who took part in the war effort, and in many lines men were rapidly replaced by women. Not only in such fields as hospital nursing and others already largely pre-empted by women, but in all forms of business and daily work women undertook their share of the national burden. To mention only one, we may note that after a year of war about 65,000 women were employed in banks, or one quarter of the total personnel. We should also include all those men and women, a large part of them teachers in the schools, who served without pay in the thankless and dull work of the rationing boards. There was no glamor about it, and no uniforms, with often unpopularity and sour looks as the only reward, but it was democracy at work and service freely given for the cause of the nation.

In the summer of 1942 the outlook was grim. More and more the war was becoming global and almost every nation had become involved. For example, on June 3 Hungary, Bulgaria and Rumania declared war on us, and on the same day Mexico declared war on the Axis. This was but a sample of what was gradually happening everywhere. The issues were so vast, so vital, so fundamental that no self-respecting nation could remain aloof. Hitler's record of broken pledges and lies, those lies on which he had intended, so he frankly told all peoples in his book *Mein Kampf,* to build his new world order, had shown the futility and inanity of trying to remain "neutral." Every man on earth had to be for or against him. To that extent he had come to dominate the entire human race as one had never done before him. Much as all of us who belong to the freedom-loving nations may hate him and all he stands for, there is no use in minimizing his influence and power. To do so is only to endure the fate of nation after nation which has thought it need not suffer from the strife but could carry on its life by the simple method of standing aside.

We may now turn again to the military events, fortunately as yet at long distance from our own shores, though distance, even if it saved us in our homes, entailed excessive difficulties. As one went about America it was hard

29

to picture it in the condition of other countries, with bombed and pulverized cities and ruined countrysides. We had only the choice of that or of holding the enemy over- seas, though both for the British and ourselves these mili- tary enterprises thousands of miles from bases was as ex- hausting, Churchill said, as holding a heavy "dumbbell at arm's length." Yet such efforts were also exhausting our enemies, whose resources were less than ours for a protracted struggle.

In the spring and early summer there was bad news for the Allies from many theaters of war, Egypt, Lybia, Russia and elsewhere, but the outlook was also brightened by successes. In the first week of May we won a decisive victory over the Japanese in the naval battle of the Coral Sea, in which our only loss was the sixteen-year-old air- craft *Lexington,* which went down gloriously, as against Japanese losses of a new aircraft carrier, three heavy cruis- ers, one light cruiser, two destroyers, four gunboats and four transports sunk, as well as nine other important war vessels damaged.

Exactly one month after the Coral Sea battle began the Japanese and Americans again met in that area of Midway, where we once more inflicted losses on the enemy far in excess of our own, losses, moreover, which their resources did not permit them to repair. Not only were we at last beginning to pay off scores for Pearl Harbor but our weight was also beginning to tell and we had learned valuable lessons. The chief was the importance of land-based airplanes to operate in conjunction with the fleets. This pointed the way to immensely increased production of planes and the need for seizing bases already occupied by the enemy. As to the first, we may note that orders were given for these, and other material, to automobile manufacturers equivalent to the production of 15,000,000 cars and trucks under normal conditions, or the output for the whole best three years of peace-time production. We shall mention later the bases we seized, and merely add here the statement made by the British Prime Minister before the House of Commons early in the year 1943, which lies just beyond this chapter, though the speech referred to events in 1942. Churchill said that the "ingenious use of aircraft to solve intricate tactical problems" as shown in MacArthur's generalship in the Pacific, should be carefully studied by all concerned with the technical problems of the war. We had at least gone a long way from that black seventh of December in Hawaii.

Nevertheless, general news was bad. The Nazis were pressing the Russians hard; Tobruk had fallen to the Axis after a long siege with 25,000 prisoners; and the Allies were slowly losing, for the time, the battle of shipping against the German submarines. Argentine reversed her policy in July and seemed to align herself in sympathy with the Axis, although in August Brazil openly declared war against Germany and Italy. In October Under-Secretary of State Sumner Welles was to issue a thinly veiled rebuke to both the Argentine and Chile for their complacency with regard to the activities of Axis agents within their borders.

Although we were sending large contingents of troops to Ulster and England, our military activities continued to be centered in the Pacific. In August we attacked the Japanese in the Aleutians simply with the idea of holding them, wearing them down, and preventing them from extending farther. We also, for quite different reasons, made an attack on Tulagi in the Solomon Islands and landed marines on Guadalcanal. The islands struck at formed perhaps the most vital key for operations in the Southwest Pacific. Our initial success was a major check to what had hitherto been the steady advance of the enemy, and when, after six months of hard fighting, we came into complete control, it meant that the tide had turned. Without minimizing the importance of other battles, probably the epics of Corregidor-Bataan and Guadalcanal will live longest in the annals of the heroism of American soldiers during the first year of our struggle for life against a nation which, nearly a century earlier, we had introduced to what we thought was civilization. In October, it may be noted, both Britain and the United States relinquished their extra-territorial rights so long held in China, an action deeply appreciated by the rising and nobly fighting Chinese nation.

The events of November were of the first importance. In the Far East we won another great victory over the Japanese in the naval battle of the Solomons, the heaviest "slugging match," as Admiral Nimitz called it, in which the American navy had been engaged since the Civil War. Irreparable losses were inflicted on the enemy, and their attempt to reinforce Guadalcanal was completely frustrated. Vice-Admiral Halsey was in command of our fleet. The victory was hailed by our Allies, and a statement was given out that including our losses at Pearl Harbor we had lost, all told, from our navy eight-six ships against a total of three hundred and twenty-one by the Japanese. On the evening of November 17, President Roosevelt on the radio said that the war had reached a turning point.

But we must now consider another field of operations. If, as we have already said, it is utterly impossible, because of lack of space, to treat even our own war actions in detail or to do more than mention those of our Allies, which nevertheless were of great importance to us, the reader must bear in mind that something was happening nearly every moment in every part of the world. The leaders, however, had been in touch, and as we have noted, far-reaching plans had been in the making. Roosevelt and Churchill were in constant communication. In September Churchill visited Stalin. Emissaries had gone hither and thither. Wendell Willkie, for example, had made a six weeks' tour round the world by plane, partly as a private citizen and partly as a representative of the President. Among others he had talked with Stalin and Generalissimo Chiang Kai-shek. Russia was doing marvellously and driving back the Nazis but needed help in the form of a second front opened somewhere against the common enemy.

At last, at nine o'clock on the night of Saturday, November 7, the news broke on an expectant world. A very large force of American troops, partly from those gathered in Britain and partly sailing direct from the United States, all under command of Lieut. General Dwight D. Eisenhower, landed in North Africa, together with British troops and ships. Exact figures are not yet available but the great armada apparently included more than five hundred vessels, and the immense preparations made months in advance and the exact timing of all coordinated operations mark it as the most perfectly executed expedition in all military and naval history. It was equally successful, and as we learned that we had occupied Oran, Algiers and Casablanca, some of the sting was taken out of Pearl Harbor. The combination of army, navy and air forces, as well as the cooperation between British and Americans, had been perfect, and the occupation of most of the long coast line was accomplished with a surprisingly small amount of casualties.

We had, of course, landed on French territory, and the long and difficult maintenance of relations with the traitorous Vichy government bore fruit. In Africa itself there were French leaders who assisted the operation, but Vichy itself naturally rejected our explanations. The two governments broke off diplomatic relations, the French Ambassador, or rather the accredited representative of Vichy, M. Gaston Henri-Hay was handed his passport in Washington, and we seized the remaining French ships in American ports. Among the local French in Africa who helped us were Admiral Darlan of the French navy and General Giraud of the army.

The situation was complex in the extreme, and in addition to his purely military duties General Eisenhower had probably the most difficult diplomatic problems to solve with which any American general in the field has ever had to grapple. Darlan had been a turncoat more than once and was bitterly anti-British. No one knew whether to trust him or not, and he was hated by many French but seemed to have the support of the navy, the major part of which was lying in the harbor of Toulon. Giraud had been loyal as a strong anti-Nazi Frenchman, and had made two daring escapes from German prisons. On the other hand, in London, General de Gaulle, who had become the leader of the Free, or Fighting, French, was strongly opposed to both the men on the spot. It is utterly impossible to fathom the motives of these three men as they looked forward to the future of France and to that of their own careers.

In any case, Giraud appealed to all the French in Africa to welcome the American aid. We soon held also Dakar, the jumping-off place for planes and submarines from the African coast toward all the New World. Before the assassination of Darlan, and acting it is said under

his orders, almost the entire French fleet, instead of proceeding against us or falling into the hands of the Germans, was scuttled by its officers in Toulon harbor. At
present writing the political situation of the French
among themselves remains confusing to the foreigner. We
had, however, gained a firm foothold on northern and
western Africa with remarkably small loss of life, had
opened a second front threatening Italy and Germany
across a narrow stretch of water, and prepared a place
from which to stab at the soft side of the Axis.

Meanwhile the British Eighth Army had been chasing
the redoubtable German General Rommel and his Afrikan
Corps out of Egypt, across all Libya and into Tunisia. It
is only fair to say that the way had long been prepared by
Churchill, who assumed heavy risks when the outlook was
darkest. The Prime Minister, however, took occasion to
say that the plan for the African campaign, which was an
"American show," had been prepared by Roosevelt and
that he himself was a willing lieutenant. Weather and
other conditions prevented during the remainder of the
year much land fighting and a clearing of the position,
but the Mediterranean had once again been made safe for
Allied shipping; the threat to Egypt and the Suez Canal
had passed; and pressure on Russia relieved, enabling her
to make her amazingly successful campaign against the
German invaders. The fall of Stalingrad, with over 300,-
000 German losses and the threat at the year's end to all
the Nazi armies in the Ukraine and the Caucusus, were

all part of the daring move on Vichy Africa. Germany had not only lost a large part of the supplies—wheat, oil, and so on—which she had thought within her grasp, but was becoming encircled, and Italy had become immediately and desperately threatened. Air raids by both British and American flyers became ever intensified over both the central European Axis powers, from Britain and Africa. The year, which had begun so inauspiciously and had held so many disappointments and catastrophes, ended with the almost certainty of ultimate victory, however much of cost and suffering yet remained to be borne. At the end of the year—December 12—the President stated that we had more than 1,000,000 men in overseas service.

We had not only to fight abroad. The Fifth Column was at work at home, and was well taken care of, although it is noteworthy that there was little of the anti-alien hysteria of the first World War. The ban on the teaching of German in the schools, the prohibition of German music in concerts and the opera, the discharging of German musicians and conductors, and other such manifestations, which had been so common in 1917 and 1918, were almost wholly, if not quite, absent. The fact marked, perhaps, an increased maturity and self-confidence in the American. In the autumn, in fact, we went so far as to announce that resident Italians even if not American citizens should not be considered as *enemy* aliens. This apparently greatly annoyed Mussolini.

Many arrests were made, however, particularly of Germans, and in such organizations as the blatant Bund, the Silver Shirts, and others. The most sensational case was that of the eight German saboteurs who had landed from submarines amply supplied with cash, implements and instructions for sabotaging our war effort. Four had been landed on the beach at Amagansett, Long Island, during the night of June 13, and the other four landed four nights later near Ponte Vedra, Florida. All were eventually captured, and tried.

As compared with the sudden executions and mass massacres of the Nazis who claim to be introducing a "New Order" into civilization, it is interesting to note how these men were treated by a democracy. They first were accorded a long and fair court martial, with seven generals on the bench, and the finding was handed over to the President as Commander-in-Chief. Six of the culprits had been condemned to death and two, who had turned state's evidence, were given long sentences in prison. However, to avoid the slightest possibility of their not having had a fair trial, the Supreme Court convened in the first special session it had held in twenty-two years, to hear their case. The Court upheld the judgment of the court martial and on August 8 the six met their end in the electric chair in the District of Columbia jail death-chamber.

At the end of November three naturalized American citizens of German birth were sentenced to death for treason in shielding and hiding one of the saboteurs, and

38

the wives of the three to twenty-five years in prison and $10,000 fine each. With the exception of the conviction (with death penalty) of Max Stephan, a tavern keeper in Detroit, for aiding the escape of a German aviator who had been a prisoner in Canada, these were the first convictions for treason by the United States since 1791. John Brown, the pre-Civil War Abolitionist was hanged for treason at Harpers Ferry in 1859, but under the laws of the State of Virginia and not under a Federal statute. There were a good many other arrests, and prison terms were meted out, but the number was infinitesimal in proportion to the totals in our foreign groups, even if we include somewhat wholesale removals of Japanese from certain districts along the California coast. Two points having important bearing on the making of the American may be noted. One was the loyalty of the vast majority of those among us, aliens and new citizens alike; and the other was the willingness with which all, old Americans and new, accepted the draft and other wartime measures. We had had our "draft riots" in the Civil War, our anxieties over foreigners in the first World War. In this war the people stood together and behind the government.

There was considerable trouble with labor. The A. F. of L. and the C.I.O. failed to get together. A conference called early in the year by the President to enable a wartime pact to be made between employees and employers also failed, the stumbling-block being the demand by labor unions that employers force their men to join the union which might show a majority in the plant. There was also much bad feeling about the length of the work-week, mostly forty-hour with overtime up to the limit of forty-eight hours. Service men (and their wives, parents and others), who knew they were risking their lives and living hard twenty-four hours a day could not see why workers at home on high wages and in safety should demand such special treatment. Moreover, the people at large, staggering under terrific taxation and being urged to make every sacrifice felt that the burdens and sacrifices should be borne by all with some degree of equality. The A. F. of L. appear to have been more aware of the needs of the situation, and willing to consider themselves as American citizens first and union members second, than the C.I.O. Further, it was believed by many that even the "overtime pay week" was too short for a nation fighting for its life. President Roosevelt maintained that the worker began to slow down after 48 hours, yet the Co-ordinator of Empire and Allied Requirements of the British Supply Council, reported that after three years' experience it was decided that the maximum output for men was reached at between 60 and 65 hours a week, and for women at between 55 and 60 hours. We should hardly like to say that the Americans cannot stand as much as the British. Strikes were numerous but had the days been those of peace instead of the hardest war we have ever fought, they would have been of less importance. The loss of man-hours due to strikes was less than in 1940 or in 1938. (In 1937 there had been the steel and automobile strikes, in 1939 and 1941 the two great bituminous coal strikes of the C.I.O.) This does not, however, quite tell the story. The loss of

A PICTORIAL PRESENTATION OF THE FARMER'S PLIGHT

Seibel in The Richmond (Va.) Times-Dispatch

INCREASING NUMBERS IN THE ARMED FORCES LEAVE THE
FARMER SHORTHANDED

man-hours in one plant might long delay the production of parts for most important war implements made in some other plant, and the loss of man-hours in the comfort and safety of America might mean the loss of many man-lives in far parts of the world.

In November came the Congressional elections. There had been grumbling for a long time. The shock to national pride given by the unnecessary disaster in Pearl Harbor had rankled. The administration had to bear the brunt of the resentment felt. It is true that the Secretary of the Navy was one of the two Republicans whom the President had added to his Cabinet, but Mr. Roosevelt had first come to national prominence as Assistant Secretary of the Navy, and that branch of the services was supposed to be his special "pet." There were many other grievances. Many persons felt that the war was being waged in favor of the New Deal and its experiments. Many were tired of these and of the red tape which tied so many rambunctious Americans to their chairs when they wanted to be "raring" on their hind legs. As a sample of the red tape and complexity of questionnaires, Congress was presented by a well-known firm with a questionnaire which demanded answers to "Form No. 1–1071–PLOF–5–NOBU–COS–WP." In connection with this, Senator Byrd told Congress that the instructions to farmers for filling out applications for the use of trucks was 24,000 words long. Business men were complaining that so much of their time was being taken in studying and filling out questionnaires that they had none left for war production. Moreover, the government's labor policy, or perhaps lack of policy, had disgruntled others. The plans for industrial mobilization so carefully worked out since the previous war had been discarded in favor of sudden opportunistic ideas. American life had come to be based on the car, not merely for pleasure but for every sort of business. The public was bewildered by the conflicting statements of members of the administration as to why they were so suddenly shut off from normal supplies of gas. One day they were told by X that it was to save oil, and the next by Y that it was not that but it was to save rubber. The confusion over rubber, not wholly cleared up by the Baruch-Conant Report, made a deep impression on the man in the street. We are not trying to appraise the essentials of the national situation but merely to suggest some of the straws in the wind which indicated that the ordinary turnover of a mid-term election might be more than normal.

It was. Briefly, as Senator George (Democrat) of Georgia said, the returns constituted "a 'Stop, Look, and Listen' sign painted in red." The Democratic majority in Congress, which for some years had been wholly abnormal, was reduced to a new low, with the House composed of 221 Democrats, 209 Republicans, and 5 of other parties. Moreover the Republicans had come into control of twenty-three states, including New York (for the first time in twenty years, where former District Attorney Thomas E. Dewey was elected Governor), Ohio and California. Their party made a clean sweep through a part of the country containing 75,000,000 people, and they controlled states with a large majority of the votes in the Electoral College, looking forward to 1944. There was a tremendous overturn in the farm states of the Middle West, where the veteran Senator Norris was defeated in

Nebraska. One of the odd features of the election was that the candidates whom President Roosevelt had backed were defeated and those whom he had opposed were elected, yet the result cannot be considered to have been a repudiation of either the President or his war policies. In so far as the President personally was concerned it seemed to be merely another underscoring of the fact that the American voter does not like, indeed distinctly resents, outside interference with his local choice. It was one of the smallest turnouts of voters in elections in recent years, only about 26,000,000 going to the polls as compared with twice that number in 1940. However, the result was emphatic, and developed three men who may well be considered as in the running for the Presidential candidacy in 1944, Governors Dewey of New York, Bricker of Ohio and Stassen of Minnesota.

One thing appeared certain, which was that even if the New Dealers were not to face a wholly hostile Congress during the ensuing two years, the people had demanded that the balance between the Executive and Congress be restored more nearly to normal and that Congress would hearken. One bone of contention would be the limitation of salaries to $25,000 after taxes, which Congress had previously declined to vote and which the President had decreed in an Executive order. This, as well as a limitation of all incomes to a net of $25,000, as was later to be asked by the President and sponsored by Mrs. Roosevelt, had been a plank in the Communist party platform of 1928 and demanded later by the C.I.O. It was to make trouble in the coming year. In December the President took action that wiped out the W.P.A. which also had long been the object of criticism. In a nation whose man power was urgently needed to the fullest extent either at the front or behind the lines, there had for some time been little need to expend public money in "making work" for unemployed.

An interesting and recurring item of news throughout the year was the number of split decisions in the Supreme Court and the way the different judges voted. As we noted in the preceding chapter, the Court had been largely appointed by the President, although he delayed several months in appointing a successor to Justice Byrnes who had resigned. The difficulty in which the Court began to find itself because recruited so much from political office instead of from the bench of other courts or from distinguished jurists in private life, was notable one day late in November when, with only eight members, the Chief Justice and three Associate Justices all had to disqualify themselves leaving only four out of a supposed nine in that august body to pass on a case.

Without attempting to detail all the cases of the year we may note that—although during the years that Mr. Hughes was Chief Justice there were from ten to twenty dissenting verdicts in a year—in the first six months of 1942 there were fifty-two, of which fourteen involved votes of five to four, the old bugbear to which the President had so greatly objected. It was remarked by one observer that if in the old days the Court was made up of "nine old men" (which it never was), it had got to be like the Quiz Kids! All that this indicated was, as has been shown over and over in our history and a fact to which we called attention in an earlier chapter, that, fortunately for the republic, judges on the bench develop an independence of the appointing power which placed them there, just as Chester A. Arthur wholly ceased to be the local spoilsman politician handing out Custom House jobs in New York when he suddenly found himself elevated to the White House.

One of the dramatic events of the year, so filled with drama, was the rescue of the celebrated flyer of two wars, Eddie Rickenbacker. The fifty-two-year-old ace and his seven companions had last been heard from about 1500 miles out from Hawaii, flying for an undisclosed Pacific area. Three days later the navy began a search, which criss-crossed hundreds of thousands of square miles of that vast ocean. It seemed hopeless. The traditional needle in the haystack was nothing compared with trying to locate eight men in a life raft or two in the illimitable stretches of the greatest ocean of the globe. All, except one, Staff Sergeant Alexander T. Kacmarczyk, who had succumbed and been buried at sea, were found after twenty-one days' search, and "Captain Eddie" was brought back to the United States to do good work.

At the end of the preceding chapter we spoke of the vastly important gift to the nation of his art collection,

TROOPSHIP OF THE SKY

A COLUMN OF SOLDIERS AND JEEPS OF THE U. S. ARMY BOARDS A NEW
GIANT CURTISS–COMMANDO (C–46) WHICH CAN SPEED TROOPS, MOBILE
EQUIPMENT AND FIELD ARTILLERY TO SCATTERED BATTLE ZONES

Harris-Ewing Photographic News Service

CAPTAIN EDDIE RICKENBACKER, RESCUED IN THE PACIFIC AFTER SPENDING 21 DAYS
ON A RAFT, TALKS TO SECRETARY OF WAR HENRY L. STIMSON

now in Washington, by the late Andrew W. Mellon. In 1942 the museum he founded was enhanced by the gift by Mr. Peter A. B. Widener of his noted collection, long known to collectors and connoisseurs all over the world. It was estimated to have cost Mr. Widener $50,000,000 and it was a free gift to the people but the peculiarities of our tax system were disclosed and the state of Pennsylvania charged a gift tax of 5 per cent. President Roosevelt estimated the value as $3,900,000 and the nation paid Pennsylvania a tax of $195,000.

The most notable among the deaths of the year was that of Brigadier General Hugh S. Johnson, who died at the age of fifty-nine. Known as "Old Ironpants," he had had a distinguished career in the army but had first become familiar to the entire nation as head of the N.I.R.A., or the "Blue Eagle," during the depression, and later as a columnist after he had turned against the New Deal. A man of tremendous energy, dynamic force, and vitriolic language, he was charming in his personal life and a force for clear thinking throughout the whole country.

The war's first year, and longer, though we cannot anticipate, was for America a year of defensive rather than aggressive action. It had begun with a colossal disaster, and although in the second half we won notable victories against the Japanese in the Far East the actions were all parts of a defensive delaying movement rather than of advances made against vital centers of the enemy's power and resources. In North Africa we initiated a carefully planned and most skillfully executed campaign against the Axis in Europe, in a real offensive, but it was, when the year ended, still only a beginning. At home, our industry had accomplished marvels in transforming civilian production into war production but that, again, was rather in the nature of preparing for future action. We had voted and spent tens and tens of billions of dollars. We had contributed heavily to the resources of our Allies. We had raised great forces, we had piled up long records of distinguished courage and ability shown by those forces, both as individuals and as units. As was said in a review of the year, we had done everything possible to prepare for victory, but we had yet to begin the march to victory. Our preparations were so vast and costly that they enhanced the sense of confidence and national pride, but the feeling of ultimate victory would have been less certain at the beginning of 1943 had it not been for the British Eighth Army's brilliant pursuit of the German forces under Rommel across a thousand miles of Africa, and the astounding successes of the Russians. It is well to consider this when some of our leaders are busy planning the post-war world according to their ideas. There will be others—the Chinese, the British and the Russians among them—who have borne the burden of the war far longer than we and who have contributed infinitely more in suffering, who may sit with us at the table of the post-war world. We shall all have to work together.

CHAPTER II

THE RECORD OF 1943

THE year 1943 is the most complex for any recorder to recount in the entire history of the United States. It marked a complete change-over from civilian life to total war. The war itself, not only total but global, reached, let us hope, a turning point in favor of the Allies and freedom, and for the whole human race. At home there were important events, political, economic and social, which may have permanent effects on the life of our nation.

As I have pointed out before, it is impossible to write *history* within a few weeks or months of such stupendous events. We are obliged to forego the chronological method and must devote ourselves to such major topics as the home front, the fighting front, and certain scattered matters, if we are to make the year intelligible at all. I may add that *all* the threads on all the fronts are, of course, inextricably intertwined and that events and acts have mutually influenced one another.

On the home front we may begin, as usual, with the messages of the President to Congress on the state of the nation and its needs, and we shall follow first the political aspects of the year, although politics, obviously, were closely intertwined with economics at home and war abroad.

During the entire preceding year, the President had not only been under terrific strain but he had been in a false position. Ever since the dastardly attack on Pearl Harbor by the Japanese, December 7, 1941, the President had had information about the extremely dangerous situation both of the United States and of its Allies. He *knew* but he could not *tell* all he knew. The public knew he knew and was not telling, so that a false and annoying relation was formed between him and the people. An enormous improvement in the Allied condition had come about by January 1943, and the President's message to Congress on the 7th of that month reflected his growing confidence. In the first part of that message he gave an admirable survey of the war to date. In the second, he reviewed the stupendous production of war materials by the nation. As the figures he gave out were, naturally, those for 1942, we shall reserve the figures for 1943 until later. In the third part, he looked to the future and our post-war aims. These included the permanent disarming of the Axis aggressors, as well as plans for employment and "assurance against the evils of all major economic hazards—assurance that will extend from the cradle to the grave." It was this part of the message which caused most criticism but, on the whole, both the tone and substance of the message afforded a happy contrast to some of his speeches the preceding year, and the way seemed open for better relations between the Chief Executive and Congress, as well as between him and the public.

That instead of this, Congress was to revolt more and

FULL SPEED AHEAD IN 1943
A cartoon by Harper in *The Birmingham Age Herald*.

more, as 1943 progressed, was apparently due to the fact that although the nation was practically wholly united on the questions of war it was greatly divided as to domestic issues. Both the fine qualities of Mr. Roosevelt, and his defects, were to add to this division. I am citing no personal opinion of my own but that generally held, I be-

51

lieve, even by his followers, when I say that although a fine leader in the war and as regards our foreign relations, the President is not good as an administrator. To the natural differences of opinion on domestic matters was added the confusion of mind caused by the overlapping authority and conflicting orders and opinions of the innumerable Boards and officials.

On January 11, the President submitted his message on the Budget, in the form of an 881-page book, most of which detailed only how $4,000,000,000 should be spent for the ordinary running of the government, though the total amount asked for was $109,000,000,000, of which $100,000,000,000 was for war. He estimated that by the end of the fiscal year, June 30, 1943, the national debt would be $210,000,000,000, but stated that the nation was "thoroughly solvent," and that "freedom from want for everybody, everywhere, is no longer a Utopian dream." The Secretary of the Treasury announced also that government expenses had risen $19,000,000,000 during the past year, and income taxes about 129.5 per cent. Methods of raising the huge new amounts needed were barely suggested and were left to Congress.

During the month the President made his journey to Casablanca to confer with Churchill but, for the sake of clarity, we may defer mention of his journeys abroad until we discuss the fighting front.

In spite of the conciliatory references to Congress in both the President's messages, trouble with that body began almost immediately, and wholly on domestic issues.

A Tammany leader from the Bronx, Edward J. Flynn, who had also been National Chairman of the Democratic Party, became the center of a scandal in New York City because the large courtyard of his country estate had been paved with paving blocks belonging to the city. Other charges, also, were made. Whatever their truth, the situation became embarrassing for the Democratic Party, and rumors spread that Flynn was to resign as Party Chairman and to be appointed Minister to Australia. On January 11, in an editorial the New York *Times* said: "Our prestige abroad, and our morale at home, would both be [so] harmed by an action so cynical" that it refused to believe the appointment would be made unless the President himself announced it. Unhappily, the President did. Public opinion, both at home and in Australia, was aroused against the appointment, and the Senate balked at confirmation. The fight was bitter and partisan but, also, it was felt by the public that in the world crisis only our best men should be sent as Ministers to the great Dominions, and that in the case of Canada, and now of Australia, domestic politics, none too savory, had played too great a part in foreign diplomacy. On January 31, within a few hours after the President's return from Casablanca, Flynn, after consultation with Democratic leaders, and less than twelve hours before final Senate action, withdrew his name. The withdrawal was immediately accepted by Mr. Roosevelt. It was a distinct rebuff to the

President by the Senate, and important as marking the first of a series of such rebuffs which the Houses of Congress were to deal him on domestic issues. Perhaps Flynn was, as Mrs. Roosevelt said, a good and honest man, and the paving-block incident one of "those things that are sometimes done by friends" and that "should not have been brought out," but there is no question but that the people and the Senate did not like the appointment. Mrs. Roosevelt added that the attack was engineered by enemies of the Administration, but the majority leader of the Democratic Senate said that the appointment might not pass and that, if it did, it would do so perhaps by only one vote.

The next rebuff came from the House. By a majority of six to one it provided for a committee of seven to investigate all the New Deal agencies and bureaus, to determine which might have exceeded their legal authority. In February, Congress decided that the President himself had exceeded his, and there occurred one of the bitterest fights since the President's effort to pack the Supreme Court. By an Executive Order, Mr. Roosevelt had proclaimed (October 3, 1942) that all salaries must be limited to $25,000, after taxes. In a Report, filed with the House, on the President's request for an increase in the limit of the national debt from $125,000,000,000 to $210,000,000,-000, it was recommended to add a rider to the Debt Bill which would substitute action by Congress on incomes for the fiat of the President. Representative Disney of

Oklahoma, who presented the amendment, stated that the Committee found not only that the President had not been given any authority for his action in the earlier anti-

OLD HENPECK WILL TAKE JUST SO MUCH

A cartoon on the growing rift between the President and the Congress, pictured in a cartoon by Hutton in *The Philadelphia Inquirer*.

inflation measures but that the intention of Congress had been "to the contrary."

In an historically remarkable communication between the Executive and the legislature, the President offered to withdraw his edict if Congress would pass a measure, dictated by him, limiting all incomes to $25,000 for a single person and $50,000 for a married couple. Owing to the high surtaxes, to keep $25,000 net meant an income, before taxes, of $67,500, and the President said it was inequitable that anyone should get that much while the men in the forces got only $600. The country immediately asked, if $25,000 was inequitable, how about $10,000, $5,000, or the wage scale of every miner, factory worker and laborer at home? Hospitals, small colleges, and other social institutions, felt that they might face extinction from loss of support. Many of the public felt that if the President, without and even against, consent of Congress, could fix the income of everyone, he could do anything. In a word, both the country and Congress were in turmoil. The opposition did not come from the small number of citizens affected directly but from the people at large. In March, the House accepted the Disney rider by a vote of 268 to 129, and ten days later, on the 23rd, the Senate killed the President's salary order by the phenomenal vote, on a domestic issue, of 74 to 3. It was, perhaps, the heaviest rebuke which Mr. Roosevelt had received during his three terms of office.

Another remarkable example of the rift between the President and Congress occurred toward the end of February. In the preceding October, Congress had given the President authority, under certain restrictions, to fix minimum prices for farm products. Mr. Roosevelt issued an order in which Congress considered he had again not only exceeded his authority but had gone contrary to the

A CONFERENCE OF THE GENERAL STAFF

Left to right: (seated) Lt. General Henry H. Arnold, Air Force; General George C. Marshall, Chief of Staff; Lt. General Lesley McNair, Army Ground Forces; *(standing)* Maj. General Joseph McNarney, Deputy Chief of Staff; and Major General B. B. Somervell, Army Service Forces.

Madame Chiang Kai-shek, at a reception in Washington, during her visit to the United States to further "all out" aid to China.

WAR ON THE HOME FRONT

Top: A Diesel engine being lowered into a submarine in a shipyard somewhere in the United States *Bottom:* Woman war worker applying sealing compound to the underside of a tank.

clearly expressed intention of the legislature. A new Bill which was a distinct rebuke to the Executive was introduced, and passed the Senate by the again remarkable majority, for a domestic issue, of 78 to 2. Not only that. Among the 78 rebuking the President were those who were numbered among his closest friends and advisers and who were regarded as the strongest New Dealers, such as Senators Barkley, Wagner, Guffey, and Senator Thomas of Utah.

In April, the Senate, by unanimous vote, deprived the President of the power, which he had held since 1934, further to devaluate the dollar. On May 26, the Senate wrote into a Bill a provision to prevent the Executive from using money for projects for which Congress had refused appropriations. On the other hand, on June 21, the House passed the requested $71,500,000,000 Army Appropriation by a unanimous vote of 345 to 0. Yet again, on the other hand, Congress, only a few days later, passed the Smith-Connally Bill, badly drawn and unsatisfactory as it was, over the President's veto. The overriding of the veto merely showed the intense dissatisfaction of Congress and the country with the Administration's labor policy or, rather, with its lack of one, just as all the instances above cited showed the complete willingness of the people and legislature to back the war policy in spite of their growing resentment against the handling of domestic affairs. It would seem impossible to read any other meaning into the record.

Meanwhile, and throughout the year, the threat of inflation, due to increased national income and a diminished amount of goods to be bought, evidently did not arise

"KEEP 'EM UP—WHILE I MAKE UP YOUR MIND!"
A cartoon published in *The Philadelphia Inquirer* during the so-called miners' "truce."

because of larger income for the rich, whose income had had been cut drastically—50 to 90 per cent—but because of the millions who were receiving larger incomes than they had ever known before, and who paid low taxes, or none. Nevertheless, the year was marked by a series of strikes in essential war industries. The number of man-hours lost in proportion to the total means nothing, since the effect depends on what the men involved were engaged in: making lip-sticks, steel, planes, ships, or providing fuel or steel, and so on.

Strikes occurred in motor works, ship-building plants, coal mines, steel works, rubber manufacture, rail transport, and other essential industries. On the whole the rank and file of labor were sound Americans, but the same cannot be said of many of their leaders. The Wagner Act, and certain decisions during the past few years by the Supreme Court, seemed to have put such leaders almost outside any possible legal control, either by government or their own union members. The most impertinently flagrant example was, perhaps, that of Petrillo, the head of the Musicians Union, who said he had nothing to negotiate because he intended to end entirely the business of transcriptions for radio. In other words, one individual labor leader stated bluntly that he planned to destroy an industry, and, thus far, he has been upheld by the law and the courts.

Throughout the year there were constant strikes and threats in the field of coal mining. On May 1, 530,000 miners struck, under the leadership of John L. Lewis, and the Government took over the mines. After an apparent settlement, the miners struck again, and Congress enacted the Smith-Connally anti-strike bill, passing it over the

President's veto, as already noted. Lewis consistently defied the President and Government, as well as public opinion, and when, toward the end of October, what he had called a "truce" expired, the miners went on strike again, following Lewis and not the President. The Government again took over the mines, but the war effort was seriously damaged and great numbers of innocent citizens suffered severely in their homes for lack of fuel.

The highly skilled rail unions having threatened, in December, to tie up all transportation, the Government, on the 27th, took over the roads, which under private management had done a magnificent war job. William Green, leader of the American Federation of Labor, criticized the seizure on the extraordinary ground that, though the men had voted to strike, they would not actually have done so. In other words, this leader bluntly said that, under his leadership, one of the finest bodies of skilled labor in America had merely tried to bluff the Government into paying higher wages by a threat of tying up, in mid-winter, all domestic transportation, thereby stopping transport for all war production and the export of matériel needed for 10,000,000 Americans in the armed forces, at home and abroad. Nothing more need be said. In spite of brave words about "holding the line" against inflation, establishing wages, prices and markets, the Government kept yielding to any labor leader who had brass enough to defy it and public opinion, regardless of the safety of the nation and of the future of organized labor itself, in the eyes of the nation, especially when the armed forces shall have come home.

The trouble was due to the fact that there was no clear-cut government labor policy. The Secretary of Labor faded out of the picture almost wholly. Other officials and Boards overlapped in their vague jurisdictions. The President took up each case as it came and often overrode his own appointees. Perhaps, as Vice-President Wallace told the Political Action Committee of the Congress of Industrial Organizations on January 15 of the following year, but referring to facts of 1943, "Many things which some of us have not been able to understand, have been explained by the fact that the President is keeping his mind on [winning the war and the peace] to the exclusion of anything else." No one man could possibly run the war, our foreign relations and all the domestic concerns of a people of 135,000,000 engaged in a war for survival. The extraordinarily complicated chart of various agencies, boards, etc., all heading up to the President, as compiled by the Office of War Information, explains much of the confusion which came to exist. As a result of this confusion and of the lack of clearly defined powers and responsibilities, the country itself became bewildered by a succession of resignations on the part of top-flight officials, and by quarrels between them, and even between Cabinet members, in public. As an example, we may cite the resignation of Chester C. Davis, whose appointment a few months earlier had been hailed by the country, and who, in resigning, expressed his opinion sharply as to the way things were being run. Among other examples was the open, and almost scandalously vituperative, quarrel between Jesse Jones and Vice-President Wallace, which ended in the President's removing them both from some of their official positions.

As far as can be judged from the acts of Congress, the polls taken of national opinion, and the election in November, the President was heartily supported by large majorities in his war and foreign policies but opposed for the increasing tangle into which domestic affairs had been brought. Also, showing the enormous advance, since the days of Woodrow Wilson, toward an international outlook, the Senate, a few days after election, voted 85 to 5 (and of the 5 opposers 2 were Democrats) to join in some form of international organization to maintain peace and security after the war, thus greatly strengthening the hands of the President in his negotiations with foreign nations. His own foreign missions, and especially that of Secretary of State Cordell Hull to Moscow (all of which will be mentioned in the section on the Fighting Front), were applauded and confirmed. In fact, I doubt if any other president since Washington has had such united and non-partisan support in his war and diplomatic policies as has Mr. Roosevelt.

However, even in war, the citizens, while supporting the Government abroad, reserve the right, and properly, to differ on domestic issues and policies. This was clearly

ALL'S NOT SO QUIET ON THE HOME FRONT
A cartoon by Draper in *The Richmond Times-Dispatch*.

revealed in the election of November 1943, although only
seven states and a few hundred municipalities voted for
candidates for important offices. The Republicans claimed
that the election should be fought on domestic issues,

63

whereas the White House made a personal issue of two of the leading candidates, W. C. Bullitt, former Ambassador to France and Russia, who ran for Mayor of Philadelphia and was defeated by over 64,000 votes; and Lieutenant General Haskell, who ran as a Democrat for Lieutenant Governor of New York State and was defeated by the Republican Joe R. Hanley by 450,000 votes. In New Jersey, Republican Walter E. Edge defeated the Democratic candidate, backed by "Boss" Hague, a supporter of the Administration, by 128,000 votes, and in the border Southern state of Kentucky, which had gone Democratic by 106,000 votes in 1939, the Republican candidate for Governor, S. E. Willis, won by a majority of a few thousand. The chief points to be noted are that the drift away from Roosevelt and the Democrats, so notable in the more important election of 1942, was continued; that the farmers were notably leaving the Democrats; that there was a split in the labor vote; and that the Negroes were in part going back to their former Republican allegiance. This was the comment of a backer of the Administration.

We may now turn to some other aspects of the Home Front. Rationing of certain foods and of other commodities began early in the year. The system was willingly accepted by our citizens and, on the whole, worked smoothly for a people who, above all others, were unaccustomed to red tape and to limitations on their own desires. It was a new and not a happy experience for Americans to be told what they could or could not buy even if they had the money. The tremendous job of registration and the handing out of ration books was handled by the teachers in the schools, who deserve much credit for this heavy extra duty. For the most part, at least, members of the local "ration boards," who had to do much, and often unpleasant, work among their neighbors, were unpaid volunteers. There was practically no grumbling on the part of the public, who willingly accepted the nuisances, and the cuts in living required, in a whole-hearted spirit of "win the war." As time went on, there were some "black markets," as there have been in every country, and some chiselling and hoarding, but not much, in view of the vast numbers who voluntarily submitted to the regulations.

In that respect, the Home Front made an admirable record. The chief complaints were with regard to the extreme shortage of gas for cars, mainly in the East, and the rationing, in December, of coal for heating homes, both of which, many felt, had been badly handled by the Administration. The life of all America, especially outside the big cities, had been built up in recent years around the car as an unfailing means of transport, and the sudden curtailment of this means, which was the only one in innumerable small towns and country districts, spelled real hardship, as well as abandonment of homes and disruption of accustomed social ways. The fact that the Government, through Fuel Administrator Ickes, had advised people to change their heating systems from oil to coal, undoubtedly was the cause of much of the resentment felt, in the colder sections of the country as winter set in, when coal was rationed and even unobtainable. The resentment mounted also against John Lewis and his miners, who had won an extra $1.50 a day by the year-long strikes and bickerings, at the cost of danger to the nation at war and of the discomfort and even death of many citizens.

In spite of strikes on the part of some labor, both labor and industrial management did an astoundingly fine job during the year. The chief credit for this must go to business and the individual American. When, at a dinner during the Teheran Conference, Marshal Stalin raised his glass to toast the marvel of American production which had saved the war for the Allies, that head of a nominally Communistic country (although far from it now in fact, despite American Communists, who lag behind Moscow in their ideas) was really toasting private enterprise and individual initiative.

The vast American industrial machine for production had been built up on that basis, and the sudden conversion, in amazingly short time, from the huge output of peace-time goods for 135,000,000 people to an all-out production for war was due to the adaptability both of the executives and of the men in plants, large or small, all over the land. General H. H. Arnold, Commanding General of our Army Air Forces, in his Report to the Secretary of War, spoke of America as having had a "most valuable secret weapon" in "the self-reliant, resourceful American soldier." These qualities do not develop overnight. They are built up by a whole life and way of life, which calls them forth, day after day and year after year. As the General also said, elsewhere in his thirty-page Report (dated January 4, 1944), and which every American should read, "Only in America would a piano company believe that it could convert to building airplane wings in a few months, and do it. A tire manufacturer built fuselages and tail surfaces. A former pickle plant turned out airplane skis and floats, and a manufacturer of girdles and corsets began making parachutes."

In 1939, our total production of army and commercial planes had been 2400. In the fiscal year 1940 the Army Air Force received only 886 planes of all types. When, after the fall of France, May–June of that year, the President asked for 50,000 planes annually, the figure seemed fantastic. A year and a half later, on the very anniversary of Pearl Harbor, American manufacturers completed their one hundred thousandth plane! This was only one item in that marvel of American production which Stalin toasted with fervor.

By the middle of 1943 we had built the greatest naval fleet the world had ever known, building in June of that year alone as many naval units as had been built in the whole first eighteen months of the defense program. The increase in our merchant shipping was even more startling. Especially in the shipyards of that genius discovered by the war, Henry J. Kaiser, ships were being built, from keel-laying to final fitting out, in a few weeks each. In spite of a shortage of manpower, we raised 5 per cent more foodstuffs than in the previous record year. We made 50 per cent more munitions in 1943 than even in 1942. With some 10,000,000 persons in the armed forces, the nation did its best to maintain a working force of 65,000,000, including 3,000,000 women new to their jobs. As we have said, at various times during the year over 600,000 coal miners went on strike, 350,000 steel workers, and 1,450,-000 rail workers voted to strike, and there was a spate of smaller, but essentially important, strikes, in many other key lines. A great deal of the record is obviously not good but, in general, the average American, from the lowest employee to the highest and most harassed executive, showed up well. On the whole, they did a job, in business, industry and agriculture, which they can be proud of and which augurs well for the future.

With output directed primarily to supplying the needs of a total war, the production of civilian goods had to be greatly curtailed. This, combined with another factor, the enormously stepped-up national income, naturally raised the specter of inflation. The President had frequently pointed to the danger, and talked about "holding the line" but, under pressure from labor, he failed to do so and, before the end of the year, even the so-called "Little Steel Formula," designed to keep wages in relation to the cost of living, was scrapped.

It is unfortunate, with so much talk of a "planned economy," that no statistics are accurate, and that even those

GOING UP!
A cartoon on the rising cost of living in *The Cleveland Plain Dealer*.

of the various government bureaus and departments vary greatly among themselves. However, such as are as good as I can get, indicate that since World War II started, a little over four years ago, wages of factory workers have increased 82.4 per cent and, as living costs in the same period rose only 27 per cent, the increase in "real wages" was very substantial, estimated at 44.1 per cent between August 1939 and June 1943. Specific examples from among factory workers have been given by Congressional Representative A. J. Engel of Michigan, as a result of study in 47 war plants. This study reveals such wages as: for a machine-gun assembler, from $4700 to $8741 a year; for a filer of machine guns, from $4200 to $8000 a year; and so on. Representative Engel also noted that an advertisement of the United States Employment Service called for "Dishwashers, waiters and kitchen men. Wages $250 a month, board and lodging. Olympic Commissary."

There is, however, a great difference in the position of the workers in this war, as compared with those in World War I. This should be stressed, for it may prove an important factor after the peace. In both wars, wages rose to hitherto undreamed-of levels, but in this war they have, to an amazing extent, been *saved*. I am a trustee of one of the oldest and largest of the Mutual Savings Banks of the country, located in a war-plant district, and I have had opportunity to watch this saving process, at first hand. We have been getting, *every day,* from eighty to ninety thousand dollars of workers' savings. I have also watched the rise in life-insurance policies, more than 50 per cent of those I follow being taken out by persons who never before had had insurance. Again, in the concerns I know about, here, from 90 to 100 per cent of the employees have voluntarily accepted a 10 per cent deduction from their wages for war bonds. Mortgages are being paid off so fast as to make a serious problem. As far as we can make out, there are two forces at work. First, people really learned a lesson from the sudden and severe depression of the 1930's. Then, also, owing to rationing and the scarcity of civilian goods and pleasures, people have not been able to spend their money. This means that there is a tremendous dammed-up demand for goods—homes, furniture, cars, washing machines, etc.—which will be released when the men come home and we turn from war to civilian production. This is a very marked, and important, characteristic of this war. Another point to be mentioned is the great drop in instalment buying. Owing partly to government regulations and partly to lack of goods, "consumer credit" throughout the whole nation dropped approximately 50 per cent in the two years, 1941–43. The release from this burden of debt on goods bought, already enjoyed, and partly worn out—a debt which emphasized the depression of the 1930's—will be another factor in the release of buying power, demand for goods, and increase of employment, when this war is over.

Another marked difference between conditions in this and in the last World War is symbolized by the difference between "War Debts" and "Lend-Lease." In the last war, we sold war supplies of all sorts to the Allies and ran up

71

bills as any merchant would do, creating the so-called "War Debts," only a fraction of which were ever paid and which were the cause, later, of much bitter international feeling. "Uncle Sam" was no "Uncle Shylock." It was just the way things were done then, as was emphasized in the famous remark of President Coolidge: "They hired the money, didn't they?" Perhaps the happiest augury for a better international order, when this war is won, is "Lend-Lease."

This time, the Allies have pooled their resources, genuinely pooled them. Accounts are kept, to some extent, although they are complicated, but no one is worrying very much about the final day of balancing and settlement. In fact, except for statistics, there may be no such day, and no one is worrying very much about that, either. The goods and services "lend-leased" embrace almost everything which we, or others of the United Nations, need to win the war. The United States, as the richest, both in cash and in available material resources, of the nations fighting for freedom, naturally heads the list on the ledger, but when, in March, Congress renewed the life of the Act, it raised no question about repayment. The vote was unanimous in the Senate, and 407 to 6 in the House. Under the able management of Edward R. Stettinius, Jr. (formerly Chairman of the Board of the U. S. Steel Corporation), who, at the end of 1943, was transferred from Lend-Lease to the post of Under-Secretary of State, Lend-Lease had not only proved one of the most successful

for the common cause. Hitler, whose method was to divide his victims and kill them one by one, had wrought this miracle of unified and unselfish joint effort. Almost all the nations have contributed. "Lend-Lease" accounts for about 12 per cent of the total war cost for us and for about 10 per cent of the same total for the British, but it is impossible to calculate exactly. British, Russians, Chinese, and others are getting things from us, and we are getting things, of different sorts, from them. We have given (we might as well, all of us, look at it that way) our billions here in the U. S. A., but the United Kingdom had given, up to June 30, 1943, over £2,250,000,-000. Canada, with less than a tenth of our population, had, after paying cash for all she got from us, made a free gift to our Ally, the United Kingdom, of $2,000,000,000. It is impossible to keep accurate accounts. The items are too multitudinous and never before was there any world undertaking so decentralized. The British—to cite only one nation—are using our ships and railways, and we are using theirs. We, in some places, are sending food to them, and some of our boys in the forces are eating meals at the cost of the Australians. The American forces in England, according to our Government, get 90 per cent of their medical supplies and hospital service from the British. So it has been, all over, in a bewildering complex of friendly transactions. What has been needed has been supplied, whether *to* or *by* Americans, British, Russians, Chinese, and all the rest. The world has never before known any-

74

thing like it. Americans may well feel proud that they inaugurated it. Let us hope that this extraordinary experiment may not be spoiled, at the end, by any resurgence of a huckstering spirit. Obviously Lend-Lease has not abolished nationalism and, after the war, we shall again compete for trade, but perhaps the example of what we have been doing, so potently and so successfully, will not be wholly forgotten.

We may mention here a few other planning schemes, on the Home Front, looking toward post-war conditions —plans of differing qualities and potentialities.

Other countries, notably Britain, which produced the Beveridge Plan for Social Security, and various other social services which have attracted much attention, were also looking ahead. In our country, the N.R.P.B. (National Resources Planning Board), to which the President in 1938 had appointed as Chairman his then seventy-five-year-old uncle, Frederic A. Delano, produced a Plan which aroused much criticism and perhaps contributed to the abolishment of the Board by Congress in March. The Plan called for a combination of governmental and private capital in industry, but also for "free enterprise," for a wide extension of social services, for continuing Federal controls of business for an indefinite number of years after the war should be over, and, incidentally, proposed a new "Bill of Rights," including such incompatibles as the "right" to security and the "right" to adventure, the "right" to the "amenities of life," meaning almost everything anyone could require, and at the same time "the right to live in a system of free enterprise, free from compulsory labor," etc. As Governor Dewey said of all the plans of all the planners, everyone seemed to believe that the post-war era could be made one "of full employment in which nobody has to work." Anyway, Congress cut off further payments to the N.R.P.B.

Another effort, this time at international planning, occurred in May. Our Government invited representatives of the United Nations, and of eight associated nations, to meet at Hot Springs, Virginia, to consider post-war food problems. Of this Conference, which might set the pattern for other important inter-Allied conferences, less is known historically than might be desired. For some reason, the Administration decided to exclude all members of the press. The American press, in contrast with the British press bureau, Reuter's, and the Russian press, kept scrupulously to the lines laid down by the Government, as it had already proved and was notoriously to prove later in the year, but the Standing Committee, representing 560 American and foreign journalists formally accredited to Congress, protested in vain against exclusion from any contact with the proceedings of the Conference as "the denial of legitimate news to the American public, and an abridgement of the freedom of the press." At the end of the meeting, June 3, a summary of its results was handed out, which indicated in a general way that food was important to man; that there would be shortages after the war; that some sort of organization should be set up to control production and prices; and that the governments should consider the matter further. The real results of the Conference may have been more important than the public could learn, with the army patrolling the grounds of the hotel where it was held.

Another international conference of representatives of the United Nations was held at Atlantic City, in November. It was organized under the name of the United Nations Relief and Rehabilitation Administration, and was added to the alphabetical jungle of administration organizations as U.N.R.R.A. This had as its province not only the problem of food but the general rehabilitation of devastated countries and, unhappily, a large part of the world has been devastated and will become more so. To indicate the magnitude of the problem, we may note that in Europe alone, over 20,000,000 persons, exclusive of war prisoners, had been torn from their accustomed homes and means of living. Forty-four of the United Nations were represented. A preliminary report, out of date by the time of the meeting, had been made in 1941, and Great Britain, Canada and the United States had all agreed to do their full share of the financing.

Although there were innumerable problems as to priorities, financing, the nature of population shifts, the obligations of each nation, organization, and so on, this meeting of delegates from forty-four nations proved more efficient, friendly and democratic than any other such

77

international gathering in history. A permanent war and post-war organization was set up, with ex-Governor Herbert H. Lehman of New York State as its Director. U.N.R.R.A., the first international post-war "operating agency" of the United Nations, expects to be in full working form by the spring of 1944. Although the "Big Four" —the U. S. A., Great Britain, Russia and China—obviously have large powers, the smaller nations are protected by the provisions that every nation shall have equal voice in council and committee meetings, and representatives of the smaller nations were appointed to chairmanships of many important committees. A sort of "world community chest" of $2,500,000,000, to be made up by the uninvaded nations, was set up for the period of transitional reorganization, estimated as extending for perhaps two years after the ending of war. Each nation agreed to contribute on the basis of one per cent of its national income for the fiscal year ending June 30, 1943. The quota of the United States for the whole period was $1,356,000,-000. As I have often pointed out, governments, political traditions, and "constitutions," written or unwritten, evolve from the necessities and natures of people and not from the blueprints made by theorists. The fact that U.N.R.R.A., arising out of the basic needs of so many different nations—nations of different races, languages and backgrounds—was, in 1943, organized so easily and democratically in a three weeks' meeting which might, a generation ago, have ended in an explosion of nationalistic ambitions and jealousies, may be another of the year's good auguries for the future. It was not the "Parliament of Man" or "the Federation of the World," as envisaged by the Victorian poet Tennyson, but it was natural and instinctive, not theoretical or synthetic.

Before leaving the Home Front and turning to the overseas Fighting Front we may mention a few points on which we cannot here enlarge. There were further changes in the personnel of the Supreme Court, so that by 1943 a large majority of the Bench had been appointed by Roosevelt during his unprecedented number of years in office. There were some important legal decisions, of a radical nature, with regard to labor and property, but perhaps the most important situation evolved as a result of so many appointments by one President, with his own ideas as to the sources from which the Justices of our highest judicial tribunal should be drawn. This was, that owing to their previous positions and activities, an unusual number of them had to disqualify themselves from sitting as judges in cases with which they had already, in one way or another, been connected, so that even a legal quorum of judges could not always be secured. This extremely dangerous situation, for so it might prove to be in some highly emotional and important case, led to various suggestions, such as changing the number required to deliver valid judgments, or, by others, that appointments should, with such possibilities in view, be made with more care.

Aside from the strikes and serious labor disturbances which occurred during the year, there were, from time to time, riots in various cities such as Los Angeles, Detroit, New York, and elsewhere. Although Mexican Spanish were, to some extent, involved in California, Negroes in Harlem, New York, and so on, the riots do not appear to have been racial, and were due, rather, to hoodlumism and to the general unrest, particularly of the younger generation, incident to war unsettlement. Indeed, in spite of the melting-pot nature of the United States, and the fact that the homeland nations of many of our citizens were fighting against one another, it may be set down as one of the encouraging features of the war years to date that racial dislikes and bitterness have been less in evidence than in any previous war.

A week before Christmas, the President returned from his extended trip and from the conferences in Africa and the Near East, and on Christmas Eve addressed the nation and the world over the radio from his home at Hyde Park. As was probably natural (but it underlines what we have said about his foreign and domestic policies), his chief interest was in foreign policies and in winning the war. Winning the war is, obviously, our first and most important concern, but to win on the Fighting Front we must have a united and smoothly working Home Front. The President made no mention of the strikes, not even of the railroad strike looming a few days ahead, but he did say that he thought "the New Deal," as a political slogan, was outmoded and belonged to the past and that, as he put it, "it was too narrowly domestic to fit the Administration's concern with a global war."

We may now turn to the Fighting Front. It would be stirring to write about individual actions, and of American heroism as displayed in them, but such actions have been too multitudinous to be set down in a few words if any general picture is to be painted.

It is obvious, in a global war, where forty-four nations are allied on our side, that what has happened in those nations is of importance to us. Looking ahead of the year 1943, we may note that the Argentine, the one country in the two American continents which had not joined all the others in breaking with, or fighting, the Axis, finally came in, to make the opinion of all the nations of the New World, from the North Pole to the South, unanimous. Later events, however, were to disturb this.

Also, we have spoken of the "Big Four," which includes Russia, and as there is some misunderstanding of that country, due perhaps to the Communist Party in our own, we may cite a few points. The tremendous help given to the Allied cause by the massive effort and ability of Russia is well known, but some of her domestic changes are less so. Some know that the "Comintern" was scrapped; that family life and marriage were put on their former Christian basis; that the Church was re-established; and so on, but the economic implications of the "Stalin Constitution" appear still not to be understood.

Interpreting the new Constitution, Professor Trainin, one of the leading Soviet jurists, says that "only efficient work can secure the progress of society. . . . Everyone possesses an equal right to work. But does it follow from this that everyone has the right to equal compensation for his work? Certainly not. . . . That is why the Constitution establishes the principle of compensation *according to the quantity and quality of the work done.* He who gives most to society receives most for his work. . . . Innovators . . . by introducing new methods of work . . . raise the productivity of labor by as much as 1000 per cent. . . . The Stalin Constitution now safeguards the rights of citizens to personal property. . . . Citizens have the right to personal ownership of their incomes from work, to their savings . . . [etc.]. They have the right to inherit personal property." I need not quote more. Apparently Russia, in twenty-five years, has gone full circle from Communism back toward capitalism, and this has been one of the major factors in winning this war for liberty against the Huns and Hitler's "honorary Aryans," the Japanese. Clearly, in a world now so closely interwoven any important changes of viewpoint among the peoples of the Allied nations, fighting for their lives, are of importance to us. We cannot discuss them all, but the fact that a nation of such vast population, resources and vigor as the Russian Soviets is now steering in these new directions is of such significance for the future of our own and of all Western civilization that it must be mentioned.

Our necessarily too brief account of the Fighting Front must be broken into even briefer sections. First, we must mention the international conferences which laid the foundations for Allied strategy and understanding, and which were, perhaps, even more disastrous for Axis prospects than any single action in the military field. The latter, again, must be divided into the Oriental and Western sections.

There were six major conferences during the year, and several minor visits paid by President Roosevelt, such as his stopping off, on his way home from Casablanca, to visit the Presidents of Liberia and Brazil, and his visit to President Comacho in Mexico, in April. Comment on the major Allied conferences must perforce be limited. The fact that they were held, and in a spirit of cordiality, mutual confidence and good-will, was in itself a stunning blow to Hitler, whose only hope and chief policy was to split his self-made enemies. As for Japan, the British, on a number of occasions during the year, gave their most solemn pledges not to lay down their arms until the Empire and the United States together had completely defeated that nation.

The conferences were, of course, concerned with the war, and largely with matters of concerted global strategy in all its aspects. Obviously, information could not be given to the enemy, and the communiqués issued had, therefore, to be brief and uncommunicative. We know a little more about some of the conferences, but not very much.

The first was held in January, between Prime Minister Churchill and President Roosevelt, at Casablanca in

SHADE OF VON TIRPITZ—"I, TOO, COUNTED ON THEM"
A cartoon in *The New York Times* in June, 1943, as Allied shipping increased.

North Africa. There, with the Tunisian campaign still unfinished, was planned the future invasion of Sicily and Italy. In May, Churchill came to Washington, and there was a conference in the White House. In August, the two leaders met again, in Washington, at the President's estate

84

at Hyde Park, and in Quebec. In the latter city the decision was taken to invade Europe in 1944. In October, Secretary of State Hull and Foreign Secretary Eden went to Moscow for conferences with each other and with the Russian Foreign Commisar Molotoff, as well as with Stalin. These talks were enormously fruitful, and when Hull returned to Washington he was met at the airport by the President and, later, received a great ovation from Congress when he reported to both Houses.

In November and December came the climax of the series. Roosevelt and Churchill went to the Near East, with elaborate diplomatic and military staffs, meeting first at Cairo with the Chinese Generalissimo Chiang Kai-shek and, later, at Teheran with Marshal Stalin of Russia. At these meetings plans were finally drawn for an all-out offensive in all quarters of the world. At the various conferences there were also formulated plans looking to the future. At Casablanca, the two leaders conferring there rejected peace feelers from the Nazis, and made the first of their demands for "unconditional surrender," a term which General Grant had made famous in our Civil War. It was after Quebec that demands were made for the punishment of the leading war criminals in the Axis countries, and at Cairo, in concert with China, it was decided to strip Japan of all territories she had forcibly annexed since 1895. At the end of the year many local problems, such as notably the troublesome Polish-Russian frontier line, were still left open for future adjustment.

Incidentally, we may here note certain new international alignments that came into being during 1943.

January 16: Iraq declared war on the Axis.

January 20: Chile severed relations with the Axis.

April 26: Poland and Russia severed diplomatic relations.

July 25: Mussolini fell from power.

October 12: Portugal gave the United Nations use of the Azores.

October 13: Italy re-entered the war as a co-belligerent of the Allies.

Military operations of the year can be sketched in skeleton form only. We may mention the Pacific theaters first. The Japanese, who, after Pearl Harbor, had seized islands in the Aleutian group off Alaska, threatening attacks on our mainland, were finally completely driven off in 1943. In January, we took Amchitka, sixty-nine miles east of Kiska. By May 31 we had secured possession of Attu, and in August we landed unopposed on evacuated Kiska, thus completing the operations.

In the farther and southwestern Pacific, army, navy, marines and air forces cooperated in the hardest kind of jungle and other terrain fighting, on islands—the Solomons, New Guinea, and others—scattered over great distances. For those who played their gallant parts in these undertakings such brief references as can here be made must seem, as indeed they are, utterly inadequate. Of all the fighting, perhaps two affairs stand out most markedly.

The first was the Battle of the Bismarck Sea, March 1–4. A Japanese convoy had been spotted making for New Guinea. For three days 162 Allied planes struck almost continuously at the Jap ships, their land-based fighters, and at their planes on the ground at various near-by airfields. Our losses were 1 bomber and 3 pursuit planes, with a total casualty list of 13 men, whereas the enemy's known losses were 61 planes, 22 ships, and an entire division of 15,000 men and their officers.

On November 22 occurred the other best-known feat of the year, though it came near being a disaster. This was the battle of Tarawa, which Lt. Colonel Evans F. Carlson, in command of the Marines, described as the toughest job ever tackled by that branch of the service in its 168 years of fighting all over the world. This time, the amphibious expedition was against certain small islands of the Gilbert group, northeast of the Solomons. Through a series of mishaps, impossible to foresee, landing on the little atoll of Tarawa proved an extremely difficult and bloody affair, the Marines having to wade ashore for some 300 yards in the face of murderous mortar and machine-gun fire. Practically all of the 3000 to 4000 Japs on the island were finally killed, but our own losses were very heavy.

Under the leadership of General Claire L. Chennault, our planes are making themselves felt in China, but the main problem in that sector is that of supplies. Ever since the Japanese got Burma and cut the Burma Road, all supplies have had to be flown in. The difficulties of supply are almost incredible but are being met, as well as possible, largely by American fliers. First, supplies have to travel 10,000 miles by sea; then, with many intervening difficulties of transport, they have to be carried by plane, often flying by instrument and in atrocious weather, over mountain ranges 17,000 feet high, from Assam to the Chinese forces. If a mistake is made flying in one direction, there is a crash into 22,000-foot peaks, while a mishap, flying the other way, lands the flier in Japanese Burma.

In the European theater we may mention first the operations of our fliers based on Britain. The heavy bomber command of the R.A.F. was designed for night missions, while the American Flying Fortresses and Liberators were planned for daylight precision raids. As the year advanced, operations by both the Anglo-American forces became more and more effective and frequent until, by its end, they were of almost daily and nightly frequency, weather alone interfering. Not only had Berlin, the capital of Nazi misrule, met almost complete destruction, but vast havoc had been wrought on key points of German transportation and military production. As the production of the United States and its Allies grew by leaps, that of Germany declined, but it would appear, though there is a school of military thought which takes a contrary view, that air power—enormously effective as an auxiliary—cannot alone end a war. Throughout the year, Russia, which had been winning magnificent vic-

TWO GREAT CONFERENCES OF 1943

Top: The Cairo Conference. *Left to right:* Generalissimo Chiang Kai-shek, President Roosevelt, and Prime Minister Churchill. *Bottom:* The Teheran Conference. *Left to right:* Premier Stalin, President Roosevelt, and Prime Minister Churchill.

U. S. MARINES GO OVER THE TOP AT TARAWA

Leathernecks storm a Jap-held airport, in taking the two-mile-long atoll, a decisive step in the attempt to crack Japan's central Pacific defenses.

tories on the eastern front, at great cost both to herself
and to the enemy, had been calling for a second land
front on the west. By the latter part of 1943 the menace

COMING EVENTS CAST THEIR SHADOWS BEFORE
As Marcus in *The New York Times* pictured the Churchill-Roosevelt conference.

of the submarine had been so largely met and overcome
as to make comparatively safe the transport of vast numbers of men and huge quantities of supplies, and we may
now turn briefly to the progress of our overseas land

89

forces. Obviously, all the Allies are working for the same end, and if we speak chiefly of the Americans, it is not that we wish to ignore the great achievements of others but merely because of the nature of these annual additional chapters in what is primarily an American history.

In the preceding chapter, we spoke of the North African campaign, and of the long pursuit by the British of the German and Italian armies under Rommel, across the whole stretch of northern Africa. We spoke of the landing of the joint Anglo-American expeditionary forces for the Battle of Tunisia, as it is called. In the winter and spring of 1943 that battle took on a new form, and was finally decided.

Early in February, General Eisenhower was given supreme command of all forces in North Africa. Meanwhile, Rommel's German Afrika Corps, with its Italian auxiliaries, had steadily retreated to the Mareth Line in Tripolitania. On the arrival there also of the British Eighth Army under General Sir Harold Alexander, the British, too, came under the command of Eisenhower, and thereafter the British and Americans—in Africa, Sicily, and Italy—were to work in the closest harmony. It was reported, somewhat later, that an officer said to the American commander: "Well, the two teams work together pretty well." His immediate reply was: "Two teams? There is only one team here." The answer did not spring from any egoism on the part of Eisenhower. It simply stated a fact, and a happily remarkable one.

Those of us who served overseas in World War I and recall the heartburnings over efforts to keep the British, French and American units and armies separate, can better appreciate the extraordinary spirit of unity and comradeship in which British and Americans got together during the North African campaign and its sequels. If much credit is due to Eisenhower's personality and tact, much is due also to the officers of both nations in the army, navy and air services, who, in this post or that, from bottom to top, worked as though it were all just "one team." Credit goes also to the men of the rank and file, who came to know and appreciate each other's qualities as fighters and comrades. Allies have fought side by side in earlier wars, but never before has there been anything quite like this, or like the spirit of Lend-Lease of which we have already spoken.

The junction of the veteran Afrikan Corps with Von Arnim's command in Tunisia gave the enemy strength for offensive strokes, and in the third week of February the Germans broke through the Kasserine Pass and threatened the whole Allied position. In earlier wars, "battles"—Waterloo, Gettysburg, etc.—were often a matter of hours or, at most, of a day or two. In this war, they are of enormous scope and may, as their names, "the Battle of Britain" and the "Battle of Tunisia," indicate, last for months.

According to the official report of General Marshall, Chief of Staff of the U. S. Army, the last phase of the

Battle of Tunisia opened on March 20 when, under terrific attacks from the air and land forces, the enemy began retreat. Axis communications for supplies and reinforcements from Italy were largely cut off by attacking planes. Week after week, the enemy yielded one point after another, retreating finally into the Bon Peninsula. By May 10 the last resistance had been shattered. All Axis forces surrendered and the entire African continent was freed of the enemy, who had lost all their African colonies—German and Italian—and all their armies and supplies. 242,415 German and Italian troops, with all their equipment, were surrendered. A French army, which had newly been created, celebrated its first birthday by capturing nearly 50,000 of the enemy. The Mediterranean was again open to Allied shipping.

As we have stated, the decision to invade Sicily and thence the Italian mainland, when Africa should be cleared, had been made at the Casablanca Conference, in January. That invasion was, therefore, the next step. One interesting point had been revealed during the Tunisian campaign. Many of the German troops were picked and seasoned men from crack regiments, who had been told to fight to the last man. They did fight well and bitterly, as General Arnold, commanding all American Air Forces, stated in his Report for 1943, but, he added, "when it became clear to them that they would lose the battle, they gave up at once." The Italians, who had never had their heart in the war, and who hated the Germans, gave up readily. In Sicily, it was to be shown that they did so even gladly.

In the next move of the Italian campaign, the coordination of air, sea and land forces, which had stood the Allies in such good stead, was continued and, although the first land troops disembarked on the shore of Sicily on July 7, by August 17 the last Axis troops had surrendered, or fled across the Strait of Messina. By September 14, the Allies were ready to invade Italy itself and, on that date, landed on the beachhead at Salerno. The Battle of Tunisia had changed into the Battle of Rome, which is still in progress, and can better be considered in our next year's chapter. In the long-drawn-out battles which characterize World War II the daily moves cannot be detailed and they acquire little significance for the layman until the work of months can be seen in perspective and as a whole. Nor can we here recite the military actions in other sectors, such as the Near East. Such outlying sections by no means constitute "side-shows" but all of them help to form the pattern of global strategy which this war demands.

All the military action and industrial production, whose outlines we have been able merely to suggest rather than to describe in detail, called for a great extension of governmental functions and of expense. They would have done so, in any case, even if war were not notoriously costly and wasteful. Again, during this greatest of all wars, we have been indulging, for better or worse as individuals may regard it, in the added luxury of a social revolution.

We may note the cost and complexity, in two brief ways. It has been estimated that by the middle of the year now under review the cost of the war reached the astronomical figures of over $12,000,000 an hour, $289,000,000 a day or $7,000,000,000 a month. Once every few years, for the benefit of our readers and in order to enable them to understand the news in the papers, we have given a list of the more important Government agencies, with their alphabetical designations. Below is the current list, far from complete.

ABNPHSBM—Advisory Board on National Parks, Historic Sites, Buildings and Monuments
ANMB—Army-Navy Munitions Board
APB—Aircraft Production Board
ARA—Agricultural Research Administration
BAE—Bureau of Agricultural Economics
BLS—Bureau of Labor Statistics
BWC—Board of War Communications
CAA—Civil Aeronautics Administration
CAB—Civil Aeronautics Board
CCC—Commodity Credit Corporation
CCPA—Committee for Congested Production Areas
CFB—Combined Food Board
CMA—Coal Mines Administration
CPRB—Combined Production and Resources Board
CRMB—Combined Raw Materials Board
CSAB—Combined Shipping Adjustment Board
DLC—Disaster Loan Corporation
DPC—Defense Plant Corporation

DSC—Defense Supplies Corporation
FBI—Federal Bureau of Investigation
FCA—Farm Credit Administration
FCC—Federal Communications Commission
FDA—Food Distribution Administration, also Food and
    Drug Administration
FDIC—Federal Deposit Insurance Corporation
FEA—Foreign Economic Administration
FEPC—Committee on Fair Employment Practice
FHA—Federal Housing Administration
FPA—Food Production Administration
FPC—Federal Power Commission
FPHA—Federal Public Housing Administration
FSA—Farm Security Administration, also Federal Security
    Agency
FTC—Federal Trade Commission
FTZB—Foreign-Trade Zones Board
FWA—Federal Works Agency
HOLC—Home Owners' Loan Corporation
ICC—Interstate Commerce Commission
IWC—Inland Waterways Corporation
LOPM—Liaison Office for Personnel Management
MAB—Munitions Assignments Board
MRC—Metals Reserve Company
NHA—National Housing Authority
NIC—National Inventors' Council
NMCB—National Munitions Control Board
NLRB—National Labor Relations Board
NPPC—National Power Policy Committee
OCD—Office of Civilian Defense
OCIAA—Office of Coordinator of Inter-American Affairs
OCR—Office of Civilian Requirements

ODT—Office of Defense Transportation
OEM—Office for Emergency Management
OES—Office of Economic Stabilization
OFAR—Office of Foreign Agricultural Relations
OPA—Office of Price Administration
OPRD—Office of Production Research and Development
ORD—Office of the Rubber Director
OSRD—Office of Scientific Research and Development
OWI—Office of War Information
OWM—Office of War Mobilization
OWU—Office of War Utilities
PAW—Petroleum Administration for War
PRC—Petroleum Reserves Corporation
REA—Rural Electrification Administration
RFC—Reconstruction Finance Corporation
RRC—Rubber Reserve Company
SEC—Securities and Exchange Commission
SFA—Solid Fuels Administration
SWPC—Smaller War Plants Corporation
TFDRL—Trustees of the Franklin D. Roosevelt Library
TVA—Tennessee Valley Authority
UNRRA—United Nations Relief and Rehabilitation Administration
USCC—United States Commercial Company
WDC—War Damage Corporation
WFA—War Food Administration
WLB—War Labor Board
WMC—War Manpower Commission
WPB—War Production Board
WRA—War Relocation Authority
WRCB—War Relief Control Board
WSA—War Shipping Administration

I N the previous chapter I stated that the year 1943 was
the most complex in our history for any recorder to
recount, and that it might prove to be the turning
point in favor of the United Nations and freedom. It did
prove to be the latter but I am not sure that it was the
former as I undertake, in a limited space, to tell the tale
of 1944 during which the global war extended and intensified, and in which we had, here at home, an epochal
Presidential election. We begin with domestic affairs.

During the second week of January, Mr. Roosevelt sent
two Messages to Congress; one, of four thousand words,
was the one called for in the Constitution, which states
that the President shall "from time to time give to the
Congress information on the state of the Union." Ever
since the first term of George Washington this has been,
each year, the first message transmitted from the Executive to the Legislature. The other, of eight thousand words,
was in connection with the Budget for the ensuing year.
The two, and one other, may be considered here together,
because, even if somewhat vaguely, as might be natural
in a year with a Presidential campaign at the end of it,
they expressed in combination the ideas of the Administration as to the present and the future.

Considered as one, the Messages were interesting both

for what they said and did not say. For example, Mr. Roosevelt gave some startling figures as to the cost of war and normal government expenses. The war, he said, including the pre-Pearl Harbor defense program and post-Pearl Harbor operations, had cost $153,000,000,000 to the end of December 1944. This was six times the cost of World War I, $41,000,000,000 more than all the money spent by the Federal Government from 1791 to 1932 (when Roosevelt was elected), and represented nearly $1200 for every man, woman and child in the United States. Moreover, the President estimated that the actual war-cost would rise to over two hundred billions by June 30. In addition, Congress was asked to appropriate ten billions for the ordinary peace-time government agencies.

The war-cost, the President correctly said, mirrored "a gigantic effort," adding that in the output of munitions alone our production now almost equalled that of all the rest of the world combined. He expressed satisfaction with the progress of the war in its military aspects but added that our very victories were tending to slacken the war effort at home. He complained that Congress, with a national election in view in a few months, was loath to lay heavy enough taxes but he did not suggest that the Administration, obviously for the same reason, was equally loath to adopt a firm stand on labor, though he did mention some strikes, such as those in the coal and steel industries, and the threatened rail strike, which would have completely hamstrung the entire war effort and cut off the stream of supplies going to our forces overseas.

As we noted at the end of the chapter on the previous

year, Mr. Roosevelt, at a news conference, had discarded further use of the term "New Deal" as no longer adequate to cover the situation and his plans and interests. His several January Messages may therefore be taken to express his own new orientation. In general, they were vague, but some aspects stand out. They were not conciliatory to Congress; they were somewhat hostile to business; and they handled labor with delicacy.

To come to some of the details, he proposed a so-called "five-point plan."

1. The President asked for a law "which will tax all unreasonable profits, both individual and corporate," and added that the tax bill being considered by Congress "does not begin to meet this test." The bill then being considered called for a tax rate on "excess profits" of 95 per cent and was so worded that practically no one in the country could have a net income, after taxes, of more than $25,000, a measure advocated also by the Communist Party.

2. The President said that for "two long years I have pleaded with the Congress to take undue profits out of the war." There had been since 1942 a renegotiation law, administered by Presidential appointees, with no right of appeal.

3. He asked for a cost-of-food law which would place a floor under the prices farmers would receive and a ceiling on the prices consumers would pay, which virtually meant a subsidy to farmers of about $1,100,000,000 a year.

4. He asked for a re-enactment of the 1942 statute stabilizing farm prices, without which, he predicted, there would be "price chaos by summer."

5. He asked for a national service law which would "make available for war production or any other essential services every able-bodied adult in the nation." We might add that ours is the only leading nation in the war which has not passed some such service legislation.

The President also considered post-war problems. He spoke of the difficulties of reconversion from a war to a peacetime economy. He envisaged a vast government spending program, including the building of 34,000 miles of super-highways, and asked for a new eight-point Bill of Rights.

There have been a number of new Bills of Rights suggested either to supersede or overlay the original so-called Bill embodied in the first ten amendments to the Constitution, but this one received the official endorsement of the President in his Message on the Budget. It included the right to a job; to earn money for adequate food, clothing and recreation; of farmers to a decent living; of business men to be free of unfair competition; and the rights to a home, to protection in old age, during sickness and unemployment, and to a good education. It was not explained how all these desirable ends, described as "rights," were to be obtained or who was to pay for them. As was to be expected, public reaction to the several Messages was very mixed, depending on whether they were regarded from a merely political or from a serious economic standpoint.

Unfortunately the country, for the second time in its history—the first time being during Lincoln's second campaign—was confronted with a national election in the midst of the crisis of a war for survival. An important difference lay in the fact that, apart from whatever contrasts there may have been in the temperaments and ambitions of the two men, election had meant only the normal second term for Lincoln but it meant a fourth term for Franklin Roosevelt. In any history of the year, this situation deserves comment.

As long as the two-term tradition lasted, which was about a hundred and fifty years after Washington's inauguration, the President was independent, especially in his second term, nobody expecting any other. But now that a President has been elected for a third and a fourth term, this situation has changed. Just as a Representative in Congress, wholly dependent on pleasing the pressure groups which deliver the votes in his limited constituency, has to "go along" to a considerable extent, so now the incumbent of the Presidency, if the number of terms and perhaps the ambition to fill them are unlimited, is going to be forced to do so also. All of these factors, including the popular election of Senators, have been contributing to change our form of government from one made up of fairly independent thinkers to one of officials, of all grades, peculiarly sensitive to pressure and vote-getting.

Of course, there have always been group and sectional interests, such as the manufacturing tariff group, the farm bloc, the "Silver States," the Prohibition group, the veterans, and many others; but the more efficient political methods of pressure groups, combined with our gradually changing form of government, have been tending greatly to enhance the power of "pressure politics."

There is one more point which is a key to help unlock the history of 1944 and possibly of a good many years to come. If it is true that our entire government (Executive, Legislature and even Federal Judiciary) is going to be increasingly affected by pressure, it is important to know from whence that pressure may come, so as to get a sense of direction. Two trends have been notable in America in the past half-century or so—industrialization and urbanization. No American group, occupational or of about the same economic or social level, has ever voted unanimously alike. There have always been currents of individual and conflicting interests.

Where pressure comes in is in being able to deliver enough votes of voters who, from opinion or discipline, can swing the *balance* of an election in one important district or State. Capitalists may be high-tariff or free-trade, depending on what their capital is invested in. Industrial workers want high wages (which means high prices for manufactured goods), but low food costs. Farmers want low prices for manufactures but high prices for their food products; and so it goes. Business men are not united, but very vulnerable because of large fixed investments in plants. Farmers are scattered and notoriously independent. The big chance to build consolidated groups is among industrial workers and in the big cities, so that we have developed the powers of the trades-union leaders and of the city bosses and city machines, which are too well-known to name. All these factors are not new. Many have been operating for a long time but as they all combine, together with the popular election of Senators, an indefinite number of terms for the Executive, and a Judiciary largely the appointees of only one man and party, we are beginning to see more clearly the "shape of things to come." All have come about naturally. Even a fourth term *may* have been essential under the conditions. However, 1944 marked a more or less climacteric year, and now we touch on some of the high-spots more definitely.

Before going on to discuss the labor problem we may speak of a spectacular break between the Executive and the Congress in February. There was nothing especially novel about this. There has always been a tug-of-war between these two branches of government, dominance passing from one to the other depending upon the abilities and ambitions of each. But this conflict had new elements which have sprung from new conditions.

Briefly what happened was this. According to competent observers bad feeling between the President and Congress had been on the increase for some months. We are too near the events to appraise them with full historical knowledge, and can merely report them. After many months of delay Congress, in mid-February, passed a tax law. It was, indeed, inadequate, but that does not explain the extraordinary tone which the President adopted. He had originally asked for over $10,000,000,000 and the Bill, according to Congress, provided $2,300,000,000 or, by the Treasury computation, about $100,000,000 less. The President, denying the validity of both sets of figures, cut the result by another billion, and more. In his brief but almost unexampled Veto Message, he attacked the integrity of Congress and the ability of his own Secretary of the Treasury. He described the measure as "not a tax bill, but a tax relief bill providing relief not for the needy but for the greedy." Party leaders and the stanchest followers of Mr. Roosevelt were amazed and angered.

Without going into further details, we may say that he had attacked and impugned the motives of his strongest supporters, such as Morgenthau of the Treasury, Democratic Senate leader Barkley, Doughton the Democratic head of the Ways and Means Committee of the House, and others. No one could quite understand.

Some commentators suggested that the President, who was increasingly referring to himself less by that title than by that of "Commander in Chief," was deliberately seeking a break with Congress and the support of the soldier vote for a fourth term. Chairman Doughton said in the House that, knowing the President as he did, he could not believe he had written the Message. It had, he added, "none of his usual dignified, courteous, and helpful approach in matters of state. I see in this document the hands of a group of individuals not in any sense responsive to the will of the American people." In the Senate, Barkley, in an excoriating speech, resigned from his position of Majority Leader and said that the President's message was "a calculated and deliberate assault upon the legislative integrity of every member of the Congress." He said also a lot more! The Presidential veto was defeated in the Senate by a vote of 72–14 and in the House by 299–95. Mr. Roosevelt, evidently frightened by the terrific repercussion of his words, in all directions, begged Barkley to remain, and Barkley was upheld by the Senate, of which his party unanimously re-elected him as a real Majority Leader rather than as a rubber stamp for Administration policies. As a whole, the resounding episode probably did good and helped to restore proper balance between the Executive and leaders in Congress.

On the other hand, the amount raised in taxes by the Bill was, as we have said, inadequate. Both the President and the Secretary of the Treasury had properly asked for more but they had made no helpful suggestions, for political reasons which are part of the story of the trend of the times to which we have referred. They could not agree with each other, or with Congress, as to the sources from which additional revenue should be drawn. The President apparently thought only in terms of increasing the income taxes on individuals in the higher brackets and the profits tax on corporations, both of which had risen to points which endangered future economic progress. He would not consider a sales tax, which would spread small taxes over great numbers of people. Morgenthau had, on one occasion, rightly said that "we know where the bulk of the new money lies and where, therefore, lies the greatest danger of inflationary pressure. Today, four-fifths of all the income of the nation is going to people earning less than $5000 a year." That, of course, was true but, well, shall we put it in plain English and say the Administration wanted votes as well as money?—which brings us to another angle of the trend—its labor policy.

In regard to the Government's labor policy, good, bad or lacking altogether, as it sometimes has seemed in 1944, all three branches of the government—the Administration headed by the Chief Executive, the Congress, and the new Supreme Court as almost wholly reconstituted by the President during his twelve years of office and appointing power—have to bear their respective shares of responsibility. What does the record reveal?

First of all, our shift-over from peacetime production

of peace goods, in the most peace-loving perhaps of all the nations, to a wartime footing which has made the United States the greatest military power on the globe has amazed the world. Allowing what you will to government, there were other and very vital factors playing their parts. We are a democracy, with the highest standard of living of any people. That simple statement involves a good many subsidiary points. We can note some.

In a real and successful democracy, men and women learn to be self-reliant and to be *citizens,* not robot subjects. Our democracy has been steadily growing in maturity, and although in this war we have drafted over ten million citizens into the armed forces to face intense hardship, discomfort and death—or worse—there have been no "draft riots," as there were eighty-two years ago during the Civil War. The high standard of living for all has its implications also. There has, for many centuries past, always been "Big Business," but in the Old World, Big Business meant for the most part big fortunes for the few and high-priced goods for narrow markets. In the New World, owing to many favoring circumstances, "Big Business" came to mean "more goods for more people," lower-priced and higher quality, which, mostly in the preceding and present generation, have spelled our American form of large-scale mass production. From this and democracy came our "know-how" on the part of executives, our vast capacity to produce, and the sense of citizenship on the part of the people at large, and thus the "miracle of production," as Stalin called our achievement in this war. I do not like labels, but taking "labor" in its popular sense as applying to those who work in a factory or elsewhere for daily or weekly wages, I do not think there is any difference, on the whole, in sense of citizenship or patriotism, between "labor" and other elements in the community; and, what is more, I do not think there is a "Labor Vote." We all believe in democracy, self-government and America. (Leave out the fringes.) Now we come to our problem again as it is being revealed.

Early in the war, labor made a "no-strike" pledge for the duration. It has not been wholly adhered to by any means. In 1944, the year here under review, there were many ghastly examples to the contrary. But there have been such in other countries also as, notably, in England, which has been as a whole the most steadfast in its five years and more of war. Perhaps the answer to many things is Mark Twain's remark that "there is a lot of human nature in man." All in all, in America, labor has behaved well, but there *have* been inexcusable strikes endangering the lives of our forces overseas and threatening the success of the war effort. We need not list them all.

One of them, the one which caused the most resentment at home and perhaps among the armed forces, was that of 1800 foremen at the Wright Aeronautical Corporation in New Jersey in November, stopping work on the making of B–29 bombers. These foremen were highly paid and presumably especially intelligent. The Administration has persistently minimized the strikes by speaking only of "hours of man power" lost but it is obvious that it makes a great difference at what stage in the production of critical material the man-power hours *are* lost. The Foremen's Association of America, which is unaffiliated, was also included earlier in the year, in May, in a strike which made an estimated 60,000 idle in war work in Detroit.

Trying to stick to the facts and avoiding theory or personal prejudice, what do we find with regard to the increasing labor chaos as the war approaches its climax? First, let me repeat, what is only opinion and not capable of statistical proof, that I believe labor, in the accepted sense, to be as patriotic as any other group. It has, however, second, become split into conflicting parties, the A. F. of L., the C.I.O., and so on. We have not a long tradition of Trade Unionism or a strong Labor Party, as in England. Many of the strikes were "jurisdictional" rather than against employers or the public. "Labor Leaders," so-called, big or little, good or bad, have tended to play their lone hands much as the non-social-minded capitalists of, say, the 1870's did. Third, there has been the effect of government measures, including those of all three governmental branches.

The Wagner Act (1935) had given labor vast privileges denied to employers. The Smith-Connally Act, adopted by majority votes of both parties in both Houses of Congress in June 1943, has had fantastic results. Under this law, ostensibly designed to prevent strikes in wartime in essential industries, the government itself must count the ballots of the workers and, so, if the vote is for a strike, makes itself to a certain extent the official sponsor. On the other hand, there cannot be a strike against a government-operated plant, so that the strikers can force the government to take over operation if they choose, as happened in the case of the coal strike in the spring. The Smith-Connally Act was not a law against strikes but, practically, a law to enable the workers to decide whether or not they should force the government to take over. These facts are pertinent, because although they proved important in 1944 they may prove even more so in 1945.

We come now to the general attitude of the Government as a whole. We have mentioned Congress, which in spite of all criticism has refused to amend either the Wagner or the Smith-Connally Acts. The Supreme Court has trailed along, in spite of a continued succession of the formerly much criticised 4–5 and other split decisions. With regard to what is more particularly called "the Administration," we have mentioned the tendency to minimize news of all strikes. When John L. Lewis defied the President and Government, he "got away with it," and the President admitted he could do nothing. In the course of the year, the two disputes which attracted the most public attention were those with James Cæsar Petrillo, of the Musicians Union, and with Montgomery Ward & Co., both of which we must mention, as they held attention during most of the period covered by this chapter, and indicate trends following earlier legislation and policies.

We may note, by way of introduction, a victory scored by John L. Lewis and his mine workers. Originally, the Wage-Hour Act of Congress was supposed to stabilize wages, except for a few workers receiving sub-marginal pay. The "Little Steel Formula" was one of its accompaniments. However, late in March, just before the deadline of April 1, Lewis got an increase under the subterfuge of "portal to portal pay," although the Union had agreed in 1940 with the operators that such a method of computation would "result in complete chaos." The actual time of each miner was not figured but an "average" time for all was agreed upon, which simply meant a rise in the wages of all, and was approved by the Supreme Court with an eloquent plea by Justice Murphy, who had been appointed to the Court after his term as Governor of Michigan following the sit-down strikes in that State and a period in the Cabinet. In the previous year, 1943, when Lewis had refused to obey an order of the War Labor Board, the President had been asked what he would do, and he answered with the query whether he should write a nice little note on pink paper, saying, "Dear Mr. Lewis, I hope you will sign the contract."

The lesson had apparently not been ignored, and so, enter Cæsar Petrillo, head of a labor union, the American Federation of Musicians, so-called. The case goes back some years. Let us make it as short as we can without distorting the facts, and those are all we have to report. According to the War Labor Board, in its findings as of March, the "union" appears to be a very loose organization of followers of Petrillo, of which only one out of three depended on music for a livelihood. Petrillo had claimed that "canned music," *i.e.,* phonograph records, juke boxes, and so on, were depriving musicians of their living, and had demanded, as early as June 1942, that the companies concerned pay specified sums of money to the union for its "employment fund." Under Petrillo's ultimatum and orders, the making of records had stopped August 1, 1942. He allowed no member of the union to take part in such production, and apparently he had so built, himself up, with the help of all departments of government, that he could prevent any musician not a member of his union from getting any job at all.

Since 1937 his musicians' wages had increased 50 per cent to 110 per cent, running as high as $18 an hour. Unions are not liable for accounting as are business enterprises but the N.W.L.B. estimated (1944) that the union (subject to Petrillo) was receiving $3,000,000 a year outside of wages. The size of the prize that Petrillo was after may be indicated by an estimated juke-box business of $200,000,000 a year and the fact that the three major phonograph companies had been making 130,-000,000 records a year.

What happened down the line? In 1942, Thurman Arnold, then Assistant Attorney General of the U. S., filed a suit in an Illinois District Court asking for an injunction to prevent Petrillo from carrying out his ultimatum. The old Norris-LaGuardia Act of Congress forbade injunctions in labor disputes. The Department of Justice lost its case. Later, through Elmer Davis, the War and Navy Departments *asked* Petrillo to *allow* the making of records because their absence was having a bad effect on the morale of service men at the front. Petrillo said No. The U. S. Senate investigated the situation and cross-examined Petrillo, only to get the same answer. In June, 1944, the War Labor Board issued an order to Petrillo to desist. Same answer. On October 4, the President of the United States telegraphed to Petrillo asking him please, even if he thought the decision wrong, "to accept the directive orders of the National War Labor Board. What you regard as your loss will certainly be your country's gain." The country gasped at this, but again Mr. Petrillo refused to rescind his ultimatum.

It is all a much longer story, including the opinion of a Circuit Court of Appeals that there had been conspiracy and coercion, and the decision of the Supreme Court that, in view of Congressional legislation, there was nothing to be done about it. Later, two of the leading recording companies capitulated and paid royalties to Mr. Petrillo or to his union. We had reached the point where one labor leader, motivated by the lust for money or power, could tell the entire American people what music they would hear and how, and defy the Government. Executive policy over a period of years, the Courts, Congress and the W.L.B., all have had a part in this.

The other leading case of the year, which shared the limelight, was quite different. Montgomery Ward & Co. is one of the largest businesses in the country, one of two leading old-established mail-order houses which reach into almost every village of the land. They got into trouble with the W.L.B. in November 1942, for having refused to sign a contract with the C.I.O. union as ordered by the Board. We have noted that when Lewis refused to sign and called an order of the Board "infamous" he was allowed to have his own way, and Mr. Petrillo has certainly had his.

A business, however, according to legislation and court rulings, is in a very different position from a labor union, both as to obeying laws and accounting for money handled. When the W.L.B. applied to the President to help them enforce their order against Montgomery Ward there was also a very different reaction than in the cases of Lewis, Petrillo and other labor leaders and unions. The President immediately sent a telegram which read, in part, "As Commander-in-Chief in time of war . . . I direct Montgomery Ward & Co. to comply without further delay." They complied. Although they had always, on principle, opposed the closed shop, they signed the contract demanded by the C.I.O. for the year, as ordered.

When the contract expired, the W.L.B. demanded that it be continued together with the "check-off" and other points which did not deal with wages. The company, whether wisely or not, refused until a poll of the employees had been taken. The issue became somewhat confused, although the main lines remained clear. The President again intervened, and Sewell L. Avery, Chairman of the Board of Montgomery Ward & Co., defied the order. The Post Office refused to deliver mail to the mail-order house, and the President ordered the army to take over the property. Avery, the sixty-nine-year-old Chairman, still defiant, was seized in his private office, carried out bodily and set in the street by soldiers of the army detailed for the unpleasant job. The W.L.B. had been unwise. Montgomery Ward may have been ill-advised, but the pictures in the newspapers of soldiers carrying an old, nationally known and respected business man out of his office to dump him on the street, as contrasted with the treatment accorded Lewis and Petrillo, raised a storm of protest and comment.

The whole thing was a mess but brought to light many complications in our present form of government and in our current Administration. We were supposed to have three departments of government, acting as checks on one another, the Executive, Judicial and Legislative. Owing to accidents of death and to the unexpectedly long term of office of the President, who would have been in office for sixteen years had he lived out his fourth term, the Supreme Court, which is the pinnacle of the Judicial system and the court of last resort, has been almost wholly made up of appointees of the Executive. During the past dozen years, Congress has abdicated many of its powers to the Executive by giving him almost unlimited powers and creating "Boards," or what you will, whose members are appointed by him. Many of these have assumed not only Executive and Legislative powers but also Judicial. Some of the most careful students of America and its institutions have pointed to this "government by commission" as perhaps the most dangerous element in current American public life.

In addition, we are at war, a deadly war in which all our national ways and institutions are at stake, a fact that too many Americans still appear to ignore. The war powers of a President are ill-defined but are supremely important and essential. They have in the past been variously interpreted by such war Presidents as Lincoln and Wilson, but no President before ever had such powers as had Mr. Roosevelt, either just taken by himself or conferred upon him by Congress.

However, the Montgomery Ward case brought all these points more or less into the clear. The confusion of government by commission became evident. For example, the War Labor Board held that this particular labor dispute was a war issue, yet the War Man Power Commission had refused to classify the company as an essential war industry. On the other hand, the War Production Board had decided that the company was sufficiently essential to the war effort to warrant granting it priorities for materials. The entire muddle placed before the public some of our difficulties, especially as regards the extent of the President's powers.

A new angle was brought out by Attorney General Biddle, who took the Montgomery Ward case to court and surprised the public by asserting in his argument that no court, in wartime, should seek "to substitute its judgment for that of the Executive." He held that there was an "aggregate" of constitutional powers in the hands of the President in wartime which would enable him to deal in his own judgment with any situation. He added that "no business or property is immune to a Presidential order"; "that the Government does not need a court order . . . to take possession." He went on that way, and the strongest Democratic newspaper supporter of the President said that people could not be blamed if they did not believe him when he said that they "were just seeing things under their beds."

Things were getting too bad. The President had been away on vacation. After his return, and on May 9, the army was taken out of Ward's and the property restored to its owners and management. In December, the President again ordered the seizure of Ward properties in seven cities, the crisis once more centering around problems of the closed shop and enforced union maintenance, not those of wages or production. On almost the last day of the year, Avery asked for a chance to appeal to the courts.

Meanwhile, the situation in organized labor had become increasingly confused. In May, John L. Lewis had finally refused, after long negotiations, to merge his union with the A. F. of L. That feud remained with more bitterness than ever. In an open letter, Lewis accused the A. F. of L. through its President, William Green, of "base hypocrisy, approximating moral turpitude." On the other hand, the C.I.O. entered politics in a big way, having organized its Political Action Committee (to become known in our alphabetical world as the P.A.C.), in which Sidney Hillman, a Lithuanian who had come to this country in 1907 at the age of twenty to become a labor leader of the new school and an Administration favorite, was a chief figure.

Lewis, in earlier years, as recounted in a previous chapter, had gone into politics with his half-million contribution to the Democratic campaign fund, only to quarrel with the President later. Some of what might be called the "elder statesmen" of the labor movement were deeply opposed to political action. In September of the year under discussion in this chapter, for example, Matthew Woll repeated his oft-given advice that the sphere of labor action was on the industrial front and that "Labor cannot and must not stake its whole future upon the success or failure of any political campaign."

However, new days, new ways, and as early as the middle of May, Hillman's P.A.C., claiming to act for an "overwhelming majority of the C.I.O.'s five million members" called for a fourth term for Roosevelt, which brings us along to the election, for this was most emphatically an election year and, considering the fourth term, the most crucial we have ever had.

We shall come to details in a few more lines but first there are a few general things to be said about this re-markable 1944 campaign. We have spoken of its being a war year. Undoubtedly the old saying about the danger of changing horses when crossing a stream influenced many voters. No one can say whether, except for the war, there would or would not have been a fourth term. Such discussion is guesswork not history, but there *was* strong opposition to it, as was clearly indicated by the resignation early in June, on the eve of the national conventions, of James A. Farley as Chairman of the New York State Democratic Committee. As Chairman of the National Committee, he had been largely responsible for Roosevelt's election in 1932, and had remained loyal as Postmaster General. He had opposed a third term and could not approve a fourth. As a wholly loyal member of the Democratic Party, he could only resign.

The action was symptomatic of the many crosscurrents in the campaign then starting. We have mentioned the increasing power of labor, especially Hillman's P.A.C. of the C.I.O. In his bolt, Farley found company in many Democratic leaders of the South, who, however, disliked the New Deal and the Vice-President, Henry Wallace, even more than the thought of a fourth term. Hillman and much of radical labor was insistent on having Wallace. If Roosevelt ran again, it was becoming evident that his running mate would have to satisfy both labor and the Solid South.

Another complication was the soldier vote. Nearly ten million men overseas, mostly of the younger generation, raised a tremendous question. For months, there was discussion in Congress and in State legislatures as to how proper and constitutional legislation could be framed so as to enable this overseas vote to be taken and counted. Ill-feeling was aroused and no wholly satisfactory adjustment reached which might serve as a future precedent for the nation as a whole. What was done might have caused great confusion had the vote been as close as in the Hayes-Tilden election of 1876 but, luckily, it was not, for such a contested election might have had terrifying consequences in the midst of our life-and-death struggle for national existence against enemies then far from beaten.

We need not detail the platforms of the two parties, but it is important to speak of certain aspects of them. Most important of all for the future of the United States and perhaps of the world, both parties agreed *in the main* on matters pertaining to the war and its conduct, and on the future assumption of responsibilities by this nation. That was something new. Party politics had stopped at last at the water's edge. Second, both parties vied with each other in offering baits to the public, such as extension of so-called security in the way of old-age pensions, medical relief and so on. Finally, labor, as a pressure group, loomed large.

The twenty-third National Republican Convention, with 1057 delegates, met at Chicago, June 26–28. Thomas E. Dewey, Governor of New York, was nominated for the Presidency by a vote of 1056 to 1, a fifty-four-year-old Wisconsin farmer, Grant A. Ritter, insisting on voting for General MacArthur, who had flatly stated he would not run. For Vice-President, the Convention nominated John W. Bricker, Governor of the often politically pivotal

Senator Harry S. Truman of Missouri. Writing to Chairman Hannegan, the President accepted the nomination for a fourth term, stating that he did not want it but that all the men in the armed forces had their Commander-in-Chief—who was himself—and that *he* had as commander above him the American people, and so, although he would "not run in the usual partisan, political sense," he *would* run. The campaign was on, and developed more or less according to the usual pattern and procedure.

A considerable change had occurred, however, during the time since the President had run at the beginning of his first term. In that fateful 1932, his support had been widely distributed among all sections of the people —farmers, many business men, labor, the disillusioned of all sorts among those out of work and discouraged, conservatives who agreed with Mr. Roosevelt's then campaign speeches as to the necessity for simplifying government and reducing its cost. By 1944, many of these followers had, for various reasons, fallen away, and those in reputed control of large blocks of votes, such as city bosses and labor organizations, had come to loom large.

At the end of August 1944, Sidney Hillman was called before a Congressional Committee of the House to explain about his two "political action" committees. His testimony was explicit and there is no reason to question its honesty but it raised important questions for American political life. Among other things, the investigation revealed that the Corrupt Practices Act excludes from its provisions both political conventions and primary elections, which latter are in many sections tantamount to election itself. The P.A.C. almost put over Wallace as

Vice-Presidential candidate in the Convention, against the wishes of a majority of the Democratic Party and of the President himself. The second loop-hole is the definition in the Smith-Connally Act of a labor organization. Hillman drew a subtle, and apparently legal, distinction between contributions for political purposes by a Trade Union and contributions by its *individual* members through *another* fund, though he was responsible for both.

Trade Unions are getting to be Big Business. No Union stands higher than the International Ladies' Garment Workers, of which David Dubinsky is the able leader. In June, he led the way for real accountings by unions, and advised others to follow. He showed that his international union, with its locals, had well over $16,000,000 of liquid assets. This indicates the financial power which unions *can* use in contested elections if the loopholes claimed by Hillman hold good.

On October 7, a few weeks before the election, Philip Murray, President of the C.I.O., and Hillman, chairman of the C.I.O.-P.A.C., issued a statement calling on all local union officers and shop stewards to get out the vote for Roosevelt. Compare this demand with any similar one which might have been issued, but could not, by the heads of any of our great business corporations. When asked, in connection with this unprecedented election order, how many of his claimed five million voters would vote for Roosevelt, Hillman merely said he did not know but that the number who would vote for Dewey was "so infinitesimally small that I don't care to estimate." The point is *not* that it was labor. It is whether *any* pressure group, farmers, labor, business corporations or other, should have such power to elect members of Congress, and the Executive, who in turn appoints the Judiciary, or whether that power should still reside in the people at large irrespective of their occupational groupings.

We can record the election briefly. Apparently the "soldier vote," as counted, did not differ greatly from what might have been expected had the men been at home. In any case, the total vote was not close enough to raise the dreaded problem of long delay. Within a few days after election, the figures showed a total vote cast of 45,568,024, of which Roosevelt polled 24,333,633 and Dewey 21,-234,379. Any changes in the popular vote subsequently counted, owing to minor difficulties, did not alter the result substantially, and the sweeping plurality in the Electoral College of 432 for Roosevelt and 99 for Dewey remained unaltered after missing districts, belated soldier ballots and other readjustments were accounted for.

Mr. Roosevelt had won his victory but from the longer historical point of view there are a number of points to consider. There had been twelve years in which to build up patronage and political machinery. There was the war and there was the "swapping horses" argument. The vote of the Electoral College, in our antiquated system, was impressive—432-99. Yet it was the lowest Roosevelt had polled in his four elections. In 1932, it had been 472-59; in 1936, 523-8; in 1940, 440-82. Moreover, his party majorities in both Houses of Congress, except for a slight rise as regards Representatives, in 1944, have been steadily declining, bringing them to 241 but as contrasted with 313, 322, and 333 in his first three Congresses.

The popular vote also deserves mention. As the best

practical solution of a difficult problem in self-government, we have accepted the verdict of the majority until
it changes, but it is well to remember what our great
proponent of this rule, Thomas Jefferson, said of it in
his First Inaugural Address. He wrote that "though the
will of the Majority is in all cases to prevail, that will, to
be rightful, must be reasonable: that the Minority possess
their equal rights, which equal laws must protect, and
to violate would be oppression." In the election of 1944,
the "Minority" who voted against Roosevelt numbered
roughly 21,500,000 out of a total of 45,500,000. They
form a very important section of the total picture.

There was another significant feature about the popular vote. Not only had the winning party, playing for
sixteen years of office, gradually lost strength as a whole
but the sources of that strength had changed. Both geo-
graphical and statistical studies of the vote indicate that
there had been a big shift since 1932 and 1936. The
farmer of the Middle West, notoriously progressive, was
leaving the fold. The "Solid South" remained, for racial
reasons, but the party lines were dividing as never before
on narrow economic lines of cleavage. A huge mass of
votes came from the industrial cities and centers of the
North and West, garnered by city bosses and trade-union
political leaders. This is new and worth noting. It was
stated that the vote in seven big cities alone gave Mr.
Roosevelt 185 electoral votes, and the C.I.O.-P.A.C.
proved its importance. The two-term tradition was clearly
buried for good, and both the character of the electorate
and the nature of the Presidential office had altered.

Although Mr. Roosevelt's fourth term would not begin

until the following January, there had been many rumors of impending changes in the Cabinet after election. There was only one, though that was of supreme importance and had nothing whatever to do with politics or with the too frequent bickerings among high officials in the Administration. Solely on account of health, the Secretary of State, Cordell Hull, found it essential to resign on November 21, after an almost completed twelve years of service in that high office, a period of public duty unequalled by that of any other incumbent of the office in our history. He had struggled with frail health from the time when, against his own desires, he yielded to Mr. Roosevelt's insistence, in 1933, that he leave his seat in the Senate to head the Cabinet and assume duties which were to prove the heaviest that any Secretary of State has ever had to carry.

This, fortunately, is not an obituary but merely a reference to the most important resignation during the years of Roosevelt's Administration.

Cordell Hull was born of a financially humble family, in a log cabin—or shack, if you will—in a "cove" of the Tennessee mountains. He once told me, as I recall, that he had never seen a railroad train or a newspaper until he was twelve years old. He rose, through a succession of offices, to a leading position in the United States Senate. I was in London at the time of the Economic Conference, and well recall the ill-feeling aroused there when the conference was "torpedoed," as they called it, on orders from America. Mr. Hull was our chief representative, *in London*. I remember that several leading Englishmen expressed their feelings to me about what had happened, but they all said, "At least, you Americans can be proud of having sent us, as the head of your delegation, a *very great gentleman.*" The little barefooted boy of the mountains had made a reputation as a noble and distinguished statesman in many lands besides our own, and was perhaps the most beloved and respected member of the Administration at home, both by those who agreed with all his ideas and those who might not.

The President appointed as the new Secretary of State, Edward R. Stettinius, who had had a notable career in business and had given it up, at much cost to himself, to enter government service, and who had occupied many important posts, including that of Lend-Lease Administrator and, more recently, Under-Secretary of State. Joseph Grew, a career diplomat and former Ambassador to Japan, was made the new Under-Secretary, and five Assistant Secretaries were also appointed, and confirmed by the Senate. On the whole, this appeared to be a good team for the heavy international work facing America during the war and afterwards.

Stettinius had made a particularly good record as Administrator of Lend-Lease and a fine impression on Congress whenever called upon to discuss that important measure, which has done so much to bind the Allies together and to co-ordinate all their operations, both through our Lend-Lease to them and through their reverse Lend-Lease to us. Nothing like it had ever been done in the case of any previous military alliance, and the favor that it found with the people and with Congress was indicated when, on April 19, 1945, the House of Representatives extended it to July 1, 1948, by a vote of 334 to 21, the few dissenting votes being all Republican and 20 of them from the Middle West. A good deal of stress has been laid on the twenty billions or so that we have "Lent-Leased" to our Allies, but not enough on the reverse process.

We may note a few points regarding this from President Roosevelt's Message to Congress of November 24. By the end of June, he reported, the British Commonwealth had given *us* about $3,400,000,000. In the first six months of 1944, the British Isles had supplied our overseas troops with well on to the equivalent of 4,000,000 ship-tons of supplies. Our army in the European theater of war was supplied by the British with about 63 per cent of its Quartermasters' supplies and with 58 per cent of those for our engineers. In the Pacific, Australia and New Zealand gave us 1,850,000,000 pounds of food alone, and over 20,000 small ships and boats for our Philippines campaign. It has not been all one-sided, and the pooling of supplies has gone hand in hand with the extraordinary pooling of aims and of effort.

On the home front, things did not run so smoothly. We had been unprepared for war, but thanks largely to the individual initiative bred by democracy, to our extraordinary productive capacity, and to the "know-how" of our great corporations, we had done a marvellous job. In many ways, however, it is easier to transform a peacetime production to a wartime one than *vice versa*. With war, people are willing to sacrifice and to cut their standard of living; there is one big job, to win the war; one big customer for all goods, the Government; business and investors have not made money out of this war, but cost-sheets, like the machinery for many peacetime goods, are thrown out of plant windows; there is no choice as to type of goods; the Government decides those things.

But when peace comes, it is different. Producers will again have 138,000,000 potential customers with differing tastes, hungry to enjoy what they have been foregoing. Plants which have discarded their peacetime machinery are cluttered with machines and tools serving Government needs only. If, after the war, the Government is not to remain the sole customer, the sole buyer and distributor of goods, the problem becomes enormously complex. During the year, efforts were made to prepare for a transition to peace, and for the readjustment of individual lives, so that we might be better prepared for these than we were when the reverse transition to war and its shortages and rationings had had to be made.

The most important of these efforts was blueprinted in the Report made to the President and Congress in February by John M. Hancock and Bernard M. Baruch. It dealt not only with the whole problem of industrial conversion but laid special stress on the human elements involved in eventually transferring 20,000,000 service men and special war-workers back into their places in a peacetime economy. Its 131 pages cannot be summarized in a paragraph, but its importance as an example of industrial statesmanship of the highest order, as well as proof of the ability of its drafters, was generally proclaimed.

The size of the problem was indicated not only by the numbers of individuals affected but by the note that we were at that time producing war goods to the amount of $50,000,000,000 a year, a production which would almost wholly cease with the final end of the war. The Report came out solidly for private enterprise, and said, "There has been too much loose parroting of the slogan, that if individual enterprise fails to provide jobs for everyone it must be replaced by some of the other systems that are around. The war has been a crucible for all the economic systems of the world, for our own, for communism, fascism, nazism—all the others. And the American system has outproduced the world." However, the Report was switched on to a siding by both the Administration and Congress, and the year passed with no constructive work done, though in the campaign both the President and Wallace talked of the necessity of "sixty million jobs." With the end of the German war at least in sight, we are still as unprepared for peace as we were for war when Pearl Harbor was attacked.

We may now turn briefly to the Supreme Court which, as we have noted, had become almost the creation of one President. It affords an interesting example of the well-known fact that a man's job and environment have a great influence on his thinking and character. The newly constituted Court *is* new, and it will take time for the new Justices to work out their lines. Most of them, when appointed, had had little or no experience on the bench; of the nine Justices appointed by Roosevelt, only two had any previous experience as judges: Rutledge had been appointed as a Judge of the Court of Appeals for the District of Columbia in 1939, and Black had served eighteen months as a police judge, but independence, if not too great concern with the need for a continuing tradition, appeared early.

For example, on January 31, the Court divided 5–4 in

a decision denying the right of parents of the sect of Jehovah's Witnesses to send their nine-year-old children out into the streets to sell pamphlets in favor of the sect. In a rough estimate, the *U. S. News* called the box-score of the split decisions: in civil liberties cases, the individual won 9 and lost 6; in the regulation of business, the Government won 17 and lost 10; in tax cases, the Government won 6 and lost 5. Moreover, the Justices did not vote *en bloc*. Even Justices Murphy and Roberts have been found on the same side. Nevertheless, the confusion was dangerous for respect for law and the Constitution. In the 1942–43 session, 176 dissenting opinions had been written as against a majority opinion in 171 cases. It began to appear that the Court was not to interpret the law and the Constitution but to form a third House of the legislature.

Justice Roberts may be considered a conservative but certainly Justice Felix Frankfurter cannot, yet on February 2 they joined in a statement that the tendency, as displayed so far, was such as to leave the lower courts "on an uncharted sea of doubt and difficulty without any confidence that what was said yesterday [by the Supreme Court] will hold good tomorrow." Justice Roberts pointed out that the law must gradually change to meet changing conditions but that it must not become a mere game of chance with no precedents to go by.

The change in the Court was well illustrated in a decision, 8–1, handed down April 3, reversing a unanimous decision in 1935. The decision, which may prove to be a momentous one, invalidated the rule of the Democratic Party in Texas to the effect that Negroes should not be allowed to vote in primary elections. In the previous decision, the Court had held that party rules were not governmental acts; but the new decision (Justice Roberts alone dissenting) held that a State cannot cast "its electoral process in a form which permits a private organization to practice discrimination in the election."

Decisions during this session of the Court confused considerably the problems of taxation. One of the main reasons for forming the Constitution was to allow a free flow of commerce between the States and to abolish tariff barriers across State lines. With 3,000,000 square miles and 138,000,000 population, the United States was to become the greatest contiguous free-trade industrial area in the world, and to prosper accordingly. Little by little, by such subterfuges as use-taxes, regulation of interstate truck traffic, food-inspection laws, and in other ways, this free trade has been in steady process of being whittled down. Four decisions of the Supreme Court in 1944, regarding taxes (although the Court split differently in the different cases), helped to break down the original intent of the Constitution. Relief appeared to lie rather in legislation by the States or by Congress than in the Court, and the same was true of a most important decision in June declaring that insurance companies were engaged in interstate commerce, reversing a continuous course of highest judicial decisions for over seventy-five years, to which all insurance companies and their policyholders had adjusted themselves and their affairs, thus vindicating what had been said by Justice Roberts about a Court decision coming to be like a railroad ticket, good for only one train on only one particular day.

Before we turn to the inexpressibly complex international aspects of the year, including the war, we may note some of the Americans distinguished in various ways who died during 1944. The year took such a heavy toll that it is impossible to give to each the notice he deserves. Alphabetically arranged, there were: George Ade, humorist; Jules S. Bache, financier, art collector and benefactor of New York; Raymond Clapper, news correspondent, killed in a plane crash in the Pacific; Irvin Cobb, belovèd humorist and lecturer; Norman H. Davis, public figure and head of the Red Cross; Charles Dana Gibson, artist; Dr. Walter A. Jessup, head of the Carnegie Foundation; Frank Knox, Secretary of the Navy; Judge Kenesaw M. Landis, czar of American baseball fairplay; Manuel Quezon, President of the Philippines; Brigadier General Theodore Roosevelt; Alfred E. Smith, ex-Governor of New York and Presidential candidate in 1928; Ida M. Tarbell, writer; William Allen White, editor; Wendell L. Willkie, leader and Presidential candidate in 1940. In a chapter already much too long, it is clearly impossible to pay proper tribute to those cited, all of whom were great Americans in their several ways.

We must now turn to the war and the international conferences of the year. We have heard much of our "forgotten wars," in this mondial one. They are far from being forgotten, but the acts of *this* vast drama *are* too numerous to be considered with any of the detail warranted by the heroism displayed by the individuals and forces in the various sectors.

Let us start with the Pacific. The war in that area has been perhaps the most difficult of all wars for a layman to understand, and it might be well for more of us to remember that, in military matters, we *are* laymen and not trained strategists. The water distances for transport, across the greatest of the world's oceans, are so enormous; the number of islands and mainland ports so great; the economic and military importance of them so different; the expansion of the Japanese was so rapid, after the destruction of our fleet at Pearl Harbor and the capture of the Philippines; that altogether it combines to make the most complex and little understandable picture of a combat zone that we have ever known.

Gradually, however, by late January, a pattern began to emerge. The apparently unrelated campaigns in the mountains and swamps of New Guinea and on the Solomon Islands began to make sense. We were headed for Rabaul and the open sea. Admiral Halsey and General MacArthur in different spheres were working together for a common end. We may mention two points. For one thing, although it was not announced until the end of August by Secretary of the Navy Forrestal, we had added to our navy since the beginning of the European war 65,000 vessels of more than 9,000,000 tons displacement, and our job, he said, was only half finished. That, and our airplane production, incredible to the Germans and to Hitler's "honorary Aryan" ally (combined, both here and all over the world, with the unexpected ability of Tom, Dick and Harry to leave peacetime jobs in a "decadent" democracy and become the toughest fighting force in the world), were to change the picture and save that world for freedom.

The second point was that the road to Tokio was not

by way train, *i.e.,* it was decided not to take island by island at great cost of life and time. The so-called "leap-frog" tactics were carried out. We jumped ahead to strategic points, over others. The result was amazing to the Japs, and even to our own public. By the end of 1943, we had captured the Gilbert Islands. By January 30, 1944, we started operations against the Marshall group. On February 8, we captured in that group the atoll of Kwajalein, the toll of dead being 286 Americans and 8122 Japs, a fine batting average. American guns destroyed practically every living thing on the island.

In the Marshall group was the island of Truk, which the Japs had fortified so heavily that they considered it a sort of impregnable Gibraltar and one of their most essential naval bases. An attack by carrier-based planes, followed by battleships, cruisers and destroyers, the force under command of (now) Admiral Spruance, captured the stronghold, February 17–18. News reports stated that the Japs lost 19 ships and 202 planes. With other islands also taken, the Marshalls were completely in our possession by the 20th. In the Bismarcks, a couple of days later, we heavily attacked Rabaul and sank a convoy of 9 ships. Rabaul itself was to fall to us, and our now successive victories had their repercussions in Japan with the dismissal of the heads of both the army and navy. In spite, however, of the immensely powerful and mobile air and naval force we had built up in the Pacific since Pearl Harbor, it was not realized at home what we had been doing. A leading journal, for example, stated that no nation before had ever undertaken to defeat at a distance of 10,000 miles from its own bases another nation of

80,000,000 people, and that we would be lucky if we got to the Philippines by the middle of 1945. We were to under-estimate the speed of the Pacific war and, at the year's end, to over-estimate that of the European one.

April 7, however, we struck again at Palau Harbor, less than 600 miles from Manila, sinking 28 enemy ships, damaging 18 others, and destroying over 200 planes. Early in August, the President paid a quick visit to Hawaii. By the middle of October, our forces were back in the Philippines. On the 25th, the President announced that in a sea-air battle we had routed the Japanese fleet, which had made a three-pronged attempt in the narrow waters between the islands to prevent our vessels, together with an Australian squadron, from entering. MacArthur, who had promised when he left in 1942 that he would "come back," *was* back, and reported the most "crushing defeat" the Japs had suffered. Apparently, the whole of the Japanese fleet had been engaged, and the victory was indeed overwhelming. Even before this fight, the score for the period since Pearl Harbor was 195 American naval vessels of all types lost on all the oceans as against 750 Japanese ones sunk or damaged. It was no wonder that Rear Admiral Clark said that "we're strong enough now out there to go wherever we want to go whenever we want to go." This statement was highlighted when on June 15 we began attacking the Japanese homeland with our new B-29's—the first air attacks since Doolittle's one raid on April 18, 1942.

In spite of that, it was to be a long job yet and a hard one, but the change from 1942 was amazing. America had become not only the greatest air power in the world

THE MIRACLE OF PRODUCTION
Our shift from peacetime to wartime production, helping to make the United States the greatest military power on the globe, amazed the world.

MacARTHUR *WAS* BACK

Accompanied by his aide and Chief of Staff, Lt. Gen. Richard K. Sutherland, General MacArthur fulfills his 1942 promise of return to the Philippines shortly after American troops landed on the last lap of the road back to Manila.

but the mistress of the seas. The Japanese navy was on its way out, wholly; the German surface navy, at least, was practically wiped out by the end of the year; one-third of the Italian navy had been turned over to the Russians and the fate of the rest was in doubt; the French fleet was largely destroyed; as compared with the British, with an estimated · 2,200,000 tons of combat ships, we had 4,500,000 tons. With such power go heavy responsibilities.

Our return to the Philippines was hailed with genuine joy by the Filipinos, who had remained stanch and loyal throughout the Japanese occupation and who completely trusted us to carry out our pledges of eventual independence under American protection. They had given us much assistance in our landings, and the whole episode was a very promising one for the possible relations between a great power and a small one. The Japanese had treated the Filipinos with great brutality, and in January our Government had released the Report prepared by the Army and Navy Departments on the atrocities committed by the Japs on our own troops before we had been forced to evacuate the islands. The details of the "March of Death" at Bataan, and other incidents, had earlier been considered too horrifying for those at home, to be published. All of these factors contributed to our satisfaction in being able to regain our foothold and gradually extend our control again over the islands.

In the previous chapter, we spoke of the wiping out of the Germans in Africa, and the transfer of the struggle from Tunisia to Sicily and thence to the mainland of Italy. It might perhaps, at the time, have seemed to the layman that the campaign in that theater had been a disappointment. For a while, the public, at least, anticipated that the Germans would be driven out of Rome, northward, out of the peninsula altogether, thus opening a way through the back door into that portion of Germany in which Hitler and other leading Nazis recently talked of maintaining their last stand.

On January 22, landings were made at Anzio and Nettuno, on the coast below Rome, with the idea of getting behind the Germans and cutting off their lines. There was also heavy fighting at Cassino. The plans did not work out as expected but in spite of the bloody struggle on the Anzio beach-head we made our footing good; Cassino was eventually blown to pieces and Rome, mostly undamaged, fell to us on June 5. From then on, progress was slow. The Germans still controlled the industrial north of Italy and the passes over the Alps, in spite of our steady edging forward. The cost, however, may have been terrific, as the Allies, partly owing to mistaken German strategy, pinned down many divisions of the best German troops in Italy, who in 1945 were to be badly needed on the Rhine.

Italy also came over to the Allied side, entering the war as a "co-belligerent"; the King resigned, though he kept his title; the Crown Prince took over; Mussolini, who had been rescued from prison by agents of Hitler, pretended to organize a government; and unrest and uncertainty continued. Troops, American, British, French and of other smaller allied groups, had fought to the limit, but somewhere in the high commands, military or political, there were missteps, and Italy was disappointing. Again, let me say, that the campaign had a very great importance, and that the men who took part in its "blood and sweat and tears" have every reason to be proud of the part they played in the winning of the final victory.

Meanwhile, for nearly two and a half years, the most painstaking plans had been in the making for an invasion of the European continent from the north by way of England. We shall speak of these plans in a moment but may here mention two incidents in connection with them. We had been piling up, as we shall note, incredibly huge supplies of men and matériel in Northern Ireland (Ulster) and in Britain. On March 10, our State Department sent a note to Prime Minister de Valera of Ireland (Eire) explaining the situation, pointing out that the Japanese and German governmental representatives in that country had the opportunity of picking up and transmitting to their home offices information of the utmost importance, and asking whether Eire would not take steps looking to their recall. The answer from de Valera was a flat "No."

The second incident occurred in the middle of June. Robot bombs, later nicknamed "Doodlebugs" by our troops in England, began to fall on London and other parts of that country, and have continued to do so up to the present writing. Jet-propelled rockets, rising to the stratosphere and descending at terrific speed with no warning sound until they hit and exploded, directed at no specific target, military or other, were, nervously as well as physically, more devastating than had been the earlier Blitz from planes dropping bombs. The rocket bomb was distinctly a new weapon. At first, they were started from the Normandy coast, the send-offs later being moved farther east along the seacoast. But the time of retribution was drawing near, and we now come to perhaps the greatest military operation in history.

The preparations began at a morning meeting in London, on July 1, 1942, when about thirty top-ranking colonels and generals sat down to begin discussions. In April of that year, we had appointed as our representative Lt. General John C. H. Lee. I can touch on only some of the aspects here, but for further details refer the reader to an article by C. L. Walker in *Harper's Magazine* for March, 1945. His article was passed by the censors in the U. S. Army and Navy, and in the British Army, Navy and Air Forces, and so may be considered accurate history. I lean heavily on it in the following paragraphs, with full acknowledgment to *Harper's*.

In the approximately two years intervening between that July 1942 and the beginning of the actual physical invasion in June 1944, what were some of the things to be considered and done? The American Army had to put over a million men into the United Kingdom by D-day. Our own, and the British forces, had to supply these men with various amounts of *more than a million different items*. In over 1100 British towns, more than 100,000 buildings had to be erected. (This, and much else, came under Britain's contribution to Reverse Lend-Lease.)

For the air forces, landing strips had to be built equalling in total length the distance from Moscow to America. At least 18,000,000 ship-tons of cargo had to be transported from America and dumped all over the United Kingdom, but dumped in such a way that it could be known at a moment's notice what was in the tens of millions of crates and packing boxes, and where these were located. For the eventual Channel crossing, more than 660 *different kinds* of landing and escort craft had to be designed and built.

For the long preliminary air bombardment, which to many civilians may have appeared somewhat haphazard, thousands of hours had to be spent in study. Not only did German war plants have to be located and picked out according to their importance for the enemy war effort, but the thing got so fine that it was estimated not only how many planes had to be used for destruction at 5000, 15,000, 25,000 feet height, but even in some plants what *wing* of the building would have to be knocked out to destroy a particularly important part or instrument being made in it. Further, there was the question of what type of bomb would be best for each particular job, and there were numberless other details to be thought out and planned in advance. Nothing was haphazard.

Both ocean freight, which, with a recrudescence of U-boat attacks, seemed seriously menaced at one stage, and land transportation in the United Kingdom itself were headaches. We had to ship 3000 locomotives and 57,000 freight cars specially built in America for use on British rail lines. A month before D-day, there was not a single empty siding on any rail line in England, and the quip over there was that if American supplies kept piling up and the invasion did not start soon, the island would sink; that all that kept it above the water already were the barrage balloons! For example, we had shipped thousands of miles of four-inch pipes, the rot-proofing for 500,000,000 burlap sandbags, 2,500,000 miles of telephone wires. We had, over there, enough bridging to replace every possible destroyed bridge in France. We had 125,000,000 maps, so accurate as to show even the tides, so that the planners knew where a boat of given draught could touch a beach at any minute, any hour of any day. Blood plasma, drugs—such as sulfa, penicillin, morphine—special slings to carry the wounded—everything was ready, and emergency hospitals had been set up and time schedules so worked out that, when D-day *did* come, between eighty and ninety per cent of the wounded received expert medical attention within ten minutes. When that day came, the vast adventure started in darkness—no lights—and in radio silence. Every man knew the exact spot where he had to be at a definite *minute*. On the other side of the Channel, the plans were just as carefully drawn, so that as material was placed on the dumps on the beaches those who had to know knew that "At Dump 6, Aisle 2, Row 4, Tier 3, you will find your box of 300 spark plugs."

There has never been anything else like it, and it must be remembered also that two peoples, the British and the Americans, were working together as one, and that we had to transport all our men and matériel over three thousand miles of the Atlantic. There had been no full-scale invasion across the Channel since that of William the Conqueror in 1066. Philip of Spain had tried it, as had Napoleon and Hitler. Now the British and Americans were trying it, in "reverse Lend-Lease," against what the conquering Germans had declared to be their impregnable "Atlantic Wall." This time, success was complete, and marked the turning-point, in the European

INVASION LANDING ON THE NORMANDY BEACH

While barrage balloons hold off German strafers, boats land an almost endless supply of matériel and troops which are carried inland by long lines of trucks.

Cordell Hull Opening the Security Parley Conference at Dumbarton Oaks,
Washington, D. C.

From photographs by International News Photos

Changing Guard at Dumbarton Oaks during the Conference.

theater, of what has been the greatest war in all history.

The attack had been agreed upon by Roosevelt, Churchill and Stalin at the Teheran Conference, but the preparations had taken time. It had been time well spent. The exact date for its inception had been left to General Eisenhower, Supreme Commander. He had finally determined to set his vast and intricate machine in motion on June 5. The weather, however, was bad. The meteorologists told the General it would improve on the morrow. Whether to believe them or not? It was a terrible responsibility. Bad flying weather for the planes, a storm on the Channel, might ruin everything. He took the chance, and the scientists were right. The weather was not too good, but it had improved and continued to do so.

On June 6, 11,000 planes blasted a way, ahead, for the troops being transported on 4000 vessels, not counting the innumerable small landing craft. The biggest airborne force, up to then in history, was also carried over the beaches, and inland to behind enemy lines. The attack had been made before dawn, and that day, Churchill, paying high tribute to Eisenhower, could tell Parliament that all had gone "according to plan—and *what* a plan!"

Hitler's boasted "Atlantic Wall" was crashed. Caen was taken, after heavy fighting and considerable destruction of the historic city. The great port of Cherbourg was also taken, although the Germans, sensing the value of ports to the Allies, held grimly to Brest and others. The overrunning of the countryside was unexpectedly rapid. On August 23, the people of Paris rose, and both the Germans and the representatives of the Vichy regime were in flight or hiding. France, with troops advancing from the south as well as from the north, was rapidly becoming almost wholly free again. The Allies were advancing into Germany and approaching the Rhine. Parts of the "Low Countries" were freed, but it took time to get control of Antwerp, first its outlying defenses and then of the port itself, and we desperately *needed* ports for bringing in the matériel required by our own rapid advances and the increasing tempo of the fighting. It was these lacks which brought disappointment in the late autumn and early winter. We had, for the moment, after high hopes had been raised of a very early end to the war, reached the limit of our forward driving power. The Germans, under von Rundstedt, turned for a counter-attack. It was a perilous undertaking for them, and was in the end to prove fatal, but the deferment of our anticipations caused the year to end on a note of discouragement, not as to eventual victory but as to the amount of time required and the human cost.

During 1944, there were several important international meetings and conferences. For Americans, three stand out especially: those at Bretton Woods, Dumbarton Oaks and Quebec. The first two may be said to represent as yet "unfinished business" taking the form of suggestions and plans which have caused great discussion and still have to be passed upon, possibly at the coming international Conference in San Francisco in 1945.

The Bretton Woods Conference was participated in by representatives of forty-four nations, opening its sessions on July 1 and closing on the 22nd. Its fundamental concern was with post-war economics. The final plan dealt with two items: one, the creation of a Fund, to which all the nations should contribute, to help stabilize the wildly fluctuating currencies of the world; and, second, a Bank which would help as an investment institution "to bring about those economic conditions which are essential to sound currency stability and healthy trade." The Fund and the Bank were closely linked, but each of them has been subjected to exhaustive criticism by one school of economists or another and by one nation or another. Something will come out of it all, but the monetary, exchange and trade aspects of the whole matter are too complex to be discussed properly here, especially as it is all still in a state of flux.

The next Conference was held at Dumbarton Oaks, near Washington, and dealt with other aspects of postwar world organization. As contrasted with that at Bretton Woods, it was a four-power Conference—the United States, the British Empire, Russia and China were represented. It was to devise some sort of world organization, and, meeting on August 21, point was given to this aim by the news, on that day and the day or two following, that the Vichy government in France had disappeared and that Romania had abandoned Germany and joined the Allies. (In the following months, Hungary and Finland were also to desert the sinking ship.)

The tentative proposals made were that the above four powers, with France added, should have special responsibility and authority for maintaining peace, attacking aggressor nations, if necessary, before, and not after, these had started war themselves. Among the points suggested were the following:

1. A General Assembly of all peace-loving nations to

make recommendations looking to the maintenance of peace.

2. A Security Council of eleven members, including the above-mentioned five as permanent members and six others to be chosen by them for two-year terms. The Council would have full authority to use economic, military or other means to maintain peace.

3. An Economic and Social Council to deal with humanitarian problems.

4. An international Court to handle justiciable questions.

The decisions and plans of the Conference, like those arrived at at Bretton Woods, will have to be confirmed, probably at the international Conference in San Francisco.

From September 11 to 16, Roosevelt and Churchill, with very full advisory professional staffs, met at Quebec for the second Conference of the war held in that city. From the reports given out by each, apparently the chief topic discussed was the future conduct of the war in the Pacific, and Stalin did not attend, in part probably because Russia was still bound to Japan by a non-aggression pact. Both statesmen expressed themselves as highly delighted with the complete accord quickly reached, and there is no question but that Britain and the Empire will throw their full weight in with us against the Japs, once the European war is finished. Aside from what was agreed upon at this Conference, Churchill has now many times, in public speeches and before Parliament, made that pledge in the most solemn manner, and there is not the slightest reason to doubt his good faith or that of the people who, he has promised, will back it.

CHAPTER IV

THE RECORD OF 1945

O N January 1, 1946, Mr. Arthur Krock, the Washington correspondent of *The New York Times,* and by many considered the best informed, most accurate and sanest of Washington correspondents, headed his daily column in that journal, "The Mightiest Year in Our History." In his first paragraph he wrote:

The year now closing will be marked as the high point of achievement thus far in the nation's history and that of any people in the annals of the world. Perhaps there are contemporary historians with the skill and wisdom to subdue the rushing events of 1945 long enough to put them within the covers of a book. But if such there are the assignment would still be terrifying.

I agree. But the assignment to put them within the pages of a single chapter is infinitely more so. What *did* happen in those momentous twelve months? What are the events that I must touch upon for you, though I cannot begin to do them full justice?

The year witnessed the dying agonies of nations in the first total global war in the history of the human race. Utterly new weapons were employed on the sea, under the sea, on land, in the air and even in the stratosphere. Military operations of hitherto undreamed-of intensity and complexity were under way. Our own nation rose to a height of industrial production which would have been inconceivable a few years earlier. There was the sudden death of Roosevelt, the first American President ever to be elected to a third and even to a fourth term. Then there was the collapse of the Axis Powers, Germany in Europe, and Japan in the Orient, that came about with an unexpected suddenness and completeness. Of the previous leaders, Roosevelt, as we have said, died suddenly. Mussolini ended in ignominy, his dead face stamped on by Italian heels in a muddy gutter. Hitler disappeared. The Churchill government in Britain was overthrown. The atomic bomb opened to all mankind a new era both of terror and peaceful power. One of the innermost and most dangerous secrets of the universe had been discovered. The great New World abandoned its traditional policy of isolation and set itself whole-heartedly, and almost unanimously, to the establishment of an organization for world peace in which we should play our part with vigor and responsibility. The world capital was obviously to be located in the United States. The end of the war, or rather of the several wars, did not bring peace and prosperity, and there were dark shadows, but the events had been staggering beyond the imagination of previous generations. Clearly, such a story cannot here be told in detail.

The first concern of all of us during the greater part of the year was the war itself, so let's begin with that. Before going into even moderate detail, we may repeat that it was the first total and global war in history. This meant, for our American men (and women), that they had to go to almost every quarter of the globe—Europe, Africa, the islands and lands of the Pacific—and that they had to learn to use every new weapon which science was devising against military enemies and civilian populations. It was not at all nice, but this was what the Axis had forced us to do.

The second general point to make here is this—that, before the war ended, the world had become divided into two camps: the Axis Powers, who wished to impose their will on all the rest; and the rest, who wished to go their own ways, although those ways might be very different from one another. There is, however, a tremendous difference in being governed by another in *his* way or running your affairs in your *own* way, be they Russian, British, North American or South American. We all wanted to be ourselves and not to have to do the Prussian "Goose-step." The variety and number of nations organized against the Axis called for the greatest coalition or alliance in all history. In the minor and more local wars of the past there have been many "alliances," and their histories have usually not been too happy. The alliances in this war were the most successful ever, and this was due, in the main, to the "Big Three"—the United States, headed by Franklin Roosevelt, the British Empire, by Winston Churchill, and the Soviet Union, by Stalin. We shall speak of their meetings later.

Now, for the details of the various wars, in so far as we can consider them. There are, first, the military details, in Europe and in Asia. We may begin with Italy.

In the preceding chapter, we noted the fall of Rome. These operations had entailed very heavy losses, which could not immediately be replaced. However, after some months, the pursuit of the enemy into the north of Italy continued. By April 29 the Allies had reached the great city of Milan and on May 2, after a general collapse of the Germans, their commander surrendered unconditionally. We may note that there were, at various times, fighting with the Fifteenth Army, troops who were Americans, British, Canadian, French, Japanese, New Zealanders, South Africans, Poles, Indians, Brazilians, Italians, Greeks, Moroccans, Algerians, Arabs, Goums, Sengalese and a brigade of Jews. Never before had peoples who wished to be free to lead their own lives worked together in this way. The surrender of the Germans ended the Italian war and wholly changed the situation in Yugoslavia. We need merely mention the end of the Fascist regime and of Mussolini.

This chapter of American history is no place in which to survey the career of "Musso," but, as he attempted for a while to stride the world, and killed his hundreds of thousands, his end is of interest. He was a small fat man,

Top, left: President Franklin D. Roosevelt. *Right:* General George Marshall. *Bottom, left:* Admiral Ernest J. King. *Right:* General Henry H. Arnold.

Photographs from *Acme Newspictures, Inc.* and *Press Association, Inc.*

Top, left: General Dwight D. Eisenhower. *Right:* General Douglas MacArthur. *Bottom, left:* General George S. Patton, Jr. *Right:* General Omar Bradley.

and not at all the majestic figure he pretended to be in his hortatory press photographs. He had been captured by the Allies and had been mysteriously if not scandalously rescued from his prison by a German plane. He spent some months in a villa on Lake Como, and then, on April 28, on the eve of the German total collapse, was again captured by the Italians. He, his mistress, and sixteen Fascist aides were shot, thrown into a moving-van and brought to Milan. There they were tossed into the gutter at a street corner where Mussolini had had fifteen innocent Milanese hostages shot to avenge the murder of certain Germans. He lay in his Fascist uniform, with his head on the body of his mistress, while an angry crowd spat on them and stamped their heels into his bloody face. The next day, he and his mistress were hanged, heels up, and the career of the smallest and most miserable would-be dictator the world has seen was ended. It was horrible but was only a minor detail in the series of mass horrors to which men were to become accustomed in the year 1945. We thought we were living in a civilized era, but no other year has left on the spirit of man so deep an impression of the depths to which he could sink.

Now we move on to Germany. We had to end the chapter on 1944 with the counter-attack of the Germans under von Rundstedt in the battle of "the Bulge." This had been helped by the worst weather in many years for operations on a grand scale by our attackers. The slugging, up through the rugged mountain country of Italy, had been costly and discouragingly slow. However, it had paid handsomely. Not only had we, for months, kept a large part of the German forces outside of Germany, but we had gained control of airfields from which we could take off to attack the vital German oil sources in the Rumanian fields at Ploesti and from which also we could begin shuttle attacks, with planes from England, in the all-important wearing-down process over the German home-land.

We were getting ready for the final "kill." Branches of all services shared in the task. We had at last gained control of the port of Antwerp, which was essential for pouring in supplies through the Low Countries. The air forces had done magnificent work—night and day—in softening German supply lines, defenses and morale. The Russians were getting ready for their drive on Berlin. During the last week in December, 1944, the weather turned in our favor. In general, the Allied plan—determined at the Yalta Conference—involved the greatest pincer movement in history. The Allies were to crush Germany by drives from the West and East. The invasion of Normandy and the defeat of the Germans at the battle of "the Bulge" had prepared the way for one; and the Russian advance for the other. Hitler, who had always said Germany could not stand a war on two fronts at once, but who, by his lies and conceit, had brought it on, was soon to suffer the consequences of his own perfidy and folly.

The Rhine was a barrier to attack from the West, but

on March 7 the 9th American armored division, probing the Rhine banks, found that the bridge at Remagen had not been blown up. The facts that the German officer in command was drunk and that a young American officer had led a detachment across, with only minutes to spare, were among the dramatic events in what was soon to become "the rat hunt" through Germany. We must, however, give credit to the brilliant staff work which took immediate advantage of the chance offered. The result was the establishment of an important bridgehead on the east bank of the symbolic river and, in time, of other bridges and bridgeheads. American, British and some French divisions began to wipe up the Germans, of whom, in the Ruhr alone, about 350,000 were captured or killed. Allied troops reached the Ilbe River, April 11, overran Bavaria and on the 20th captured the already largely destroyed Nazi shrine-city of Nürnberg, formerly one of the loveliest in Germany but now a heap of rubble.

Meanwhile, Russian armies had crossed the Oder River (March 24) on a wide front, and fought their way toward Berlin. We have mentioned the execution, or murder, of Mussolini on April 28. On May 1 the Hamburg radio reported that Hitler was dead and that Admiral Karl Doenitz had been made Fuehrer. Apparently, Hitler was not yet dead, and his fate will be mentioned later, but Germany *was* crumbling. On April 25, American troops from the West and Russians from the East had joined forces at Weismar and the "Holy Soil," as the Germans

with characteristic insolence called their land, had been
split in half. On May 2, Berlin fell to the Russians. Germany disintegrated, day by day. On May 5, the German
commander surrendered unconditionally all his forces in
northwest Germany, Holland and Denmark. As 500,000
Germans laid down their arms to the British General
Montgomery, he remarked, "This is the moment." The
next day, our forces captured Pilsen in Czechoslovakia.
Other advances were made and, on the 6th, all German
forces in Austria surrendered. The German dream of a
retreat to impregnable positions in the mountains of Austria and Bohemia had vanished. At Reims, on May 7,
with chaos everywhere, the emissaries of the Doenitz German Government unconditionally surrendered all land,
sea and air forces of the Reich. The German war, which
had lasted five years, eight months and six days, was over.
Italy had collapsed, with the surrender of 1,000,000 Germans, and the Reich and its satellites were in ruins.

Throughout fanatical Germany city after city had been
destroyed. Cologne, Nürnberg, the great port of Hamburg, and others, had become mere heaps of rubble. Berlin
itself, which Hitler had proclaimed the capital of the new
Reich for a thousand years, had gone down in a holocaust
of fighting and flames. The greatest city ever to be conquered and ruined, it had had a population of nearly
4,500,000 spread over an area of more than 340 square
miles. From its radio, as a final note, had gone forth, on
May 1, a notice to Germans to stand by for important

news. First, came the deep strains of Wagner's *Götter-dämmerung,* the "death of the Gods," which should have been dubbed "the end of the Devils," and then word that Hitler had died as a "hero" in defense of the city.

He did not die as a hero, although the details of his death are still obscure. The best documentary evidence we have indicates that, after a marriage to his mistress of many years—even her name does not deserve commemoration—and a macabre wedding celebration, both took deadly poison and, with the aid of gasoline, were incinerated in the underground apartments of the vast Chancellery which was to have lasted a thousand years. At any rate, there seems to be no doubt that they died as suicides and that their bodies were burned beyond recognition. At the same time, and in more or less the same manner, died the notorious Nazi leader Joseph Goebbels, the German propaganda chief.

In fact, the fall of Hitlerite Germany was unique. Other nations have been defeated in war but never has there been such a wave of suicides. On May 25—the date is unimportant—Heinrich Himmler, the former head of the noted Gestapo, committed suicide after being captured while in disguise by the British. He was stripped naked to see whether he had any poison hidden on his person, and killed himself by chewing a small glass tube containing cyanide, which he had concealed in his mouth. One of the most hated men in the world, such was his end. There were others. Never before has a great nation and its leaders gone down in such a holocaust of destruction and infamy.

The end of the Reich was an amazing melodrama of unbelievable horrors and fantastic episodes. We need merely touch on some of them here, although in the global war in which the United States had been engaged it is hard to draw the line between what is American history and what belongs to the history of other countries. The insensate sadism of the prison and concentration camps has been recorded for all to read, and not by propagandists but by military authorities of unquestionable accuracy and veracity. Millions had perished of hunger, avoidable sickness and by fiendish torture, executed with all the efficiency of modern German science. The world had known barbarism but never before anything like this, and on the part of a people who called themselves not only civilized but the "Master Race." This was what we had fought against, and it is well to recall it, not in a spirit of vengeance but simply "lest we forget."

There were also fantastic incidents, such as the finding of hoards of loot, hidden away in caves, saltmines, and elsewhere, the plunderings of leading Nazis. There was, for example, one hoard of art treasures belonging to the bemedaled Field Marshal Goering valued as high as $500,000,000. Allowing for exaggerations in valuations the loot had still been colossal and made Napoleon look like a huckster. A trifling minor matter was the capture of Goering's private train of ten armored cars, one filled with the choicest of wines and liquors, one with his favorite music records, and others for lounging and sleeping, every room with its private bath. All this was state socialism and friends of the people with a vengeance! Well, they have gone, or are going—Mussolini, his face ground by Italian heels as his corpse sprawled in a muddy gutter; Hitler burned under the crumbling ruins of his vast Chancellery, from which he had hoped to rule the world; and the rest, dead or now being tried for their lives. The necks of a few cannot atone for the millions whose lives and happiness have been destroyed, but it is something, whether or not it may deter others in future from attempting to pursue the same mad course.

The war in Europe was over, but the best-informed opinion expected another year or two of bloody fighting in the Pacific, with possibly tremendous losses, against the fanatic and now desperate foe. On July 16, as day broke on the New Mexico desert, the innermost secret of the universe was shown to have been penetrated and solved. The dream of atomic fission became a reality. The first atomic bomb in history was successfully exploded in the lonely waste, and America found herself possessed of the most powerful weapon ever known to warfare.

We now shift to the vast ranges of the Pacific waters. The secret of the bomb was known to only a few in inner circles and even they did not know what the effects might be. The war had to go on.

The story of that war was one of infinite suffering and

of great losses. Minds were so concentrated on the European theater that many of the troops in the Pacific area perhaps felt that they were regarded as a sort of "sideshow." This, of course, was not true. Although the European war had to be won first, the Pacific war was, to us in America—facing two oceans—perhaps in the long run the more vital. At all events, that war had to go on, with the prospect of a long struggle and heavy losses.

We can only pass over it briefly, although it covered vast spaces and many land, sea and air engagements.

Both the Allied and Japanese operations in China and in the East near Burma had, according to General Marshall in his Report on Winning the War, been maintained at ends of the most precarious supply lines in history. General MacArthur's landings in the Philippines and the operations of our naval forces in the China Sea had cut the Japanese line to Burma. By the end of January, the Japs were in full retreat and by May the Burma campaign was practically ended, with 300,000 Japanese casualties, including nearly 100,000 dead, as stated by the British Admiral Lord Louis Mountbatten. In spite of the marvellous road built by General Stilwell (now abandoned after colossal cost), and the fact that in January 1945 we were transporting more than 46,000 tons of war material "over the Hump" to the Chinese forces, the enemy continued for some months to gain in the interior of China.

To touch on only a few points in what we may call the battle of the islands, we may note that on January 9 the

U. S. Sixth Army had hit the beaches of Lingayen Gulf in the Philippines, and that by nightfall the surprise attack had landed 68,000 troops in control of a beachhead 15 miles long and 6000 yards deep. MacArthur continued and, after recapturing Corregidor, Manila Bay was opened to us early in March. The General and his men had accomplished in less than two months what it had taken the Japanese more than six months to achieve after Pearl Harbor. MacArthur had made good his promise, when leaving the Philippines for Australia in the early dark days of defeat, that he *would return.*

Steadily we advanced, and the pincers closed on the homeland of Japan. The Philippines came gradually into our control. Other islands followed, notably, after a historic struggle, Iwo Jima, only 775 miles from the main Japanese island of Honshu and of vital importance to our air assault on Japan. The offensive against the Ryukyus began on March 26, when General Buckner and his forces made their first attack on Okinawa. The battle was long and bloody and did not end until three days after the killing of General Buckner on June 18, almost on the eve of victory. Meanwhile we had suffered 39,000 casualties, including 10,000 naval personnel, but almost 110,000 Japs had been killed and about 8000 taken prisoner. The long struggle had been notable for the particularly fierce suicide attacks by the Japanese, including rocket bombs, with a ton of explosive each, guided by live pilots, who inevitably died when they hit the target.

Steadily the Allies advanced here and there and closed in on the doomed Japanese Empire, now of the setting not of the rising sun. In June the Australians made an unopposed landing in northwest Borneo, establishing air bases which could be used in combination with those in the Philippines. Operations continued in the latter islands and the campaign in Luzon was practically completed by the end of June, by which time MacArthur's forces had killed 317,000 Japs and captured over 7000. As the encirclement continued, the whole Pacific Ocean from California to China was swarming with American seapower—a marvellous change from the day of Pearl Harbor. Japanese shipping—naval and commercial—had been largely sunk or driven from the seas, and what was left was rapidly crumbling. In Malaya, the Dutch East Indies and China, troops were on the move.

On April 6, by order of the Joint Chiefs of Staff, Mac-Arthur was appointed to the command of all United States Army forces in the Pacific, and he and Admiral Nimitz, commander of the Naval Forces, were ordered to prepare the final attack on Japan itself. Other appointments were made, including especially those affecting the Air Force, strategic command of which remained with General Arnold.

During July, thanks to our possession of the Marianas, Iwo Jima, Okinawa and other air bases, our superbombers, aided by the fleet and by British units, steadily shelled cities and industries on the Japanese home islands. There were two plans for gradually bringing the war to an end, but operations according to either would have been long, and costly in Allied lives.

There was, however, another plan and weapon. The experiment in the Arizona desert had been successful. From the meeting of the "Big Three" in Potsdam, General Spaatz of the Air Force received orders to drop an atomic bomb on the industrial part of any one of four named cities. He could make his own choice and drop the bomb any day after August 3 when the weather permitted. On the 6th a bomb was dropped on the military base city of Hiroshima. The effect was as terrifying as it was devastating. Most of the city was wiped out. The loss in life has never been accurately stated but apparently about 160,000 persons met almost instant death. Nothing like it had ever been known before.

Two days later, on August 8, the Soviet Union declared war on Japan. Russian armies at once were on the march. The following day, the American Air Force dropped a second atomic bomb, this time on the great city of Nagasaki. It was even more destructive than the first, the smoke from the burning metropolis rising 50,000 feet into the air, visible throughout the surrounding country for 175 miles. On August 10, the Japanese Government sued for peace on the terms of the Potsdam Convention, which meant unconditional surrender.

I may mention for the information of readers, because I have had a number of inquiries from England and even here at home, that the term "unconditional surrender" is well over eighty years old; it was first used by General Grant in the capture of Fort Donelson in the Civil War, in 1862. As, owing to a mistake, Grant's name had been entered on the records at West Point as "Ulysses Simpson Grant," which characteristically he did not bother to correct, he became *U. S.* Grant, and the initials for the first two words of U. S. A. and also for "unconditional surrender" may have had some odd influences on his career. He became known, after his Mississippi River campaign, as "Unconditional Surrender Grant." Some Britishers seem to think it was a term invented by Franklin Roosevelt at Casablanca. Perhaps even some Americans do not know its origin.

The problems of the occupation of the various conquered countries may better be dealt with in the next chapter, but we may note here that, in the case of Japan, our military power was established in a somewhat different form from that set up in Italy or Germany. General MacArthur was made the Supreme Commander; the Emperor (who had traditionally been regarded by his people as a god) and the whole Japanese Government were placed under the absolute control of MacArthur, who in the remaining months did an excellent job.

The final ceremony of surrender took place on the deck of the battleship *Missouri*—mightiest warship afloat, then lying safely in Tokio harbor surrounded by other naval units and with planes circling overhead. Among other

American officers present were Admirals Halsey and Nimitz, and Generals MacArthur and Wainwright, the last thin and emaciated from his years in a Japanese prison camp after his heroic defense of Corregidor. It was a perfect ending to exactly six years of the most horrible war in history, a war brought on by the three powers which had aimed at the conquest and enslavement of all the rest of the world. The war had come within a hair's breadth of succeeding and we all owe it to Britain, who for some terrible months stood alone, that it did not succeed. The struggle had started on the plains of Poland on September 1, 1939, and, having involved the globe, ended on an American battleship lying within Tokio harbor, on September 1, 1945.

The losses had been greater than any dreamed of in previous wars. Without trying to estimate the millions upon millions of casualties suffered by Russia, the British Empire and our other Allies, we may mention only those sustained by the United States, as given in the final Report of General Marshall, Chief of Staff, and the losses of our enemies as estimated by him. The war in Europe cost the United States in round numbers about 773,000 casualties, with 160,000 dead; the Pacific war 170,000, with 41,000 dead. On the other hand, 1,600,000 Germans, Italians and Japanese were killed; 304,000 permanently disabled; and 8,150,000 taken prisoner and disarmed.

We have spoken of the new weapons, notably the atomic bomb. There were, in fact, several weapons which helped the Allies to win, although, for various reasons, the bomb has most stirred the popular imagination and apprehension. Throughout history there have been many new or secret weapons. But no other has struck mankind so aghast as has the atomic bomb.

I think it is not merely the number it can kill at once. Speaking realistically, was it not better to end a war, once and for all, with the instantaneous and therefore practically painless death of one or two hundred thousand people rather than by the agony of millions who, otherwise, might have died from painful wounds received in battle or after months of suffering in hospitals, concentration camps, and elsewhere? We had also been taught by our enemies that "total war" meant not only intense suffering for the men in the armed forces at the fronts but for the whole civilian populations in seemingly peaceful towns and cities far behind the lines. What struck us about the atomic bomb was not the numbers killed, but the fact that the bomb indicated that we had penetrated the secret of the most powerful force in the universe, and that no one could predict the future. That is what has worried us. The future control of atomic energy by the various nations is still in doubt. At present the "secret" is *supposed* to be mainly the possession of Great Britain, Canada and the United States. How long will it remain so? We, fortunately, stole a march on the other powers by developing this secret first, but they also have been carrying on scientific investigations which might—or may yet—lead to discoveries in this field of releasing incredible energies by the splitting of atoms.

Without going into minor matters such as the improvements made in the structure of tanks, planes, guns and so on, we may mention another technical discovery, less spectacular than the atomic bomb but considered by some equally effective in winning the war, and the value of which in peacetime may be more quickly proved than seems likely in the case of atomic fission. That is radar.

Radar may be briefly defined as "direction-finding and ranging by radio." What it can do is almost incredible. In the war its uses were, among others, to locate rockets, planes, ships and other enemy offensive weapons which were far beyond the limits of human vision even with the use of any aids up till then available. The location and direction of enemy weapons could be so accurately determined that they could be destroyed without being seen —for example, ships below the horizon or planes beyond the range of vision or behind clouds. Obviously, radar's peacetime uses are likely to be many and, for the present, far greater than are those of the energy released from the splitting of atoms. All great wars, especially of modern times, have brought about discoveries in medicine, mechanics, and in other branches of science, which have had their value in time of peace but, to date, as far as this war is concerned, radar seems to promise the most.[1] The race

[1] I speak as a layman but suggest for those who wish to investigate the problem farther the 52-page pamphlet *Radar* published by the Office of War Information.

between the Axis Powers and the Allies, in improving tanks, planes and so on, would carry us into analysis too technical for this short chapter, but we may note that the balance was finally won by American mass production and the "know-how" not only of those at the head of the great corporations but of the small business men and workmen all down the line. This does not mean that "*we won the war.*" Had it not been for the amazing courage of the British in holding the front line in the "battle for Britain," and for the work of others at a time when we were as yet unprepared both in a psychological and in a military sense, we might well have had triumphant Germans controlling New York and Washington. What I mean is that we put into the scales at the critical moment just that extra weight which tipped them; and it was the plain American business man—big or little—who did it. The business man, of either category, has no *Congressional Record* in which to register his speeches, but *he* it was who did the job. That is now often forgotten, but it must not be.

We have spoken of weapons in the mechanical sense. In this greatest of all wars there were other weapons, of a spiritual and psychological sort, which the Allies possessed and the Axis did not. The first was the love of freedom. The plain fact is that neither the Germans nor their "honorary Aryan" allies the Japanese objected to being governed and regimented in their private lives. The Japanese, for example, may have regarded their Emperor as a god. Well, the British, with all their loyalty to the throne, and the Americans, with their loyalty to their form of constitutional government, have never regarded the head of the state in that way. We could say what we liked, and we have often said a lot not applicable to a god. The Allies simply could not conceive of being goose-stepped.

There was also the psychological viewpoint, which in this war may have had an unusually strong foundation in the spiritual. The wars of all history teem with alliances. But these alliances have been shifting and brittle. I need not run over them here. Any student of history knows them. Never before, so far as I know, has a Grand Alliance proved so close, strong and lasting as that of the Allies in the final and determining stages of what we call World War II but which, actually, was the concluding phase of a single war which had lasted, with an interlude, from 1914 to 1945—if it yet be over.

In the concluding and decisive years, the Alliance, chiefly of "the Big Three," held together as no previous one ever has done. You may give your own reasons, such as the spiritual one I mentioned above, the character and mental resources of the three heads of state—Franklin Roosevelt, Winston Churchill and Stalin—or whatnot. Anyway, they hung together in crisis after crisis as was the case with no other Alliance.

In respect of this team-work, there are two things to note. One is what we may call operative and the other political. As to the first, we want to call attention to the extraordinary and really amazing cooperation of American and British forces in the field. I do not know of any other two nations cooperating as closely and as intimately. In what was perhaps the most important, and certainly the most complicated operation of the entire war, the American General Eisenhower was placed in supreme command over both American and British Empire troops. At present writing, the high esteem in which he is held by both peoples would seem to indicate that he had been the major factor in bringing about this unusually close and harmonious cooperation between the two nations. Many other officers might be mentioned, but the chief fact is that there came to be such a complete harmony between the personnel—both officers and men—of the two nations as to make them practically one for the purpose of winning through to freedom and to the right to live their own lives as they wished.

There were also, however, the political aspects. In the absence, as yet, of the pertinent documents, these political aspects have been publicized chiefly through the meetings of "the Big Three." There were three meetings of special importance. In February—ending on the 12th—Stalin, Roosevelt and Churchill met at Yalta, in the Russian Crimea. Roosevelt had not been well, and, with his physical infirmities, the long journey and strain undoubtedly told heavily on him.

We do not yet know what agreements may have been

entered into at Yalta between the heads of the three states. At the time, it was announced merely that there had, in general, been agreement on the occupation of Germany when defeated, with reparations to be demanded from her, and that the Allies would remain united for peace as well as in order to win the war. From time to time since then, however, certain secret agreements have come to light, mostly in the form of territorial and other concessions made to Stalin, apparently as the price of continuing the absolutely essential participation of the vast and powerful Russian forces in the joint struggle. Stalin was in a position to strike bargains and, as an absolute dictator, the terms he made concerned only himself.

Roosevelt and Churchill were in more uncomfortable positions. They also represented great powers but powers which were democracies. These democracies had been exhibiting the enormous reservoirs of strength which derived from the initiative of free peoples, but their voters, either through Congress, Parliament, or public opinion, had the final say. We need mention here only that, as some of the secret clauses have had to be acknowledged, they have aroused a good deal of apprehension and resentment, not only because of the bargains themselves but quite as much from the uncertainty as to what may still remain hidden. The course of the war, with the successive defeats of Italy, Germany and Japan, would seem to indicate that the democracies of the world are, in the long run, stronger than the totalitarian dictatorships, but sit-

ting around a table a dictator has certain, at least temporary, advantages. It may be added that, in a life-and-death
fight for survival, every decision cannot be made a subject
for public debate, as in the case of a tariff in peacetime.
Nor can the public be even informed of every move.
Hindsight is easy. Foresight, in a great crisis, is difficult.
To me, this seems a valid excuse for whatever may have
been agreed to at Yalta. The wars were, as yet, far from
won; and civilization was at stake.

The next important conference of the Big Three, with
a change in personnel, was held in Potsdam, ending August 1. In the meantime, two important events had occurred.

On the afternoon of April 12 the entire world was
stunned by the sudden death of President Roosevelt. Not
only was he one of the "Big Three," and the leader of
America in the war and in its new international rôle but,
owing to his unprecedentedly long series of terms in the
White House, there were many young Americans who
had never known or voted for any other President. There
were many who believed this to be an unfortunate development in our system of democracy but, be that as it may,
it made his sudden passing from the scene at the rising
crisis of the war all the more of a shock.

A few weeks earlier, on January 20, he had been inaugurated for his fourth term, the first President to serve
for more than two. It has been said that today no one can
endure for more than eight years the terrific strain which

the office entails. There were those who believed, as they heard rumors about the President's health and studied the newspaper pictures of his drawn face during the campaign, that he could not possibly last out the sixteen years for which he had asked.

His health grew worse and, as I have noted, the trip to Yalta was a heavy draft on his failing strength. One may say that in the circumstances, though they were such as to make the decision difficult for him, he should not have accepted a renomination; but not even his bitterest enemy can say that, having done so, he did not give of himself to the utmost for the cause he had at heart and, like a good soldier, fight to the very end.

By April 1 the final offensives, within Germany and on the Ryukyus in the Pacific, had begun, and the President had gone to Warm Springs to rest. He was still putting in heavy days and on the one on which he died he had signed a series of state documents at about 2 P.M. and was sitting for the painting of his portrait when, suddenly, he had a severe cerebral hemorrhage. By 4:35 he was dead. Two hours and a half later, in Washington, the Vice-President, Harry S. Truman, was sworn in as President, and the ship of state sailed on. Roosevelt had been one of the most powerful men in the world and head of what had become the most powerful of all the nations.

Nothing could illustrate better the essential difference between democratic and totalitarian government than the chaos which followed the deaths of Mussolini and Hitler, and which might follow that of any other dictator, and the orderly and wholly constitutional way in which nearly 140,000,000 people, at the pinnacle of their world influence, accepted the transfer of their highest office—no suicides, assassinations, mass murders or revolution, merely a quiet ceremony in the White House, at which, in the presence of the quickly assembled Cabinet members, a simple American, who forty years before had been a clerk in a haberdashery store, and who then had served in Congress, took on the mighty burden, unsought and undesired, of serving as the head of the United States in the greatest crisis of history.

We come now to another striking example of the democratic process at work as contrasted with that of the dictator-totalitarian type. The conference of the new Big Three—Truman, Churchill and Stalin—was scheduled to meet in Berlin—or, rather, near-by Potsdam—on July 16. Truman and Churchill were there, but Stalin, without explanation, failed for some days to appear. The meeting was held over. Eventually, there was a gathering but, meanwhile, there had been a general election in Britain, the first in over five years. Churchill, head of the Conservative Party, had been Prime Minister through all that period during which the British Empire had endured the greatest test of its courage and determination in its thousand-year-long history. Churchill had proved himself a magnificent leader in war, but a democracy has the right to choose, and wise democracies have learned that great leaders in war are not necessarily the best leaders in peace. In any case, over 20,000,000 English voters went to the polls, and the result was a surprisingly overwhelming victory for the Labor Party. Clement Attlee, almost unknown outside of Britain, became head of the government, instead of Churchill, who, like Roosevelt and Stalin, had towered in world affairs. As in America, where the change from Roosevelt to Truman was effected by the former's death and not by an electoral campaign, the shift was accepted without disturbance of any sort. A free people had spoken, and the "Big Three" of the Potsdam Conference became Truman, Attlee and Stalin instead of Stalin, Roosevelt and Churchill. At the Conference, it was agreed to decentralize Germany both politically and economically; to shift the boundaries of Poland; and to create a Council of Foreign Ministers, including those of France and of China.

At the Potsdam meeting, President Truman had courteously been made Chairman, but this was the last meeting, to date, of the heads of states. On December 6, Churchill stated in the House of Commons that he had heard with "great grief" that "the Big Three are never to meet again." However, the Big Three had formerly been more than merely the representatives of powerful governments. They had been men of wide experience in international affairs and of determined minds and wills. Attlee was no Churchill; Truman was no Roosevelt; and Stalin, whose health had not been good, seemed to be relaxing somewhat the reins of power. Neither Truman nor Attlee were as well known throughout the world as were their predecessors, nor did they have their world influence.

The final meeting of the year was held at Moscow, on December 15, but was attended only by Molotoff, the Russian Commissar for Foreign Affairs; James F. Byrnes, who had become American Secretary of State under the new administration; and Ernest Bevin, British Foreign Secretary under the new Labor Government. An earlier meeting of Foreign Ministers in London had ended in a more or less acrimonious stalemate. Although the Moscow meeting was thought by many to have cleared the air, the communiqués were vaguely worded and there was much difference of opinion as to the degree of success actually achieved. In general, an Allied Council was recommended to be set up to control Japan; it was also recommended that the General Assembly of the United Nations should deal with the new problem of atomic energy; that the United States and Russia should withdraw their troops from China and Manchuria; that Korea should be placed under a five-year trusteeship; and that peace treaties with Italy, Rumania, Bulgaria, Hungary and Finland be prepared; and, finally, that Rumania and Bulgaria should be recognized by Britain and the United States. No one can tell as yet just what loopholes there may be in these agreements; what other agreements may have been made, of which we do not know; or how well those agreements of which we do know may be kept.

Turning from these successive meetings of the Big Three, which had grown gradually from the military alliance of the three greatest of the Allies, we now go on to note other international events which involved the United States.

There was, first, the meeting of representatives from practically all the nations of the New World (except Canada) to consider hemispheric solidarity and mutual defense. The result of their deliberations was the document now known as the Act of Chapultepec, from the fact that the Conference was held in Mexico City. Briefly, the old unilateral Monroe Doctrine was superseded by a joint resolution of all New World nations south of the Canadian border to unite in the defense of these continents against the attack of any foreign aggressor, and to consult together as to when such an act had been attempted or contemplated. This Act was dated March 3.

On March 5, in pursuance of an agreement made at the Yalta Conference, at which the Big Three, together with France and China, had been authorized to issue an invitation to certain other nations to join with them at a meeting in San Francisco to form the organization of the United Nations, such invitations were sent out. France declined to sponsor the invitation but the other four powers did, and invitations were sent to thirty-nine nations. The meeting was a successor to that at Dumbarton Oaks, in which France had not joined. The feeling, and the move of America toward internationalism instead of isolationism, was well expressed by Senator Vandenberg in the concluding sentences of his letter of acceptance: "It will be my prayer that the San Francisco Conference may be successful in promoting dependable peace, with organized justice, in a free world of free men. Civilization cannot survive World War No. Three."

In the third week of April the Conference got under way, after a delay due to the late arrival, via Washington, of the Russian Molotoff. Representatives of fifty nations assembled, and one of the minor difficulties, but one which was of more significance than some advocates of a hasty world federation will allow, was the necessity of gathering a fleet of taxicabs whose drivers should have a combined command of sixteen different languages! There were many knotty problems, including the status of the Argentine, the dispute with Russia over the Polish situation, and others which we have not here the space to discuss. The main point at San Francisco—before we move on again to Washington—is that a Charter for the United Nations *was,* at length, successfully drawn up and agreed upon.

Its objects may be best and most succinctly described by quoting a sentence or two from the long address by Secretary of State Stettinius before the Senate Foreign Relations Committee. He said, in small part, that:

This Charter is not the work of any single nation. It is the work of fifty nations. . . . [It] is both a binding agreement to preserve peace and to advance human progress and a constitutional document creating the international machinery by which nations can cooperate to realize these purposes in fact. . . . Members of the organization are pledged to carry out in good faith the obligations of the Charter. They are pledged to settle their disputes peacefully . . . not to use force against the territorial integrity or political independence of any state . . . to give the organization every assistance in any action it takes under the Charter and to refrain from giving assistance to any state against which the United Nations is taking preventive or enforcement action.

The amount of work and thought and, it may be said, of "give and take," had been extraordinary, and the draft of the new association of nations emerged a far better one than observers at times could have dared to hope. If the fact was remarkable that, after the slow failure of the League of Nations, fifty nations had been willing to make a new effort to build a world structure of peace, and had, within a few weeks, at least agreed upon a Charter, perhaps even more remarkable was the change in attitude in Congress from that following World War I. The month of July probably marked the greatest shift in American foreign policy from isolationism toward international cooperation in our entire history. First, on the 13th, the Senate Foreign Relations Committee (Senators Hiram Johnson of California, Murray of Montana, and Shipstead of Minnesota not voting) approved the

United Nations Security Charter by a vote of 20–0. This was breathtaking. Then, on the 19th, the Senate passed the Bretton Woods Agreement by a vote of 61–16, the House having already passed it by 345–18. (It was ratified by twenty-eight nations and went into effect on December 27.) That was the result, after about a year of public discussion and congressional debate. Finally, on the 28th, the Senate ratified the UNO Charter by the astounding vote of 89–2, the only dissenters being Senators Shipstead of Minnesota and Langer of North Dakota. The United States was the first major power to adhere to the new world order, if such it is to prove.

Many men and events had contributed. The President, Truman, unlike Woodrow Wilson, was not at odds with the Senate but had been a former popular member of that body and knew how to get along with it. Leading Senators had been prominent at San Francisco and at the meetings that led up to and followed from it. The then Secretary of State, Stettinius, who had shown his skill in negotiating and smoothing over difficulties at the Conference, had always commanded the respect of Congress. But, aside from these and other personal equations, the world had changed and America had changed. The Senatorial debates were notably lacking in the rancor and bitterness of the days of Lodge and Wilson. In any case, America had set its course in a new direction, though it must remember that documents and words of humanitarian aspiration are not enough. We, as the most powerful nation in the world in 1945, took the lead. We cannot now, like the traditionary ground-hog, go back into our hole for another sleep.

In Great Britain, both Houses of Parliament voted for the Charter unanimously, so that the two great English-speaking Allies were standing together. Just at that moment, however, we took a step which was somewhat misunderstood in Britain and which caused not only alarm but much ill-feeling. The system of Lend-Lease had been one of the most brilliant and fruitful ideas of the late President Roosevelt, or at least of his Administration, whoever may have contributed to it. As Attlee said in Parliament, when Truman unexpectedly and suddenly terminated the arrangement:

The system of lend-lease in the United States and Mutual Aid from Canada and the accumulation of sterling by the sterling area countries have been an integral part of the war organization of the Allies. In this way it has been made possible for us in this island to mobilize our domestic manpower for war with intensity unsurpassed elsewhere and, at the same time, to undertake expenditure abroad for the support of military operations over a widely extended area without having to provide export to pay for our imports of food and raw materials or to provide the cash we were spending abroad.

Those who know what Britain achieved will recognize this as a very mild statement of the case. It had always been understood that the end of Lend-Lease would coincide, more or less, with the end of the wars; but no one, not only among the Allies but even in our own Congress, was prepared for the abrupt termination decreed without preparatory warning by Truman. It is true that the President, in making his twentieth quarterly report on Lend-Lease some days later, stated that in his opinion the United States should write off an "overwhelming portion" of the more than $42,000,000,000 which we had "lent-leased" to our Allies. However, Byrnes almost immediately made his own statement, which brought confusion and left those who had received Lend-Lease uncertain as to where they stood in their economic quandary, with shortages of food and all other imported materials.

In the President's practically final Report it was disclosed that of all Lend-Lease Britain had received, roughly, 42% or about $13,500,000,000; Russia 28% or about $9,130,000,000; and China only 2% or about $198,000,000. As we have explained in earlier chapters, there had also been "Reverse Lend-Lease," and by April 1 we had received in goods and services over $5,600,000,000 from the various parts of the British Empire and elsewhere. Truman in his statement pointed out that in percentages of national income the United States had spent, including everything, no more than had Britain or Russia, but the whole affair of the termination of an arrangement which had done so much to promote harmony and military cooperation between the Allies was badly bungled at the end.

The President had also not been happy in his plans for

the domestic economy. In fairness, it must be said that he had inherited a colossal mess which had not been of his making and that he had not desired the office of Vice-President, which for the first time in our history appeared, in the circumstances, almost certain to lead to the Presidency. Washington, in more than twelve years, had become a vast and intricate network of politics and overlapping alphabetical agencies forming the greatest bureaucracy in our whole national development. The new President understood politics in all its aspects, good and bad, and a President *has* to be a good politician to get anything done. But politics in the ordinary sense had, in the preceding few years, become inextricably mixed up with those of the warring labor factions, particularly those of the Left-Wing of the CIO and its political pressure offspring. This made for complications.

Also the planners and so-called experts, in the government bureaus, made some very bad mistakes in their estimates of post-war unemployment, the rate of reconversion of industry, and so on. We may note, for example, that on August 30, 1945, John W. Synder, then Director of Reconversion, estimated that there would probably be 6,000,000 unemployed by the end of the year, and possibly 8,000,000 by spring. The Chairman of the Social Security Board expected from 5,500,000 to 7,600,000 by December. The Secretary of Labor presaged 6,000,000 to 8,000,000 by spring; Henry Wallace concurred, while Sidney Hillman of the Political Action Committee of the

CIO said 10,000,000 within six to eight months (from August 13). These "experts" figured that there would be intense deflation and that government aid (which they would manage) and public works on a grand scale would be required. On March 23, 1946 (the date lies outside the scope of this chapter but the facts are pertinent), the United States Employment Service announced that the number of requests from employers for employees of all sorts was *ten times* the number of those applying for jobs. This indicates the difficulty of a planned economy in a highly complex industrial society of more than 135,000,-000 people. President Truman did not pretend to be an authority on labor relations. These expert bureaucrats did; so what?

The new President, thrown with hardly a moment's notice into the national driver's seat, had to find his way around. Furthermore, though there had been frequent strikes and labor troubles even during the war, the end of a major war is always the signal for an outbreak of violent demands. Peace seemed to presage not so much a lowering of wages as a reduction in overtime and the "take home," and living costs had advanced to some extent, although not in general as much as straight wages. Incidentally, labor had saved more and accumulated more reserves during this war than ever before, due partly to high wages and partly to the lack of consumers' goods to be bought. Finally, there were the specters of inflation or deflation—the government experts apparently could not

Photographs from Press Association, Inc., Acme Newspictures, Inc. and U. S. Army Air Force

Top, left: General Carl Spaatz. *Right:* General George C. Kenney. *Bottom, left:* General James **H.** Doolittle. *Right:* Major General Curtis E. LeMay.

Photographs from Press Association, Inc., Kenyon and Eckhardt, Inc. and U. S. Navy

Top, left: Admiral Raymond Amos Spruance. *Right:* Admiral Chester W. Nimitz. *Bottom, left:* General Alexander A. Vandergrift. *Right:* Admiral William F. Halsey.

make up their minds which—to be guarded against.

The situation and problems in the United States, and in the rest of the world, were of acute difficulty. To many it appeared that one thing was of primary importance: that production to the fullest capacity should get under way as rapidly as possible to prevent unemployment and *de*flation and also to provide the long-wanted goods which would absorb much of the swollen bank accounts of all classes, including labor, and thus help to prevent *in*flation. This was the view of business and, after VJ-day, factories were reconverted from war to civilian production with a speed which surprised all, including the government experts.

Unfortunately, labor, or at least some of the most influential labor leaders, did not share this view, and from April onward strike after strike occurred. First, among the major ones, came the usual April coal strike which, at that time, threatened not merely to retard reconversion but the winning of the wars themselves, at that time not yet won. We need not list all the strikes called by labor but may note only the beginning of the greatest of them all, which started in November in the automotive industry. If there was one industry which, above all others, had helped to win the war, it had been this one. If there was one industry which could produce civilian goods, such as cars, ice-boxes, motors for all sorts of things, from electric fans to Diesel motor engines, and so on, faster than any other, it was this one. Its employees numbered hundreds of thousands, and their pay was the highest in the world. But the strike came, and lasted for months, costing the people of America all that time in getting back to normal consumption and production, and General Motors alone, with its employees, about a billion dollars loss. The President's "fact-finding committees" and other nostrums of the government experts had proved a costly farce.

Meanwhile, there had been the usual shifting of offices in the top positions, though the rank and file, often highly important if less heard about, tended to cling to office. In the Cabinet, after Truman's accession to the Presidency, one by one—the dates are not important—old members were replaced by new, although Ickes was not to go until 1946. In December 1945 the new Cabinet was as below:

Secretary of State, James F. Byrnes of South Carolina, who replaced Stettinius, successor to Hull.

Secretary of the Treasury, Fred M. Vinson of Kentucky, who replaced Morgenthau.

Secretary of War, Robert P. Patterson of New York, who replaced Stimson.

Attorney General, Tom A. Clark of Texas, who replaced Biddle.

Postmaster General, Robert E. Hannegan of Missouri, who replaced Walker.

Secretary of the Navy, James V. Forrestal of New York, who had previously succeeded Knox.

Secretary of the Interior, Harold L. Ickes of Illinois, who did not resign until early in 1946.

Secretary of Agriculture, Clinton P. Anderson of New Mexico, who replaced Wickard.

Secretary of Commerce, Henry A. Wallace of Iowa, who had already succeeded Jesse H. Jones.

Secretary of Labor, Lewis B. Schwellenbach of the State of Washington, who succeeded Miss Perkins.

In the above list, the members of the Cabinet are arranged in the order in which they succeed to the Presidency in case of the removal, death, resignation or inability to serve of both the President and Vice-President. As Vice-President Truman became President within the first three months of Roosevelt's fourth term, this meant that there was then no Vice-President, so that this list of possible succession is therefore of importance. Truman himself soon made an effort to correct by legislation this defect in our Constitution, but there were objections to the specific suggestions offered and as yet nothing has been done.

On November 20, the trial of twenty-one top Nazis began at Nürnberg, and at present writing is still going on, so that there can as yet be no valid comment on this trial.

In spite of strikes, and what seemed the quite unnecessary delay in getting reconversion, and the release of a much-needed flood of goods for civilian use, under way, war regulations were gradually being relaxed in the latter part of the year: such as gasoline rationing, on August 15; the rationing of shoes, on November 1; of meat, on

November 23; and so on, leaving sugar the only rationed commodity by the end of the year.

Ordinarily, the necrology of the year would call for mention and some notice of the more important individuals who had died, but 1945 was so full of deaths, natural, or in battle, by assassination, suicide, judicial process or other, that it would be hopeless to try to record them here, at the end of this chapter on the world's worst year. The principal deaths were those of the three heads of states: Mussolini by murder, Hitler by self-administered poison, and Roosevelt of a cerebral hemorrhage. After these, we could name dozens of world figures. One whose name cannot be omitted and whose death, the result of injuries suffered in an accident, was internationally mourned, was General George S. Patton, affectionately called "Old Blood and Guts" by his men. This fighting soldier, who typified much that is the best in the youth of America, played an important part in the defeat of Germany and by his gallantry and superb leadership endeared himself not only to Americans but to all who had the Allied cause at heart. We may end, perhaps, by noting, at the close of this period of horror, the passing of one of our finest and most loved men, who had kept through all the miseries and terrors he had witnessed his sense of humanity and warm comradeship, the news correspondent, Ernie Pyle, who was killed at Okinawa, on April 18. *There* was a man, and a guiding hope for a better future—somehow, sometime.

CHAPTER V

THE RECORD OF 1946

THE year 1946 did not have the intense dramatic interest of 1945. It was a period of transition. That, in itself, does not mean too much, for individuals, nations, the world itself, are always in a state of transition from one period or phase to another, and, as the French say of life, "the more it changes, the more it is the same." What lends a sinister interest to what we are living through now is the certainty that if there is *not* a change there will be a complete and horrible end of Man. Civilization cannot survive a World War III of atomic bombs. So far, in spite of the hopes for the United Nations, in spite of the trials we have suffered and the lessons we should have learned, the signs of change do not seem to be bright on the skies over a whole globe which the inventions of science have made to shrink to about the size of a baseball. There are some encouraging points, but not many.

The social and economic patterns, or curves, after every great war—to go back only a century and a half, or so— have shown a remarkable similarity. This, by my own interpretation as I have tried to explain it in other writings, is due not to natural laws, such as those of chemistry or physics, but just to human nature.

During a war, at least on the part of those wholly in favor of it, every effort is bent to win, and every hardship willingly met. Then comes peace, and, especially if it is peace with victory, a huge load is lifted off the hearts of all. They go on a buying spree for all the things which have been denied to them. But they have not won Aladdin's Lamp. Merchants have stocked their shelves. Farmers have grown used to high prices. The economy gets out of gear—wages, prices for farm produce, manufactured goods, cost of living. A readjustment has to be made, and we get the usual *primary* post-war depression. Adjustments *are* made, things look good again, and we go on a big speculative spree. But war destroys capital, and its restoration calls for time and hard work. The big boom busts, and then we have the *real* post-war depression.

For example, let us take only the American Revolution and World War I. The "shooting war" of the Revolution may be said to have ended with the surrender of Cornwallis at Yorktown in 1781. Peace was signed in 1783. There was a spree until 1785, when the primary depression and first period of readjustment set in. This lasted till 1787, when our present Constitution was drawn up, largely as a result of the intense economic difficulties and social unrest. Next came the boom, till the crash of the early 1790's.

After World War I the "shooting war" ended in 1918; peace was signed in 1919. We were having the spree. Then came the first depression of 1920–21; then the big boom until the real post-war smash of 1929. In 1946, and perhaps 1947, we are at the customary stage of this apparently inevitable cycle.

We shall speak of the labor troubles a little later, but before we start on our more or less purely domestic concerns we may repeat what we alluded to in the last chapter, *viz.,* that the so-called history of America is becoming enormously more complex. It is not only that our own political, social and economic life is becoming more complicated but that formerly isolated America has spread over the globe.

I quote a few lines from an extremely important article, "Our Treaty Procedure vs. Our Foreign Policies," by J. Sloan Dickey, President of Dartmouth, in the April 1947 issue of *Foreign Affairs:*

During the first 150 years of our national history our major foreign policies were in the main unilateral in form, negative or merely declaratory in character and restricted in scope. Today they are dominantly cooperative, *i.e.,* contractual in form, and involve positive undertakings as to men and treasure. There is no place, there is no subject, not touched by our concern.

I recommend the entire article to the readers of this chapter, but what I have quoted indicates the difficulty

THE UNITED NATIONS: ITS

GENERAL ASSEMBLY

Up to five delegates from each of fifty-one member nations, but only one vote for each nation. Its duties are to discuss any questions within the scope of the Charter, and submit recommendations to the Security Council.

SECURITY COUNCIL

Eleven members — the Big Five permanent, the other six elected for two-year terms by the Assembly. Investigates international disputes; takes action against aggressors if necessary.

TRUSTEESHIP COUNCIL

Composed of any members administering trust territories; plus those of Big Five not administering such trusts; plus as many others as are needed to ensure equal representation of members who do and do not administer trusts.

SECRETARIAT

Headed by a Secretary General, it includes administrative and research staffs serving the entire United Nations.

ATOMIC ENERGY COMMISSION

Eleven members of the Security Council plus Canada. Will "consider problems arising from the discovery of atomic energy".

MILITARY STAFF COMMITTEE

Composed of Chiefs of Staff of U.S., Britain, U.S.S.R., China and France. Decides composition and directs forces against aggressors under the Security Council.

INTERNATIONAL ARMED FORCES

To be composed of a quota of forces readily available from all members for putting down threats to peace. (Not yet organized. To be decided by Military Staff Committee.)

Special text — revised for the Board of Education, City of New York

ORGANIZATION AND FUNCTIONS

ECONOMIC-SOCIAL COUNCIL

Eighteen members elected for three-year terms by the Assembly. Will coordinate the work of specialized agencies to eliminate economic and social roots of war.

INTERNATIONAL COURT

Fifteen members, chosen for 9-year terms, by Assembly and Council, from candidates nominated by national groups in Permanent Court of Arbitration. Will meet in permanent session to decide legal disputes between nations.

INTERNATIONAL BANK

Part of the Bretton Woods plan, ratified by thirty-five nations. Will provide funds for reconstruction and develop resources not fully employed.

INTERNATIONAL MONETARY FUND

Also part of the Bretton Woods plan. Will be employed by member nations to help stabilize currencies.

FOOD & AGRICULTURE ORGANIZATION

A research and study organization to help ensure freedom from want, increased food production, improved agricultural methods and higher food and nutrition standards throughout the world.

CIVIL AVIATION ORGANIZATION

Organized in 1944 to deal with complex economic and legal problems in commercial air transport operations, and inspect travelers and cargo to prevent spread of disease.

UNITED NATIONS EDUCATIONAL, SCIENTIFIC AND CULTURAL ORGANIZATION

Drafted at London 1945, to develop international cultural understanding and to help make the world's accumulated knowledge available to all.

CHART BY GRAPHICS INSTITUTE FOR THE NEW YORK TIMES

for any historian in telling the story of the U.S.A., even of one year. One can no longer stop at the water's edge. There are the plane routes through the stratosphere, and instead of the stormy Atlantic the North Pole has become the shortest route from the New World to the Old.

We obviously cannot write the history of the world in 1946 in one short chapter, or even cover all the contacts we have had with the rest of the globe; we can touch only a few high spots.

The year 1946 was, as we have said, a year of transition. The wars in the shooting sense had ended in 1945, but peace had not come. Some of the longest industrial strikes in our history were winding their slow way but were not to end until 1947. We were, in a sense, in slack, although very turbid, water.

On the international scene we noted in the last chapter the formation of the United Nations with fifty members. At midnight on April 18 of the year we are discussing, the League of Nations expired. It had not lived in vain, if its successor, the U.N., can build better on the basis of the knowledge we gained from the failures of the League.

Any organization formed by "nations" is bound to encounter its difficulties in the individual characteristics and ambitions of nations as such; but that is a chance which has to be taken. It is better than ironing the whole world flat into one pattern and mode of thought and action, like a gigantic ants' nest. The now-dead League failed for many reasons. The United States, which had been foremost in planning it, did not at last join it. Na-

DANGEROUS INTRUDER
From a cartoon by Fitzpatrick in *The St. Louis Post-Dispatch*.

tions which had joined did not live up to their obligations. They permitted the Japanese invasion of Manchuria and the Italian invasion of Abyssinia, and other matters which led directly to the holocaust of World War II. What we can do now remains to be seen. By March, 1947, Russia, always with its satellite state or puppet government of Poland trailing along, had used its Veto Power ten times to defeat the purposes of the U.N. Security Council; it may continue to use that power to defeat the purposes of the new international organization to which it adhered.

It is too early to make a prediction, and the year 1946 in the U.N., as in so many other factors and phases of our post-war life, comes under the heading of "unfinished business." So much of the twelve months was apparently taken up with squabbles over forms, procedure, and even the site of a permanent location—Westchester, Connecticut, New York City, San Francisco and other points east and west—that the public may have lost interest, and to some extent may also have lost sight of what really had been accomplished. We have to reserve for the 1947 chapter the generous offer by the Rockefellers of $8,500,000 and the final decision to house the U.N. in a little city almost of its own within the city of New York.

A good deal of solid work in the way of handling international affairs and acute complications had been accomplished, and four new nations had been admitted to membership — Iceland, Sweden, Afghanistan, and Siam. The diversity of nations and peoples, and of the problems involved, was rather breath-taking. But we can only wait and see. "Unfinished business" again. Although the permanent home of the U.N. had not been decided in 1946, the year marked the first time that the Security Council held its meeting (the twenty-fourth) in Amer-

EACH TO HIS OWN
From a cartoon by Marcus. Reprinted by permission of *The New York Times.*

ica, at Hunter College, New York. On October 23 the meeting of the General Assembly was opened by President Truman at their temporary quarters in the New York City Building in Flushing Meadow Park. He pleaded for peace and asked that the world should not be split into "irreconcilable parts." During the session, which ended in December, the problem of the veto so constantly used by Russia was discussed, but no final change was made.

Meanwhile the so-called Paris Peace Conference had come to an end on October 14 without making any treaties with the major former Axis powers. It finished in a good deal of acrimony, and Yugoslavia walked out of the final session, indicating that even the smaller powers had a sort of veto. Molotov, for the Russians, talked rather angrily about the Western Powers, saying that they had nothing to suggest; but in fact neither did he and his nation. So ended that.

Another end came on October 16, when eleven of the chief Nazi war criminals who had been tried at Nürnberg died, ten by hanging and Goering by suicide. Those hanged were Wilhelm Keitel, Ernst Kaltenbrunner, Fritz Sauckel, von Ribbentrop (the "von" denoting aristocratic origin was his own fancy decoration), Arthur Seyss-Inquart, Alfred Rosenberg, Julius Streicher, Alfred Jodl, Hans Frank, and Wilhelm Frick. Von Papen and Schacht were held for further trial by a German de-Nazification court, and were condemned by that court the following year. The multiple trial had necessarily been long-drawn-out, but it had been fair; and when ten top Nazis were hanged in seventy-five minutes, that at least was not "unfinished business" for the year. If we consider the ends of Hitler, Goebbels, Mussolini, Ciano and other leaders in the previous chapter, the world had never before seen Nemesis so thoroughly at work.

CAN'T HANG AN IDEA
From a cartoon by Poinier in *The Detroit Free Press*.

To extend the international scene, we can merely mention certain quarters without going into the details needed to understand the difficulties everywhere. Nobody can be a specialist on every country, however wisely columnists may appear to talk on all subjects; and apart from that, to offer information on the globe today calls for not a part of a chapter but a large book.

To indicate briefly some of the sore spots in which we had economic, military or diplomatic interest remaining in the year:

The Far East was in turmoil. We have always had a very friendly interest in China, and of all outside nations I think we have ever been China's best friend. Civil war between the parties of Chiang Kai-shek and the Communists was still going on when President Truman sent General Marshall, former Chief of Staff, to be his personal representative, with the rank of Ambassador. After many months Marshall, who had formerly been fully familiar with China, had to turn in a very pessimistic report, and we began to withdraw some of our armed forces. The problem, especially after the killing of four American Marines by Chinese Reds in August, was complex; but I would trust Marshall's judgment.

In Japan General MacArthur was carrying on the American occupation with considerable success, although the end is not yet. The Emperor Hirohito in his New Year's message to his people had set the stage for the house-cleaning of the Jingo element (which MacArthur later carried out) by announcing that he was not a God. The Emperor did not deny that he was descended from the Sun Goddess, but merely that he was not himself divine. This may seem absurd to us, but it was important news in Japan. However, the Emperor went further and made perhaps the more important pronouncements that the Japanese people were not superior to all other races, and were not destined, as centuries-long tradition had affirmed, to conquer all the world in war. The trials of the Japanese war criminals went on.

Also in the Far East, the Dutch colonies continued in revolt, and rebellion broke out in French Indo-China. The great sub-continent of India itself was seething; there were murderous mobs and every indication of wide civil war between Moslems and Hindus if the British withdrew and gave "India" its complete "independence," both indefinable terms under the circumstances.

In the Near East there were also vast upheavals following the global war. The British prepared to evacuate Egypt and the Sudan, with effects on the control of the Suez Canal and the "life-line" to India. There had been trouble brewing in Palestine between the Jews and Arabs, and Britain was primarily responsible for order in that country. The situation is an extremely intricate one and can be described only as an unholy mess. The sufferings of the Jews in Europe have been very real. We all know of them, but historically and racially the rights of Spanish, Polish, Russian, American or any other Jews to any large part of Palestine are certainly very vague and intangible. The Jews themselves are by no means agreed, and I myself have had letters from Rabbis asking me to speak up for Zionism, or, in other cases, to write against it.

Meanwhile the Arabs are determined that only a certain number of Jews be allowed to come in as immigrants each year. More insist on doing so, and hence the conflicts, the concentration camps, the terrorism, and the problem of what is to be done. The Labor Government in Britain is about through with carrying it alone. At various times, notably in October, Truman had suggested, on occasion tartly, that the British settle it. We sent a delegation to London to discuss the question, but the President rejected their findings. We have given advice but have declined all responsibility, and so far have succeeded only in keeping the kettle boiling.

Then there are Greece and Turkey, to say nothing of Persia—now Iran—and its oil. The Russians threaten a thrust that way, and if the Near East is important for the British Empire it has become increasingly so for us, because of trade routes, oil and other products, and because of the need of keeping alive countries which are threatened by the Communist glacier but would like to hold to their independence.

Moving nearer toward the old Europe, we find the Balkans largely under the sway of Russia, and Poland in the U.N., seems always to vote with the Soviets as just a "me-too." Practically all these countries are dead broke, for the physical destruction of war has been followed by the most fantastic of currency inflations.

For example, take Hungary, from which, oddly enough, I have recently received the first royalties from a Hungarian translation of one of my books. Before this last war a Hungarian *pengo* was worth twenty cents in American money, or five to a dollar. On June 12,

1946, paper pengos were one *trillion* (1,000,000,000,000) to the dollar, and three days later the same number were worth only thirty-five cents. The government were printing larger notes every week. What happens to the economy or the ideology of a people under such conditions?

We have had our troubles with Yugoslavia, another satellite of Russia, through the whole year—Yugoslavs carrying forbidden weapons in our zone of occupation, American fliers shot down, diplomatic notes shuttling back and forth, and constant recrimination on both sides. I cannot linger longer over the international complications—Germany, the strident Left-wing of the British Labor Party, Franco's Spain, or Peron's Argentine. I have said enough to indicate that 1946 was indeed a year of "unfinished business," and that it is going to take on our part a lot of money, courage, and above all knowledge and brains to finish it. With the world, as I said at the beginning of this chapter, shrunk to the size of a baseball we can never again take refuge by drawing into the shell of isolation. *There are no oceans any more.* We may not like it—I do not—but we have to face the fact of a new world and of new dangers, from within and without.

The shift from war to peace was being made, and in the process some things were being finished, or practically so, in the United States. We shall speak of politics later, but here we may say that in his first message to

Congress on January 22, President Truman, in one of the longest messages ever sent—25,000 words—discussed the coming transition from almost every angle. Later in the year he proved himself ready and willing to go a long way in cutting down the war-time agencies and his own war-time powers.

The O.P.A. came almost to a complete end. All price controls were to expire at midnight of June 30. The situation as to prices was chaotic for a time, but although some went up when the ceilings were off, others in time went down. There was, however, distinct anxiety as to what would happen. I need not go into all the details of bills passed, vetoed, repassed, replaced by other bills and so on, for some months through the summer. Suffice it to say that by the end of the year, the O.P.A. (Office of Price Administration), which had done much good work and some clumsy work, as is natural in war, had practically ceased, except for such items as sugar, rents, and a few others. There was also a strong movement to turn rent controls over to the individual States locally, and sugar control was expected to end in 1947.

In August another war agency came to an end: U.N.R.R.A., as it was called to alphabeticize—if I may coin a word—Roosevelt's rather long-winded name for the United Nations Relief and Rehabilitation Administration. The State Department announced that it would ask for no further funds. The organization had had two primary objects: (1) to supply the nations liberated by the Allies with foreign exchange with which to buy goods, and (2) to handle the problems of procurement and shipping. The U. S. A. had appropriated about $2,700,000,000 for these purposes. We had also agreed to contribute through the Export-Import Bank, through the International Monetary Fund, and in other ways, about $15,000,000,000 more. The other organizations had been established. The war had been over about one and a half years.

As always happens when a huge bureaucracy has been set going with billions, there was a clamor, but Undersecretary of State W. L. Clayton was unusually correct when he stated that there was no more need for U.N.R.R.A., and that "the United States is not a limitless reservoir of wealth and goods. We have serious problems of our own." He also remarked that "the gravy train is going around for the last time." The United States had contributed 70 per cent of the total cost for world rehabilitation, in some cases to bolster up regimes such as those in Yugoslavia and Poland which were not even friendly to us. Serious scandals, which had international repercussions had also crept into the Relief administration. Both our State Department and Congress decided on sudden death for it.

Another war adventure which was being placed in the category of finished business was Lend-Lease. The idea of what came to be called by that term originated apparently with Franklin Roosevelt in 1941, and it developed into the most stupendous mutual-aid program in all history. We have spoken of it in previous chapters, and need merely say here that in effect it meant that the Allies would pool all their resources to attain victory —cash, food, munitions, everything. We were the richest nation in the world, and the burden naturally fell heaviest on us on a bookkeeping basis; but we must forever recall that we were not ready for war, and that for two years and more the enemy which nearly vanquished all of us was held at bay by "the blood and sweat and tears," in Churchill's phrase, of the British. It had been a gallant, daring, and perhaps an eventually decisive improvisation on the part of Roosevelt, and one for which all the world, including ourselves, in spite of the cost to us, must always be grateful.

In 1946, however, the time had come to wind up accounts. We ourselves had not been the only ones to "Lend-Lease." Other peoples had done the same for us in what was called "Reverse Lend-Lease." The balances were impossible to figure in dollars and cents, because money had been only part of the almost unthinkably huge and complicated set of transactions. There had been money—yes—but also materials, housing for troops, food, medicines, doctors and hospitalizations for our men as well as the Allies, transport, and everything which could be conceived in a nightmare of an expert accountant.

We opened negotiations with the thirty-four nations which had joined with us, and on December 27, President Truman informed Congress that as near as could be figured in the complications, the others had repaid in Reverse Lend-Lease, or in one way and another, about 70 per cent of the nearly $60,000,000,000 involved. Belgium was the only country which gave us more than we had given to her in her agony, but satisfactory settlements had been made with the United Kingdom, France, Turkey, Australia, New Zealand, and India. At the end of the year we were still awaiting results of negotiation with Russia, China, Greece, Holland, Norway, and the Union of South Africa. Russia was the largest remaining partner in the enterprise, having reecived over $11,000,-000,000 but so far has declined discussion, although it was claimed that she had passed on part of her share to her new satellite states. That was some of the unfinished business.

Meanwhile we had made the greatest single international loan in history. It was $3,750,000,000 to Great Britain, and it passed the House of Representatives by a vote of 219 to 155, with defeat of all suggested amendments which might somewhat have crippled it. The loan was made to enable Britain, which had become weakened in the war (which for a while she had carried on absolutely alone in the world against Germany and the other Axis powers), to regain her strength, and also to enable her to repeal certain regulations she had been forced to make to save the world, as well as herself, but which we felt might hurt us in times of peace.

Briefly we agreed that she could borrow all or such part as she needed, up to 1951. Up to then she would have to pay no interest, but after that she would pay 2 per cent on all she had borrowed, and the principal was to be repaid by 2001. If she suffered a severe depression in any year, interest would be waived for that year. On her own side, Britain made certain agreements in trade which were much to the advantage of the United States.

Although it was rather a year of winding up, one other new international commitment was entered into. This was UNESCO, which stood for the United Nations Educational, Scientific, and Cultural Organization. The 220 voting delegates meet at UNESCO House in Paris, formerly the Hotel Majestic. The plans are rather vague but far-reaching, including world-wide broadcasts, increased international freedom of the press, international exchange of students, and coordination of cultural surveys, among other things. What will come of it, aside from expense, no one yet knows, but forty-four nations joined, with the notable exception of Russia, which seemed to regard the organization as a vast propaganda machine for the capitalist powers.

During the year no final treaty of peace was made with a major power on the Axis side, although a treaty draft was drawn up with Italy, which had become a Republic in June after the abdication of the King and his flight to Egypt. The treaty, which still had to be

Photograph by Press Association, Inc.

THE SECURITY COUNCIL MEETS AT HUNTER COLLEGE

A tense situation developed in one of the meetings of the Security Council at Hunter College, New York City, when Andrei Gromyko, the Russian delegate, stalked from the chamber because the Council refused to postpone discussion of the Iranian dispute.

OPENING SESSION OF UNESCO

The Foreign Minister of France, Georges Bidault, addressing the opening session of UNESCO in the amphitheater of the Sorbonne University in Paris.

ratified by the Big Four, stripped Italy of all her colonies, considerable territory adjacent to the home peninsula, her navy, most of her air force and army, and set aside $100,000,000 in reparations for Russia. The terms suited neither Italy nor Yugoslavia, and how it is to be enforced when the more general settlement of Europe ensues is problematic.

While still considering the unfinished business of the wars and before discussing our more purely domestic affairs, we must speak of that dread menace which has come to hang over all the world, the atomic bomb. For the most part it is all still "top secret," or supposedly so; but there are two matters concerning it which attained much and continuing publicity through the latter half of the year. One was the testing at Bikini, and the other our efforts to devise some sort of international control which might lift the thought of the horrors of World War III from the minds of all mankind. We have not yet succeeded in the second point and have been only partially informed as to the first.

Early in the year, or probably earlier still, it was decided to test the effects of the atomic bombs, which had been so devastating on Hiroshima and Nagasaki, on a fleet at sea. The question to be studied, especially important for the two great sea powers, Britain and the United States, was whether sea power could survive atomic energy. As Admiral W. V. Pratt, U.S.N., explained in an article in February on "Operations Crossroads," as it was called, the United States made the experiment because we had the secret of the bomb and a great store of all types of sea craft. A problem was where to conduct the Operation. The Mediterranean, Atlantic and other waters were ruled out for obvious reasons; in the Pacific winds, weather, harbors, populations and other matters had to be considered.

The choice narrowed down to Bikini, the most northern atoll of the Ralik chain of the Marshall Islands. The spot is unhealthy and produces scant sustenance. It had a population of only about 200, and has an enclosed lagoon ten miles wide and twenty-one miles long to harbor the vessels. The weather could be depended upon, and the winds were right to carry off the destructive radio-activity over wide empty spaces of ocean. The natives were moved to another and better island home, and every possible scientific preparation was made to record results, especially the power of the blast, the effect of intense heat, and of the radio-activity on material and animals.

On July 1 the bomb was dropped. It was the fourth. The first had been in the New Mexico desert, and the other two on the Japanese Empire, ending the war. On July 25 the fifth bomb was dropped, not on the surface but in a moderate depth of water. The effects were different.

When the first bomb was exploded above water, only one ship was within 1000 feet of the explosion, but twenty others were within a half mile. Of these twenty-one, six were sunk and the rest very badly damaged. Tests on the animals (goats, pigs, rabbits, mice and so on) showed that if the ships had been manned by human beings the initial flash of the lethal radiations would have killed almost all the personnel aboard vessels centered around the blast and many at greater distances.

When the second and sub-surface bomb exploded, a column of water about 2200 feet in diameter rose to a height of about 5500 feet, and for a few moments lifted the 26,000-ton battleship *Arkansas* into the air before it plunged to the bottom of the ocean. Waves of some several hundred feet high swirled around the column, which was estimated to have contained about 10,000,000 tons of water, which had become radio-active and fell back in spray on the other ships. The activity was the equivalent of that which would have been produced by many hundreds of tons of radium, and would have killed all human beings at once or within a short time. For some days ships continued to sink, and it was not considered safe to approach them on account of the lethal radium. We need not go into further details; those here have been taken from the official reports made to President Truman on August 2 by the civilian observers and the joint Army and Navy Chiefs of Staff. It has been suspected that the tests revealed even greater dangers to mankind from this demonic weapon than were disclosed.

At present the secret in its full manufacturing entirety

is *supposed* to be known only in the United States, but we do know that Germany had very nearly discovered it for herself, and it is now said that Russia is working on it with the help of scientists imported from Germany. While, as we have said, it is mostly all "top secret," yet we have learned enough to know that another war might be horrible beyond expression, and that something must be done. Atomic energy may indeed open vast vistas for peaceful industry; but though dynamite, gunpowder, and T.N.T. are useful in peace, no one bent on war has hesitated to use them for that purpose also.

Following our discovery, use, and experimenting with the bomb, we have been doing our best to control its use by all peoples. The Report by Bernard Barurch and others suggested one approach to the problem. We have taken it up with the United Nations, but so far no agreement has been reached. It is difficult to see what arrangement can be made to use atomic power in peace, to keep other nations from learning the secret in "one world" of science, or to trust anyone. In the past generation we have seen so many solemn treaties torn up as "scraps of paper," and been told so explicitly by international gangsters like Hitler and others that the bigger the lie the more useful it is, that at present one can only dread the future. It may be said that we should not have made the discovery of atomic fission or used it, but we have unfortunately to remember that Germany came within an ace of beating us to it—and if she had, then what? We finished

HELEN OF BIKINI IN ACTION

The Baker Day explosion of the fifth atomic bomb, at Bikini July 24, 1946, as recorded by an automatically operated camera on a nearby island. This picture shows the column of water as it began to fall.

A NEW CHIEF JUSTICE FOR THE SUPREME COURT

Fred M. Vinson being sworn in as thirteenth Chief Justice of the United States by D. Lawrence Groner, Chief Justice of the United States Court of Appeals for the District of Columbia.

the gangsters of three Axis Powers—but is the world any safer today for democracy than it is for the atomic bomb? There are yet individuals and nations who care more for ambition and aggrandizement than for civilization.

We may now return to more purely domestic affairs, notably politics and economics. Both were heavily influenced by the labor situation; so we may discuss that first. The year was marked by prolonged and bitter strikes, some to run for a year or more and not to be settled until 1947. I have already noted that the primary periods of readjustment after great wars are always notable for difficulties with prices, wages, and social upheaval, partly purely economic and partly psychological. The year 1946 was bad, but on the whole, whatever may be ahead, I do not think it was as bad, from my memory, as around 1920, when I paid thirty cents a pound for sugar, bought the last barrel of flour obtainable on the East End of Long Island, paid $22 a ton for coal which was half slate, and national revolution was openly talked of. It is always well to have some perspective.

The main job of the year was to pass from a war-time program for industry to one of peace-time production. It was a colosssal undertaking. Business, big and little, with its executives and labor, had accomplished the greatest feat of production in world history, but it had entailed a wholesale turnover of goods and the machinery and tools necessary to make them. The end of the wars had come more suddenly than anyone had thought probable or even possible, and we were confronted with the immediate necessity for going into reverse. During the wars we had concentrated almost wholly on war material instead of peace demands—tanks, for example, instead of cars, bombs instead of refrigerators, and so on. We had built camps, hospitals, ships, and all sorts of things, but not dwelling houses. All of a sudden we had to supply the accumulated needs of peace, the needs of an increased population, of millions of returning veterans, need of replacements for wornout cars, of equipment of all sorts.

During the wars two things of prime economic importance had happened. On the one hand, all sorts of goods could not be obtained. On the other, labor had received immense sums in wages and there was a very limited chance to spend money as compared with World War I, when workmen wore silk shirts, their wives fur coats, and every luxury could be bought with the new high pay. In this war it was different. A mink coat, perhaps, but there was a limit to the number of mink coats any one person wanted, and most avenues of expenditure were closed because of lack of goods. So money piled up. I saw it in the savings bank of which I am a trustee in a big manufacturing city, and in the reports of other banks.

Peace came, but not world settlement, with an amazing lack of goods people had wanted—cars, houses, washing-machines, refrigerators, really good clothes, and all the rest—and with an unprecedented amount of cash savings and debts paid off. The one thing needful was *production,* not only to fill long-felt wants but to turn the superabundance of cash on hand into goods and to stave off inflation. A quick readjustment was essential. I think it must be admitted that business did a remarkable job in transforming plants and machinery in huge establishments, such as General Motors, and innumerable small ones, from war to peace; but the difficulty which may have caused us to "miss the bus" was labor with its strikes. I am a "friend of labor," as the phrase goes, and think that labor as a whole made a fine contribution to the war effort. Nor am I trying to compare what labor did at home, in safety and comfort and at high wages, as contrasted with what the ten million or more men and women of the armed forces, in discomfort, did at low pay and risking their lives. We will let that go. The fact remains that, with the plants and factories transformed, we had to *produce.* At that point labor fell down. If we have not got the houses for veterans and their wives and babies, or the goods, including cars and all the rest, that everybody wants and could pay for, the lack cannot be blamed on either capital or executive management. War profits were a myth. Let anyone look at the dividend records of the companies which did most to win the war.

We cannot go into all the details of the strikes which hampered the called-for production; we need mention only some of the long list which operated to raise prices and the cost of living. With a long-pent-up demand for things, with an unprecedented amount of savings with which to pay for them, with limited production, the answer would be obvious—*inflation*. And if the government clamped on "ceilings," then black markets would begin, as they did in some cases. With increased cost of living, increased wages would be asked, and the vicious spiral might be set in motion toward a *Pengo*.

The year opened ominously. The newspapers recorded actual or prospective strikes involving over 2,000,000 employees in leading industries, such as Western Union, Western Electric, the Bell Telephone System, steel, General Motors and others. At Stamford, Connecticut, the bitter strike at the Yale & Towne plant was threatening to become a general one, the first general strike in the history of the State. A strike in the meat-packing business was called for the 16th of January with demands for a 25-cent-an-hour increase in pay for 200,000 workers.

Meanwhile Truman, or his advisors, had lit on the idea of appointing "fact-finding" commissions to determine what increases of wages were called for and might be paid without increasing the cost of the finished products to the public, starting with steel. It cannot be said that the plan worked out. It smashed the government's so-called "wage-price policy," and with the first recommendation for an 18½-cent increase, set a pace for every labor leader, big or little, to aim at or surpass.

Naturally the factor of labor varies from industry to industry. In some, labor cost is as low as about 6 per cent

KEEPING HIM SPINNING
From a cartoon by Marcus. Reprinted by permission of *The New York Times.*

of the total cost of production. In others labor may represent 50 to 60 per cent of the total. There can be no straight line across all industries, but there is a tendency, natural in a way, for labor leaders, if one of them gets a certain rise, to try to get the same for their unions regardless. So when "fact-finding" pointed 18½ per cent in one case, that appeared to set the lowest figure for all to shoot at. Some of the broader aspects of the President-Labor situation will be mentioned when we come to the politics of the year, and we shall here continue with some of the strike news.

It was incessant, and marked by every arrogance on the part of so-called labor leaders, in disregard of the general public interest and even of our form of government. The Wagner Act and others which had been passed in the heyday of the New Deal, and which appeared to create one world of law, crimes and patriotism for capital and a much more comfortable one for labor, had been largely responsible, and Congress cannot escape its own share of blame.

To mention a few dates: We may note that the packing-house strike began January 16, causing a nation-wide shortage of meat for all. Five days later the steel strike began, resulting in dropping steel output, when it was so badly needed for cars, building, and everything people wanted, to the lowest point in fifty years. On April 1, John L. Lewis called out the soft-coal miners, and although the government under its still existent war-powers seized the mines from the owners on May 21, the strike continued. A nation-wide railroad strike precipitated by a few unions was forced to end by Truman on May 25. This strike, which would have paralyzed the whole effort of the nation to recover from the war, was one of the bad spots, because the railroads had been practically under government control for more than a generation as far as rates and other factors in operation were concerned, and the Railway Brotherhood had been almost the most conservative of unions among highly paid and highly skilled labor. A. F. Whitney, head of one of the rail unions, when thwarted in his purpose by the President and public opinion, threatened to raise a fund of millions to defeat Truman in 1948 should he run for President. We were used to the struttings of a John L. Lewis or a "Cæsar" Petrillo, but we had not expected that sort of thing from the Railway Brotherhood. On September 5, the maritime workers started a series of strikes which practically closed the ports of the nation to shipping, stopped commerce and our aid to the starving in other countries.

There were many other strikes of importance, or strikes threatened by unions which held a pistol at the head of the public, such as the Subway of New York, under Quill. The entire city of Pittsburgh, a most important producing city, was stalled for weeks with enormous loss of goods for the entire country and public and with intense discomfort to its own local inhabitants. Under the Wagner and other Acts already mentioned, labor leaders have come to consider themselves immune to the laws and penalties which control all the rest of us.

Who are the rest of us? Who is a laboring man? Who

is a capitalist? It is getting hard to say. Is a noted labor leader who is reputed to have a salary of $25,000 a year and a handsome house a laboring man, and is an old man who may be trying to get along on $2500 a year from a lifetime of accumulated savings a capitalist?

There are certain things which stand out in the strikes of this "year of transition." One is what I have just pointed to. Another is the recklessness of the leaders and their utter disregard for everybody else in the world. Two others are the needlessness of so many strikes and their enormous waste to both the workers and the public. This chapter is not an essay in economics but in history. The history of 1946, however, points a moral if it does not "adorn a tale."

We can touch on only two or three other labor conflicts, and must get on. The strike, marked by violence, which lasted more than a year at the Allis-Chalmers plant, was not over until 1947, but we can sample a few more.

There was the longest and costliest strike in the automotive industry, that against General Motors, which was ended in March. What happened? Of the C.I.O. Automobile Workers Union, 175,000 went without working and without pay for 113 days, in an endeavor to increase the company's offer of a 10 *per cent* raise to the figure set by Truman's committee of a 19½ *cent* raise. The strike was finally settled on a basis of 18½ cents, and some side benefits, but it was estimated that the workers would have to work steadily for five years to make up in lost pay the difference between the company's voluntary offer and what the strikers got. At the Chrysler and Ford plants the workers got 19½ cents and 18 cents increase by negotiation without strikes and with no stoppage of production. The General Motors strike is estimated to have cost the workers $127,690,000 (the figures of their union); it cost the company $600,000,000 in unfilled orders, the dealers $100,000,000 in lost commissions; and the public had to go without the cars and other goods that they wanted and needed.

To note another case: the C.I.O. strike at the Granite City Steel Company plant lasted 150 days, the longest in the steel industry. The company had offered 20 cents-an-hour increase, but the C.I.O. leaders demanded 26 cents. The strike was settled after about five months at 21 cents. The workers had lost an average of $1160 each, and it would take them fifty-five years to make this up from the one cent gained, which they had been fighting about. The strike cost the public 150,000 tons of badly needed flat-rolled steel. These are merely samples to show the extreme waste in strikes for companies, men, and the public—and most of us are "the public."

We cannot even mention the many other strikes which, as we have already said, occurred all over the country throughout the year. We will end with the second coal strike.

Soft coal has, of course, been essential for industry of all sorts, including to a great extent the railroads, although many are now changing over to oil on account of the frequent and unpredictable strikes of the miners and consequent lack of fuel. We have already mentioned the strike which began on April 1 and ended only in May after the government had taken over the mines.

On October 21 Lewis, in a public statement, declared that Secretary of the Interior Krug had broken the government contract with the miners on two technical points. By the middle of November the issue was joined between Lewis and the government. The problem was whether to accept the dictation, even that of Green of the A. F. of L. who joined with Lewis, or to fight for the rescue of the economic and social stability of the nation. Even strong pro-labor Senators warned Truman that the time had come. The President decided to fight. Winter was approaching. The country had only thirty-seven days' supply of coal above ground, it was said. In two weeks steel mills would have to close; in twenty days railroads would stop running; in thirty days public utilities would have to discontinue service.

Lewis did not declare a strike. He simply said there was no longer a contract, and as miners would not work without one he knew what to expect. On November 20 the mining of soft coal in twenty-eight states came to a halt, and 10,000 anthracite miners also walked out. The production of over 2,000,000 tons of coal daily for American industry, for American health and comfort, stopped. Lewis kept silent.

However, on the 18th Justice Goldsborough of the

United States District Court of the District of Columbia, issued an order restraining Lewis from cancelling the contract with Krug, and if he did not obey it to appear November 25 to show why he should not be held in

STILL TO BE WEIGHED
From a cartoon by Herblock in *The Washington Post.*

contempt of court. Four hundred thousand miners were out and remained out. Two hundred and fifty thousand other workers had been forced into idleness; millions were expected to be out if the strike continued; 25,000,-000 tons of coal had not been mined; and 1,000,000 tons of steel had not been made, according to estimates.

On December 3, Lewis was declared guilty of contempt, and the following day he was fined $10,000 and his union $3,500,000. In pronouncing sentence Goldsborough is quoted as saying: "This is not the act of a low lawbreaker, but it is an evil, demoniac, monstrous thing that means hunger and cold and unemployment and destitution and disorganization of the social fabric; a threat to democratic government itself." Lewis's lawyer shouted "shame and double shame." Lewis joined himself to that and other remarks, but two hours later gave in. He ordered the miners back to work until *March 31, 1947.* The freight embargo was lifted; the 50 per cent of train service was resumed; Pittsburgh and other centers began to produce again; lights went on; hospitals, schools and homes were saved from the threat of freezing. Another strike was over for a time.

There is an old saying that figures do not lie but figurers do. I have no intention of suggesting that the Bureau of Labor Statistics under recent administrations have falsified figures, but it is often difficult to know just what they mean. Strikes are figured in lost hours of manwork, but it is a question how far the estimates are carried. Are they the lost hours in a "struck industry" or is the estimate carried through all the ramifications of a strike in coal, steel, railroads, makers of parts essential to some other industry, and so on? In any case, the government figures, not published until April, 1947, but relating to the year 1946, do give us some idea of what happened. The Bureau of Labor Statistics then reported that in the preceding year strikes had caused a loss of 116,000,000 man-days, more than a million each in the cities of Buffalo, Chicago, Cleveland, Detroit, Houston, Los Angeles, New York, Philadelphia, Pittsburgh and San Francisco. This indicated the nation-wide extent of the troubles, and the added fact that, even as the government figured, the lost hours were three times those due to strikes in 1945.

Without going into all the rest of the strike situation in 1946, we may now turn to the political scene of the year.

Truman, who had not particularly wanted the Vice-Presidency, had been hurtled into the Presidential office in an hour or so after Roosevelt's sudden death in 1945. Such changes in position have often been extremely sudden, as for example after the assassinations of Lincoln and McKinley; but it is one of the shortcomings of our form of government that the man who thus finds himself, with hardly any warning, the most powerful individual in the United States and perhaps the world, had not been an understudy, or sufficiently familiar with all the problems he is unexpectedly called upon to handle or solve. After World War I, a President did try to have the Vice-President sit in at Cabinet meetings, but the plan proved somewhat impracticable. The Vice-President, under the Constitution, is the presiding officer of the Senate, and it is impossible to combine that job with that of an active member of the Cabinet. It has not been tried again; so the man who at any moment may be called upon to assume the office of President perforce remains more or less outside the constant inner councils of the administration.

When Truman, on the afternoon of Roosevelt's sudden death, had to take the oath of office and become the leader of the nation, he was extremely modest and even humble in the face of the task ahead of him. We Americans are a kindly folk, I often think—from living and observing in many lands—the most kindly in the world. We sympathized with Truman, wished him well, and waited.

He had, I think, about the hardest job which ever awaited a Vice-President when called almost at a moment's notice to be President. Some other Vice-Presidents, with somewhat limited experience and background, had done well, such as Chester Arthur after Garfield; but when they had to take the helm the ship of state was on a fairly steady course and the weather was not stormy. Truman came in at one of the greatest crises in American and all world history. Moreover, his predecessor, Roosevelt, for the first time in the history of the Presidency, had been elected for a third and a fourth term. His power had been great. He had been immensely popular with at least more than a majority of the electorate. A large percentage of the younger voters, men and women, had never known any other President. He had been a leading figure in the years of depression and war. He had appointed eight of the nine justices of the Supreme Court, a contingency never anticipated. He had built up his continuing power on an odd combination of pressure groups and city bosses, including labor, having taken $500,000 from the miners' union in one election and having built up John L. Lewis for a while. He had had immense "war powers," and those which were granted in the continuing "crises" which he had declared. He was the center of the stage.

Truman, although a Senator, was not a world figure or even a national figure, and had not been in a position, except on the sidelines, to see how the New Deal "clicked." But at first he seemed to feel—which was perhaps natural—that he must carry on the Roosevelt policies, where he could find them, and make the Deal click with something of the former tick-tock. The public began to feel that he was bewildered, and that he was trying to be just a "me-too" in the cast of a play in which he had not rehearsed. His stock went down rather sharply.

Gradually, however, he appeared to be learning to stand on his own. Little by little the Gallup polls and other indications pointed to a rising popularity. Also he was becoming more used to the responsibilities of his office. Between the two, his confidence in himself and his enjoyment of power and responsibility increased. He began to become more President in his own right instead of just someone pledged to carry out the known policies —or unknown, like Yalta—of his predecessor.

223

Two things were possibly effect and cause of the change in his own attitude and that of the public. One was that during the year the remnants of the New Deal Cabinet were wiped out, and the other was Truman's position as to labor. Truman is, of course, friendly to labor, as most Americans are, but under the New Deal labor had, thanks to the administration and Congress, gradually been relieved of many of the legal restrictions placed on all other citizens. Congress sensed that public feeling was beginning to shift, and although Truman vetoed the Case Bill and some other strongly anti-labor acts, he ended the year with a knock-down-and-drag-out fight with John Lewis, some years back the pet of Roosevelt. The end is not yet, but Truman and the administration won the final round of 1946. It began to be evident that Truman was no longer the trustee, so to say, of the Roosevelt political estate, but President of the United States from Missouri, and popular polls indicated that the public acclaimed the change.

As to the Cabinet: On page 182 I noted the changes in the Truman administration to the end of 1945. There were two familiar figures remaining, Harold L. Ickes, Secretary of the Interior, and Henry A. Wallace, Secretary of Commerce. There were a number of "blow-outs," so to say, in both the Cabinet and the Supreme Court during the year.

The first was especially pungent, as Mr. Ickes always was. Ickes had been Secretary of the Interior for thirteen years, and had been an able and faithful public servant, although there were many, including myself, who were far from agreeing with all that he did. He was a self-styled "old curmudgeon," and it was a tribute to his underlying honesty of intention that many who did not like some of his acts or much of his language nevertheless accepted the title with a certain degree of genuine affection.

Truman had nominated Edwin W. Pauley, a man with large private interests in oil, to be Under-Secretary of the Navy, and a feud broke out between Ickes, who opposed the nomination, and the President. The public did not like the nomination too well either, for Teapot Dome still smelled. Without reflecting in the slightest on the personal integrity or capacity of Mr. Pauley, I may say that the suggested appointment seems to have been unwise; but the President stuck to it. Ickes insisted that there was a question raised between his own veracity and that of Truman, wrote an extremely caustic letter, and handed in his resignation, which was accepted. The change did not strengthen the administration, but it did mark another step away from its being the administrator of the Roosevelt household and four terms of office. The new Secretary was Julius A. Krug of Wisconsin, who still holds the position.

In June there was another shake-up. Truman made the nominations, later confirmed by the Senate, of Secretary of the Treasury Fred M. Vinson to become Chief

Justice of the Supreme Court succeeding the late Harlan F. Stone, which placed eight Democrats on the highest Court. He also nominated John W. Snyder to take Vinson's place as Secretary of the Treasury, and John J. Sullivan to the contested post of Under Secretary of the Navy.

Before going on to the last change in the former Roosevelt Cabinet, we may speak of another occurrence in June, perhaps the most unseemly row which the Supreme Court has ever offered to a public which has always had the highest respect for it. Justices Robert H. Jackson and Hugo L. Black attacked each other violently in the press. Such terms were bandied between them as "war," "weapons of the open warrior" and "stealthy assassin." I recall in history nothing like it. Both men were Roosevelt appointees. That President had had apparently little understanding of the function and high position of the Court, for in spite of some of the magnificent services he had rendered, he had suggested at times that the Justices consult him before handing down their decisions; he had tried to pack the whole Court so that it would interpret the Constitution as he wished, and had appointed men who had rendered party service rather than men who had had experience in the judiciary. So much was this true that in a number of cases Justices could not take part in decisions because in one way and another they had already been involved in the litigation before it reached the highest tribunal of the land. Justices are appointed practically for life, in spite of the talk of the "nine old men" when Roosevelt was trying to pack the Court, and that is one of the serious dangers to the people in the break from the two-term tradition established by Washington and maintained until 1940. We are supposed to have three branches of government—the Executive, Legislative, and Judicial, each acting as a possible check on the other. But if the Executive is elected for three, four (as Roosevelt) or more terms, the Judicial branch may be wholly appointed by one Executive, as it practically is now. It is interesting, however, to observe that men remain men, and that although Roosevelt appointed men who, he thought, would decide as he wanted, there have been more 4–5 decisions than before.

In September came the final important blow-up in the Cabinet. Henry Wallace had lived in the public eye and at public expense from 1933, when he had been made Secretary of Agriculture by Roosevelt. He has long been a center of controversy, and there was considerable opposition when in 1940 Roosevelt insisted on the Convention's naming him as his running-mate as Vice-President. He served in that office until 1945, but Roosevelt had consented to drop him and had run with Harry Truman. He was then made a member of the Cabinet as Secretary of Commerce; but there had been a row with Jesse Jones, and although the Commerce Department had presumably absorbed the R.F.C., of which Jones had been head, the Senate split the two when confirming Wallace. In 1946 there was the trouble with Ickes, Wallace, and Bowles. Then in September came the speech by Wallace at Madison Square Garden in favor of Russia and against Byrnes; it was what some journals called "the Wallace nightmare." The President fumbled the ball at first, but he had to stand by Byrnes. The public that had been treated to the squabble between two Justices of the Supreme Court, now witnessed that of two Cabinet members: the Secretary of Commerce attacking the Secretary of State. Wallace had to resign and his resignation was accepted. He is now editor of the left-wing *New Republic*. With his departure the Roosevelt Cabinet came to a complete end. Averell Harriman, previously ambassador to Great Britain, became the new Secretary of Commerce. It cannot be said that the New Deal was ended, but there was a new head of state, and new faces around his council board.

Meanwhile Congress had adjourned in the first week of August. In its seventy-ninth session the legislative body had made history and had also disappointed some hopes. The honeymoon of the accidental President and of Congress had somewhat come to an end the preceding September. During the session the President had submitted in all thirty-two major programs. Of these Congress went with him on ten, refused to follow on fifteen, and compromised with the White House on seven. The two important points were that it was no longer a rubber-stamp Congress that would take orders, and also that it had reversed a legislative trend of years in international affairs. The charter for the United Nations had been accepted, as well as our participation in that organization. The huge loan to Britain had been favorably acted on, and other international agreements made. If the old isolationism was not completely dead, it was evident that the people, through their representatives, had changed their course and embarked on the new responsibilities with which our tremendous influence in the War had saddled us. This time we did not scuttle; we tried to carry. Elections proved the changed temper, and that in the fall recorded a marked reversal from the previous sixteen years.

The election was an "off-year" one, but the total number of votes cast was 35,874,568 out of a possible total of voters over twenty-one of 91,634,472. It was not only an "off-year," but there was an enormous dislocation of votes due to changes in residence during the war and the forces which were still overseas. However, in comparison with the preceding "off-year," 1942, the 1946 vote showed an increase of nearly 6,500,000 ballots cast, which indicated interest. The Republicans outvoted the Democrats in thirty states with electoral votes of 362. The eighteen states in which the Democrats won have an electoral-college vote of only 169. The Republicans gained control of both Houses of Congress for the first time in fourteen years. This did not settle 1948, but it did indicate that the trend notable for several elections was continuing.

Truman accepted the defeat of his party, in what was a political landslide, with good grace. He indicated that for the good of the country he was anxious to work in harmony with a Congress controlled by his political opponents. All of these things—the winding up of the old New Deal Cabinet; the defeat, at least temporary, of the John L. Lewis who had first climbed to power by contributing $500,000 for the election of Roosevelt; Truman's increasing grasp of foreign affairs, his ready acceptance of his party's defeat in November—all contributed perhaps to the marked rise in his popularity from the low point to which he had fallen in popular esteem at the beginning of the year.

Although this account of 1946, in which the United States was playing a part in almost every quarter of the world, is necessarily inadequate, we can mention only a few more points with which to conclude it. This is, after all, only a chapter and not a book.

We may speak first of a matter not usually touched on in history—the weather, which Mark Twain once said every one talked about, no one did anything about. The winter of 1946–47 will long be remembered as the worst in two or three generations, particularly in Britain and on the continent of Europe. Blizzards blocked roads and railroads by snow; intense cold and floods and gales killed crops and vast numbers of domestic cattle, caused intense suffering, prevented distribution of food and fuel, especially coal for manufacturing, and in every way helped further to disrupt an already disrupted civilization. In a word, the weather increased our obligations to other suffering peoples, and added to the economic and political unrest everywhere. It seemed almost as though Heaven were punishing man for the horrors which he himself had let loose in the world since 1939.

At home our national debt had risen to fantastic figures, and, in spite of efforts to cut the cost of government, that too kept rising in the number of federal employees and their pay. There were, however, marked contrasts. The salary of the Chief Justice of the Supreme Court was raised from $20,500 to $25,000; the salaries of Congressmen from $12,500 to $15,000, and so on. But although office boys in government employ were raised from $1440 to $1690, there was no increase for the President of the United States from $75,000, for the Vice-President from $15,000, or for a member of the Cabinet from the same figure. The great democracy may figure that $75,000 is a large income, as it regards salaries of some of the executive heads of large corporations with great responsibilities, but it forgets the taxes and the necessary expenses attached to the job. Later in the year it was figured that after income taxes and such expenses as he *had* to pay for the White House (although the government pays some) the President of the United States had a "take home pay," as labor calls it, of $4500 a year. It is interesting to compare that with the huge fortunes in palaces, works of art and property of all sorts accumulated by a Hitler or by any other prominent man in a totalitarian state, including possibly Communist states.

Among the notable deaths of the year were Harry Hopkins, who had been Roosevelt's most confidential adviser; Senator Carter Glass of Virginia, who had been for a generation or more a leader in finance in the Senate; the retired Justice McReynolds of the Supreme Court; General Stilwell, who had won fame in the war in the Pacific and had built the Stilwell road to China; and "Jimmie" Walker, ex-Mayor of New York City.

On the whole the year ended in a gradual emergence from war to peace but with serious labor trouble behind us and more to come in 1947. Two things stood out. Democracy had proved its worth in the war, and we had made not only enormous but sudden and unexpected transitions from an old order to a new. We took the elections in our stride. We did not collapse when Roosevelt died. The ship of state sailed on, even though the waters were rough and stormy. Moreover, we seemed at last to have grown up and to be willing to assume our role as the most powerful country, or one of the two most powerful countries, in the world. The gradual collapsing of the old British Empire presaged a new world in which we should have to play a leading role. We had cause for pride as well as for anxiety.

CHAPTER VI

THE RECORD OF 1947

THE field to be covered by each of these Supplementary Chapters, as also the task of writing them, has increased enormously since in 1933 I undertook the first one in order to keep the original four volumes up to date. After World War I, and, specifically, with our refusal to participate in the League of Nations, we had turned our backs on the rest of the globe. Our thoughts were almost entirely concentrated upon ourselves within the forty-eight states, with an occasional uneasy glance at Alaska and our outlying island possessions.

In those earlier additional chapters, there were to be chronicled the great depression of the '30s; the glittering promises of the "New Deal"; and surprising developments in politics and constitutional government. The story of those years was not simple but, from our present viewpoint, extraordinarily local. Then 1939 brought the beginning of World War II and our history veered in an entirely new direction. The history of what happened I have tried to tell, year by year, as far as mere current reporting may be considered history.

With the Spanish War of 1898, we had become a great power, to be reckoned with by other nations, but we still went pretty much our own way. With World War I, we became a "world power," but afterward shied away from what that entailed. We emerged from World War II as the most powerful of all nations except as regards military man-power, in which Russia exceeded us. In wealth, in production of goods for peace or for war, in "know how" in techniques, in inventive ability and other elements of strength no one could any longer compete with us. There was another and tremendously fateful factor, fateful for ourselves and for the whole of world civilization. After World War II we did not "shy away." We are still a bit dizzy and overwhelmed by the responsibilities and obligations which we have found thrust upon us, but, with the exception of a comparatively small number of die-hard isolationists, both the people at large and their leaders have this time accepted our new position. Popular polls and congressional votes clearly indicate this.

The steady shrinking of the British Empire to which, in spite of its faults, the whole world, including ourselves, had looked in large part for international stability and security, political and financial, in the four quarters of the globe and on the Seven Seas, left vast vacuums which must be filled by some other nation capable of taking over with the same strength and the same ideas of human freedom, individualism and personal liberty. I do not mean that we have to step in and govern those peoples whom the Empire has freed from its own control, but we are called upon to stabilize in freedom the rapidly developing new world of independent and free nations, so that they shall not fall into a worse condition than before, thus endangering their own liberty and ours.

In our recent post-war history, perhaps the most important item is the fact that we have accepted the challenge of that job. The outstanding fact in the history of 1947, made clear by a multitude of continuing incidents, may well be this—that the U.S.A. and the U.S.S.R. have become the two giant nations contending with each other for determination of the future course of world history. On that we shall have more to say later on and may merely mention here that, though *we* have no desire to expand *our* limits, Russia, already the largest territorial unit on earth, most evidently proposes to expand *hers*.

A CARTOON COMMENT ON RUSSIA'S FOREIGN POLICIES
From a cartoon by Manning in *The Arizona Republic*.

Again, the difference is ideological—to use an ugly and clumsy current word. America has been made what she is by the traditions and the immigrants brought to this land from Britain and western Europe, and especially by their hopes of becoming free and independent with a chance to say and think what they wish and to make the most of themselves as men and women untrammelled, as far as that is possible, by government or by the chains of the past. Russia is a totalitarian police state. The events of 1947 have made that clear. The new world-alignment of powers has set new problems. That is why I quoted, in the chapter covering the preceding year, a sentence from an article by the President of Dartmouth: "There is no place, there is no subject, not touched by our concern." And so we begin this chapter with our world concerns rather than with our domestic ones.

In dealing with the former, it might be simpler to discuss them country by country or topic by topic, but a chronological treatment of the year's foreign affairs will, I think, give a better understanding of the complex and constantly shifting problems to which we have had to accustom ourselves. Two points may be mentioned first, as background.

Toward the beginning of the year, January 7, President Truman announced the resignation of the Secretary of State, James F. Byrnes, and the appointment of General George C. Marshall to succeed him. Although this would ordinarily call for comment in the section devoted to our domestic and political news, the center of gravity for America had so shifted toward international affairs that the unexpected change of the head of our State Department was news of the first importance not only to ourselves but to all the world. Although unexpected, the transfer of office was not, as some papers said, "sudden." Byrnes had long been an ill man and had wished for many months to be relieved of the strain of office. He had remained only at the repeated insistence of the President. Marshall while still in China had known of his own appointment but the secret had been well kept by all three men. The retirement of Byrnes was generally regretted, but the name of his successor was widely acclaimed both at home and abroad.

The Senate acted with unprecedented speed in confirming the nomination by unanimous acclamation. That a Republican-controlled Senate should so act on the nominee of a Democratic President was notice to the world that the country was, this time, wholly united in a bipartisan foreign policy. Politics appeared at long last to have "stopped at the water's edge." This was the more welcome inasmuch as at a time when we needed continuity and unity in our relations with the rest of the world Marshall was the fourth man within the space of twenty-five months to be in charge of them.

The second factor which we may mention as background was the United Nations. It might be thought, in view of the high hopes raised by its organization, that we could more or less follow international affairs through its proceedings as recorded during the year by press and radio. In fact, however, although it has started some important projects it has been too largely preoccupied with matters of procedure, organization, and, unfortunately, violent recriminations (mostly on the part of Russia and her satellite states) to serve the purpose of a guiding thread to our story. And now we shall start on our journey. It will take us to many far parts—parts to which, a generation or more ago, "American history" did not have to travel, except in the wake of business.

For the thirteen months before he flew home to become Secretary of State, General Marshall had been in China vainly trying to bring peace between the warring factions there. His Report to the President was not encouraging. In brief it stated that the Kuomintang party contained too many dyed-in-the-wool reactionaries and the Communist party too many dyed-in-the-wool Marxists, the latter determined to make all China Communist eventually. Each party completely distrusted the other although each contained very considerable liberal minorities. These minorities, however, were without cohesion, political experience, arms or other resources. Without American aid they could do little. The Americans have always been friends of China and were formerly popular there, but the propaganda of the Communists, in Marshall's official words, "has given plain evidence of a determined purpose to mislead the Chinese people and the world and to arouse a bitter hatred of Americans. . . . Sincere efforts to achieve settlement have been frustrated time and time again by extremist elements of both sides." This is part of what, in the preceding chapter, I called "unfinished business."

We shall mention later, under domestic affairs, the President's various messages to Congress, but may mention here his Proclamation of the last day of 1946, published in the news of January 1, 1947, which did in some ways mark a piece of finished business. Although its chief effect was on home legislation, even the straddle of dates is suggestive of the increasing straddle between what was becoming domestic and what foreign in our growing complexity. The Proclamation was brief, and declared, after a few words of introduction, that "although a state of war still exists, it is at this time possible to declare, and I find it to be in the public interest to declare, that hostilities have terminated."

The President emphasized that the "states of emergency" declared by Franklin Roosevelt in 1939 and 1941, and the state of war itself, had not been terminated. The last would presumably not be terminated until Congress had authorized peace treaties with the many belligerents. The declaration of a termination of hostilities, however, had the effect of terminating immediately eighteen statutes based on the use of that phrase and, within six months or at a later definite date, thirty-three others. Some were important and some had then ceased to be so, although in one case the declaration had involved the termination of $1,500,000,000 in taxes. The Proclamation seemed, nevertheless, to indicate that Truman was then willing to relinquish *some* of the swollen power which the Roosevelt administration had accumulated. It appeared also to suggest, in spite of certain technicalities of phrasing, that the time had come for peace-making and starting the world on the way toward reorganization and recovery.

A year has gone by since then and there has been no general peace conference like that of Vienna in 1815 or that of Paris in 1918–1919. However, a start was made with the completion, after fifteen months' work, of treaties between the Allies and (separately) five of the satellite states of Hitler—*viz.* Italy, Hungary, Rumania, Bulgaria and Finland. With the exception of Finland, with which the United States had not been at war, each treaty was negotiated between the individual enemy state and, on the side of the Allies, Russia, Great Britain and Northern Ireland, the United States, China, France, Australia, Belgium, the Byelorussian Soviet Socialist Republic, Brazil, Canada, Czechoslovakia, Ethiopia, Greece, India, Holland, New Zealand, Poland, the Ukrainian Soviet Socialist Republic, the Union of South Africa, and "the People's Republic of Yugoslavia." The list is interesting as indicating, even with the exclusion of Germany, Austria,

Japan and other nations which had participated in the struggle, not only the mondial character of the conflict but also the new geography of nations and peoples to which we have had to get accustomed.

The drafting was finally completed by the Foreign Ministers Council of the Big Four (the U.S.A., the U.S.S.R., Great Britain and France) in New York on December 12, 1946, but the texts of the five treaties were not made public until January 17, 1947. It was hoped that when signed in Paris they would make possible the early evacuation by the conquerors of some parts of Europe and ease the important task of drawing up peace treaties with Austria and Germany when the Big Four should meet in Moscow in March.

It is impossible to go into the details of the terms imposed in each case. (The texts of the treaties were published in full in *The New York Times* of January 18, and fill eleven newspaper pages of small print.) In general, they dealt with boundaries, reparations, and demilitarization. Italy gave up all claim to her African colonies, the future disposition of which was left to the Big Four; ceded territory to France, Greece and Yugoslavia; agreed to pay a total of $360,000,000 in reparations to Yugoslavia, Russia, Greece, Ethiopia, and Albania; her armed forces were cut to a nominal figure and the bulk of her navy was turned over to the Allies. The other treaties, with varying details, followed much the same pattern but provided that Allied troops should be withdrawn from Italy and Bulgaria within ninety days after the signing.

It is evident from a reading of the treaties that Russia

was building up herself and the former Hitler satellite states—now satellites of Russia—which she intended to

HOPING IT WILL HATCH
From a cartoon by Seibel in *The Richmond Times-Dispatch*.

absorb into her own system. It had been hoped, as we have said, that the work of the Big Four might ease the situation for the Moscow Conference, but there are some interesting points to be noted. Except for the radio "Voice of America" the one to two hundred millions of ordinary Russians are allowed to learn little or nothing of other countries and how conditions in them compare with those existing in the Soviet republics. "The iron curtain" is very real, and radios are so scarce that broadcasts reach only a small fraction of the people. Few foreigners are allowed to visit and move freely within Russia. For example, at the end of September Russia refused visas for passport entry to the American Assistant Secretary of State Peui-foy and ten Senators for the limited purpose of "Inspecting the American Embassy in Moscow," a purpose similar to that for which the group had already visited many countries. As was said at the time, it was "a distinct shock to State Department officials as well as to Congress." Russians are not permitted to travel, and therefore get their ideas from the officially allowed and controlled newspapers, notably *Iszvestia* and *Pravda*.

A fortnight or so before the opening of the Moscow Conference, *Pravda* had an editorial in which it stated that Russia, due to Soviet socialism and the genius of Stalin, had won the war "in single-handed combat unprecedented in history." It added that the Allies had delayed as long as possible so as to weaken Russia and had opened a second front only when Russia had already won against Germany and Japan. This would seem calculated to justify to the Russians their disproportionate demands when peace terms were being fixed. Also, just before the Moscow Conference an incident occurred in the United Nations which was another movement to justify Russia's huge annexations and demands for reparations.

With the Peace Treaty of Versailles in 1919 the system of "mandated territories" had been inaugurated. The mandated sections remained under the control of the League of Nations and were in no sense transferred as possessions to the nations receiving them but were held in trust, so to speak, under strict rules. Japan had received the mandate for many small islands in the western Pacific, which she had treated as her own and which proved to be important points in her secret and felonious attack on America. The United States asked the United Nations, as successor to the League of Nations, to award the mandate to us and to grant us exclusive air, naval and military rights over these strategic points for attack upon us. There were some objections voiced and, in view of the long-sustained verbal duel between Russia and the United States throughout the whole history of the U.N., it came as a surprise when Russia readily acquiesced. Apparently, however, the Kremlin wanted to make it appear that we were a partner with her in loot. The mandated islands had altogether a territory of only 846 square miles and a total population of 48,000. The islands belong to no nation but to the United Nations and, as Japan as mandator had broken all her pledges to the League, we asked to be allowed to take her place merely for our own safety and for the good of the inhabitants. We had just fulfilled our own pledge to give the Philippines, with 115,000 square miles and 16,000,000 people, complete independence, although obviously "independence" did not mean military strength, and we should still have the responsibility of standing behind them, should they be attacked. On the other hand, Russia, after the war, had taken

—as apparently accurately stated—more than 250,000 square miles belonging to other nations, with a non-Russian population of almost 25,000,000. By unanimous vote of the United Nations Security Council at Lake Success the Japanese mandated islands were placed under the trusteeship of the United States on April 2. The episode of Russian agreement with America, unexpected and unique, had its humorous aspects. With such incidents, and many others round the globe, the Moscow Conference opened.

The Conference started on March 10, its main object being to draw up peace treaties for Germany and Austria, although Molotov tried to make a démarche at the beginning with consideration of the Chinese Civil War. The Foreign Ministers of the Big Four who participated in the conference were Marshall (U.S.A.), Bevin (Great Britain), Molotov (U.S.S.R.), and Bidault (France).

We shall speak of the failure of the Conference but may mention first, in chronological order, two items tending toward stability. On March 4, a fifty-year treaty of alliance was signed between Great Britain and France within the framework of the U.N. charter "to prevent the recurrence of the German menace" and in no way forming a bloc against the Soviet. On the same day, President Truman, who had flown on the 2nd to Mexico City on a good-will visit to President Aleman, won all Mexican hearts and a tremendous ovation by placing a wreath at the national shrine to the band of youths who fell in the final attempt to defend their country during the battle of Chapultepec, in the war between Mexico and the United States, in 1848. This was said to have been suggested by the American Ambassador. However that may be, it was a gracious act of the sort which the proud and emotional Mexicans would and did appreciate to the full. In spite of the Marxists and other followers of that belief, history is not wholly determined by economics, and this simple act of chivalric friendliness had resounding effects which may last a long time, after a century of distrust on the part of our important southern neighbor. Aleman that evening hailed Truman as "the new champion of solidarity and understanding among the American republics."

And now back to the Conference at Moscow, which, although a failure in a sense, may have marked a turning-point in the history of our civilization. It dragged its way until the patience of all but the Russians, who were doing the dragging, was exhausted. Every question, even when it could finally be brought up for consideration, was deadlocked. For example, on one fundamental point the Coördinating Committee reports that "The United Kingdom and United States delegations do not agree to reparations from current production. . . . The acceptance of reparations from current production is an absolute condition of the Soviet delegation's acceptance of the principle of the economic unity of Germany." It is reported that Bidault said: "Where are we? God knows," and that Bevin answered: "Yes, and He isn't a member of the Council of Foreign Ministers."

So it went, with a number of amusing incidents, however, such as the Russians' giving a gala performance of the ballet on the night of the Greek Ambassador's dinner, in order to keep the members of the delegations away from the latter, after the announcement had been made of Truman's plan for Greek aid. On April 23, Marshall assailed the Soviet Union for having blocked any possible peace treaty with Austria, as well as a four-power pact to keep Germany disarmed. Molotov denied the charges, and the Conference ended the next day.

On his return to Washington, after his Report to the President, Marshall spoke to the American people on the air (April 28) and said in part, "Agreement was made impossible at Moscow because . . . the Soviet Union insisted on proposals which would have established in Germany a centralized government, adapted to the seizure of absolute control." There had been very plain speaking and a full report. Moscow was no Yalta or Potsdam, and we now knew where we stood. No more evasions or secret compromises. "Bed rock," as the *Herald Tribune* called it, instead of the "quicksands" of the past. A new era in the relations between Russia and the West was opening, in which spades would become spades.

Even during the Conference, there came the first an-nouncement of "The Truman Doctrine," which hustled the Russians into their invitation to the gala ballet men-tioned above. On March 13, Truman presented before a Joint Session of the Houses of Congress a new foreign policy of vast possible import. He demanded that the Fed-eral Government should have the right and the power to intervene in the affairs of other nations when their national integrity was threatened by Communism or other totalitarian ideologies. Specifically at the moment he asked for $400,000,000 to give economic and other aid to Greece and Turkey. Russia was not named as the menace but was clearly indicated.

The President pointed out that already we were seeing totalitarian regimes forced on such countries as Poland, Rumania, Bulgaria, while others were struggling to maintain their freedom of choice. "Greece," he added, "is today threatened by the terrorist activities of several thousand armed men, led by Communists," along its northern boundaries. The independence of Turkey was also being threatened, and, he went on, "Should we fail to aid Greece and Turkey in this fateful hour, the effect will be far-reaching to the West as well as to the East."

He made it plain that our move was not a threat to Russia but only to the unlimited expansion of the Soviet system and the forcing of its way of life on unwilling peoples. For more than a century, whether under the Czars or under the Communists, Russia had been trying to control the Dardanelles and to overrun the Balkans, Greece, Turkey and the Near East. She had been held off her neighbors time and again, notably in the Crimean War, largely by the British Empire and its occasional allies. As I have already noted, the Empire was no longer able to perform the duty of world policeman in maintaining a reasonable balance between the great powers.

The part of the world in question was of the utmost strategic importance for any single nation bent on domination of the world. The huge bulk of Russia was rolling on across all northern Asia to the Pacific, and across country after country in Europe which had never been in its possession. Its strength is in its inexhaustible reserves of docile man-power, whereas that of the United States is on the sea, in the air and in its inventiveness and high production. Nobody can roll back the masses of Soviet infantry. The one point from which we can exert pressure which will be recognized by the Kremlin is the eastern end of the Mediterranean. We did not go there, however, to attack Russia, but to protect free peoples in their right to live their lives independently and in their own way. The announcement of the so-called "Truman Doctrine" was in general well received by the American people and press, although it marked the most decisive swing from traditional isolationism since the Monroe Doctrine of 1823. In Congress the support was notably bi-partisan, the most bitter opposition coming not so much from the Republicans as from a small minority in the President's own party. The bill which implemented it by appropriating the $400,000,000 was passed toward the end of May and the "Doctrine" may be said to have been then accepted as an integral part of our foreign policy and a fateful step in the willingness of the United States to assume its grim task of defending the freedom of the human spirit wherever it might desire to be free. The future is on the lap of the gods.

There had been, as I have said, opponents to the plan, but we may concentrate on one, not only for the furor which he created in 1947 but for his probable prominence, if not importance, in 1948—Henry Wallace.

Wallace had been in the Cabinet of Franklin Roosevelt for about five years when Roosevelt forced his nomination as Vice-President, and he rode into office with his chief, who dropped him in 1944 in favor of Truman. Had Roosevelt's sudden death come earlier, Wallace might have been President now instead of Truman. The disappointment must have been bitter. He was made Secretary of Commerce, but the office was shorn of much of its power when he was confirmed by the Senate. Later, after an unseemly Cabinet row, his resignation was accepted and he became a free lance. He became also a bitter opponent of the Administration and its policies. In addition, he steadily and rapidly, judging by his speeches and writings, became a defender and friend of Communist Russia. He had often been used by the Communist official papers in Moscow to indicate that American "Liberals" (words no longer have any definite meaning) favor the Soviet regime. On one occasion, during the Moscow Conference, he advocated that America make a large "non-political" loan or gift to the Soviets to help restore their devastated regions.

In *The New York Times* of March 18 there was a full-page address by Wallace, apparently paid for by his backers, the "Progressive Citizens of America," in which he violently attacked the Truman plan for Greece and Turkey and said that Truman "proposed, in effect, that America police Russia's every border. There is no regime too reactionary for us, provided it stands in Russia's expansionist path."

On April 7, he took a plane for England for a European speaking tour. According to *Newsweek,* he was handed, as he left, a beautiful embossed scroll signed by such Americans as Senator Pepper, Louis Adamic, Guy Tugwell and Elliot Roosevelt—a "Henry Wallace Scroll of Greeting" to the liberals of Britain. Arrived, he at once launched into a fierce attack on America. He accused us of wanting to stretch an American empire round the globe. He even called America's course "a wild and mad nightmare of ruthless imperialism." He said that "no powerful idea—and Communism is a powerful idea—can be countered by a gun." The comment in America was hot. In the Senate, both Democrats and Republicans denounced him. For example, Senator Vandenberg (Rep.), head of the Foreign Relations Committee, said, "it is a shocking thing when an American goes abroad to organize the world against his own government"; and Senator McClellan (Dem.) of Arkansas said, "I wonder if he [Wallace] is not trying to establish himself as a favored Communist Quisling." Having been, by the grace of Roosevelt, Vice-President for four years and a Cabinet member for many, his name carried more weight in Europe—never too well posted on American domestic politics—than it did at home. There was talk of a cancelling his passport or of proceeding against him under the Logan Act, but a longer length of rope was decided on.

In the spring, came the further shrinking of the British Empire by a complete withdrawal from Burma and India. India at once split into three parts—the present state of "India," Pakistan and the Princely states—with ensuing bloodshed and terror.

Throughout the year we continued to try to enforce the treaty with Russia regarding Korea. That little but very important nation on the Pacific had been promised independence, with the right freely to choose its own form of government, but meanwhile it had been split into northern and southern parts, the first occupied by the Russians and the latter by the Americans. There was constant friction between the Communists in the one part and the Americans in the other, and Russia consistently blocked all efforts to carry out the promises made to the

Korean people, even to the extent of refusing to allow a delegation of the United Nations to inspect the Russian zone. The deadlock continued into 1948 and we need not go into the details here. We may note, however, that for Russia the importance of little Korea was largely in relation to Soviet plans for controlling the great Chinese province of Manchuria, a territory approximately as large as France and Germany taken together. Manchuria is the most highly industrialized part of China and also extremely rich in such raw materials as coal, iron ore and oil. There are possibilities there of eventually far greater production than in our own Pennsylvania-Great Lakes section.

From time to time Russia was accused of not living up to her agreements in other nations, and on June 5 Truman denounced as "an outrage" and a breach of the Yalta agreement her actions in Hungary, where the government was overthrown with Soviet connivance. The State Department was more guarded in expression, but a strong note of protest was forwarded.

On the same day that the President denounced Russia, Americans got their first view of what has come to be known as "the Marshall Plan," a project of enormous importance. At Harvard, where he had gone to receive an honorary degree of Doctor of Laws, the Secretary of State made a historic speech.

After endorsing the statement made by Truman at Washington earlier in the day to the effect that our aid to Europe was necessary, Marshall added that Europe "must have substantial additional help or face economic, social and political deterioration of a very grave character." He went on to say that help should no longer be on a "piecemeal basis," but that the initiative must come from the countries of the Old World in drafting their needs and in evincing among themselves a spirit of union and cooperation, and that then we would help as far as we could. He denied that the United States would foist a plan on any country that was unwilling to accept it or that the plan was directed against "any country or doctrine," but he added significantly that we would give no aid to "any government which manœuvres to block the recovery of other countries," and that any which sought to benefit politically by perpetuating human misery would meet "the opposition of the United States." In a brief but extremely lucid speech he pointed out the completeness of the breakdown of the European economy in such matters as currencies, investments, banks, insurance companies, exchange between the industrial and the food-raising sections, and called attention to a vast complexity of factors which were retarding recovery and confidence and were even more important than was the obvious physical destruction of machinery, buildings, railroads and the loss of manpower.

Meetings were held in Europe and the plan gradually took shape. In his Harvard speech, Marshall had said that the extraordinary complexity of the interlocking problems and the mass of facts presented to the public would confuse its judgment, but as discussion continued in Congress, in the press and everywhere else, the unanimity in favor of some such form of help was not only remarkable but another indication that Americans were growing up to a comprehension and acceptance of what the Secretary called "the vast responsibility which history has clearly placed upon our country." The amount suggested as necessary gradually grew to $18,000,000,000 to be distributed over a five-year period, with the deadline for beginning set as April 1, 1948. The final action of Congress with regard to this project will be recorded in next year's chapter.

June 5 was a day of historic importance. On that day, in addition to the items already mentioned, the Senate confirmed treaties with four countries—Italy, Hungary, Bulgaria and Rumania. The first was passed by a roll-call vote of almost 8–1, and the others without a call but by an almost unanimous shout. As proof of the bi-partisan character of our present foreign policy, which I have noted as indicating a most amazing change in our political climate, there is the fact that the treaty with Italy, presented by a Democratic President, was voted for by 42 Republicans and 32 Democrats. We had come a long way from the days of Wilson and 1919.

For centuries the problem of the Jews has been an extraordinary one, affecting both themselves and the peoples among whom they have lived. It is impossible to discuss it here in all its controversial aspects. All that we can do in the space at our disposal is to comment on the question of Palestine, one of the most difficult among the political and racial puzzles of our time. The Zionist movement, which claimed that the Holy Land was the "Homeland" of the Jews, has been active in various forms for a long period, but it may be noted that even now not all Jews are united in favoring it. There are able Jewish leaders and Rabbis who are opposed to it. I know of no other problem which involves such a complex play of forces of all kinds—racial, economic, political, passionately emotional, and others—as that of Palestine. It was coming to a head in 1947 and we have no idea to what it may lead. It is beyond our scope here to go into the bloody events already occurring in 1948. In the case of so complicated and controversial a subject, we must, however, outline the background of the past few years.

During the latter part of World War I Britain signed the ambiguous Balfour Declaration to the effect that she would "facilitate . . . establishment in Palestine of a national home for the Jewish people . . . it being understood that nothing shall be done which may prejudice the . . . rights of existing non-Jewish communities in Palestine." (Lord Balfour was an interesting philosopher but by no means adept at drawing up intelligible State Papers.) When, after the Peace and the formation of the League of Nations, the system of Mandates came into effect, Britain received, though not too willingly, the Mandate for Palestine, and the full-of-trouble pledge of Balfour was written into the Mandate. Although any account of this problem is "charged with dynamite" and likely to suit nobody, it would appear that, as compared, for example, with the complete disregard by Japan of her pledges for the Pacific islands mandated to her, the British had done their best to carry out the difficult and fuzzy-worded Mandate given to her. (In the post-war world after World War I, the United States, although asked to do so, had refused to assume responsibility for any Mandate.)

When, early in 1946, the League of Nations voted itself out of existence it passed a Resolution that League members holding Mandates should "continue to administer until other arrangements have been agreed upon between the United Nations and the respective mandatory powers." Britain was anxious to be relieved of the responsibility and obligation to solve an almost insoluble problem and, after consultations with the United States and other nations, which led to no solution, Britain, in May 1947, laid the matter before the United Nations, with a request to report in September.

Meanwhile, as far back as 1939, when war was again threatening in Europe, Britain had restricted Jewish immigration into Palestine to 75,000 over a five-year period, although after the war she raised it to 1500 a month. At the time of the hearing before the U.N. it was estimated that there were 1,300,000 Jews on the European continent who had survived the Nazi terror. The Jews and Arabs were represented, the former by Rabbi Silver and the latter by Henry Cattan, a lawyer from Jerusalem. Silver spoke of the "desperate urgency" of the human problem of increasing the immigration quota, whereas Cattan said that linking the refugee problem with that of Palestine would make "both problems infinitely more difficult." Meanwhile Jews embarking from ports, usually not named in the newspapers, were trying to enter Palestine against regulations, and were often intercepted by the British and taken to camps in Cyprus. The situation became increasingly tense.

A little more background is called for. One estimate of the time placed the number of Arabs at 1,200,000 and the number of Jews who had been there, or who had

recently entered, at 600,000. Viewed historically or otherwise, who, after two thousand years or more, can be said
to hold title to all or even part of the Holy Land? Also,
it was later said that the Soviet was sending Jews and,
with them, Communist agents. We have spoken of the
"vacuums" left by the withdrawal of the British Empire
from various strategic parts of the world. To mention
oil is to suggest machinations on the part of that pet
bugaboo of the demagogue, "Big Business." But the fact
remains that at the eastern end of the Mediterranean, in
the Near East, are the greatest reserves of oil outside those
in Russia and the dwindling ones in the United States.
Oil is not just "big business," as a large part of America,
with its oil-burners, its motor age and its planes, has discovered during the last few years, and if our supply, as
some alarmists predict, will be used up in twenty-four
years, what becomes of our whole life? Also, if Russia
moves into the Near East and adds its oil reserves to her
own, how could we defend ourselves in war? Again, the
Arabs are not just "Arabs." They could set the whole
Moslem world against Western civilization. The leader
of the Arab Higher Committee, organized in 1936, was
the Grand Mufti of Jerusalem, who fled from Palestine
to Berlin during the war because of his Nazi sympathies
and is now directing policy from Cairo, though Mr.
Cattan spoke for him at the U.N. When I mention oil
it is not because I believe in the economic interpretation
of history. The Arabs threatened a "holy war," and that
is something different and equally important.

One or two more points. There are about 40,000,000
Arab sympathizers in Arab League countries. If it came

to a complete instead of a sniping and guerrilla war, it is quite obvious who would be wiped out. It would not be the 40,000,000 Arabs, unless the United States and other nations became engaged in war against them on the grand scale. It would be the Jews. The Arabs and Americans have always been friendly. The Arabs have regarded us as helping them toward democratic ways and a higher standard of education and living. Yet they are now turning against us in bitterness because, under Truman, the United States took the lead most energetically in inducing the Assembly of the U.N. to vote for the partition of Palestine.

Here oil comes in again. It is the greatest, and an enormous, asset of the Arabs. They *have* to sell it to get the money to import modern machinery. They had planned to make a two-way trade with the United States, and on November 7 Truman, in his Report on Foreign Aid, counted on getting from the Near East 15 per cent of the oil called for by the Marshall Plan. If we go to war with the Arab League, Russia will step in and get the oil, in exchange for Communism, although, as I have said before, we are committed to hundreds of millions of dollars of expenditure in Greece and Turkey to protect the Near East *from* being overrun. The Palestine problem is extremely complex, as complex as human nature itself. We Americans like simple answers, but there are some world problems to which there are none.

To conclude the record as regards Palestine during the year 1947, we mention the meeting of the General Assembly of the U.N. on November 29 at which it was voted, 33 to 13, with ten abstentions and with Siam absent, to partition Palestine into two states, one Jewish and one Arab. The Arab delegates walked out of the meeting. For once, Russia voted with the United States in favor of the plan but with some uncertainty as to just what they meant to do in the future. The intricate problem of the boundary lines between the two states was postponed. There are 4,770,000 Jews in the United States, of whom 2,035,000 are in New York City, and New York State has the largest vote of any in the Presidential Electoral College. The whole problem has an almost infinite number of angles, and we must now leave it until we come to the record for the year 1948.

During 1947, the Palestine question was perhaps the most discussed of all international problems which might bring on war. Otherwise, what was important was precisely what was *not* done and—to make an Irish "bull"—*how* it was done. For the most part, it was a year of almost complete frustration for the U.N. I recall no other case in history of international meetings where the leading figures of great and small nations poured out such a torrential volume of scurrilous, insulting and mendacious adjectives and nouns without war resulting. Perhaps that in itself was something. Perhaps time will bring an improvement in manners. The Russians won the prize with the almost unbelievable remarks of such men as Gromyko, Vishinsky, Molotov and others, but even they were outdone by the Yugo-Slav, Dr. Bebler, who threw into the delicate negotiations over Greece, and over what the Balkan states were doing, such mollifying terms as "assassination," "quislings and traitors," "a slanderous and infamous document," and added that those who had reported on the situation were "without shame." As the Belgian Prime Minister Paul-Henri Spaak observed, "If the force of an orator can be measured by the number of his insults, Dr. Bebler has reached the summit of eloquence."

Fortunately, in spite of provocation during the two sessions held—one regular and the other a special one called to consider Palestine—representatives of other member powers kept their discussions of affairs on a higher level. Russia, nevertheless, and her satellite states, managed to block almost all progress toward world settlement. Only once has there been practical unanimity. Vishinsky had been vitriolically denouncing as war-mongers the United States, Great Britain, and many of their leading statesmen, as well as other countries such as Greece. He had presented a resolution denouncing in especial "war-mongering in the United States, Greece and Turkey," but feeling ran high and, for once, there was a unanimous vote of 56–0 on a compromise denouncing "war-mongering" by any country.

The veto power, however, was the strong weapon of the Soviet. When the U.N. was formed, the four great nations insisted on a power of veto and it is likely that we ourselves would not have joined with an indefinite number, possibly before long more than seventy, of small and many of them powerless nations, if we had had to be completely controlled by their collective decisions, with no right on *any* occasion to say "No." The veto power, however, was expected to be used very sparingly by anyone, and only *in extremis*. In 1946, the United States and Britain used it twice, but they have not used it since then.

France has used it only once. Russia, during the two years, has used it *twenty-two* times. This has very definitely clogged the machinery of what was intended to be an instrument for the adjustment of world problems and for the maintenance of peace, but which has largely become an amazing world sounding-board for speeches made by representatives of the Soviet and its satellite nations.

In September, Secretary Marshall had proposed that there be a limitation of the veto power and that a "Little Assembly" of the U.N. be set up to remain in session and to prod the Council into action. Vishinsky replied in a violent speech of more than an hour and a half, denouncing the United States as preparing for a Third World War "to satisfy the limitless desires of its influential circles . . . which is the crazy idea of world domination." Nevertheless, after a tempestuous session, on November 6 the American plan for the "Little Assembly" was voted 43–6, with six abstentions. Russia and her satellites said they would boycott it and they have done so ever since.

Without entering upon the details of other and minor matters we must note that throughout the year it was the constant opposition by Russia to plans proposed by the other great powers which has thus far prevented any settlement of the problem of control of the atomic bomb in war. Incidentally, in an unexpected move which surprised all the Allied capitals, Russia suddenly signed peace treaties with five former satellites of Germany—Italy, Rumania, Hungary, Bulgaria and Finland—with all of which (except for Finland, with which, as I have noted above, none of the Allies other than Russia had been at war) treaties had already been signed by the others of the Big Four, in Paris, February 10.

We may now mention, much more briefly, certain other world matters which were a part of our history in 1947.

On June 30, after four years of service, the United Nations Relief and Rehabilitation Administration, commonly known as U.N.R.R.A., came to its legal end. It had spent nearly $3,000,000,000, of which the United States had contributed 72 per cent. The seventeen countries receiving food, clothing and other supplies had been Albania, Austria, China, Czechoslovakia, Hungary, Finland, Korea, Yugoslavia, Greece, Italy, Poland, White Russia, the Ukraine, San Marino, the Philippine Republic, the Dodecanese Islands and Formosa.

On August 14, we crossed off from Italy's account with us approximately $1,000,000,000 of war debt and also lightened her burden in other ways, such as freeing $60,000,000 worth of blocked property and returning to her 28 of her captured freight ships. In October, the first comprehensive report of our foreign relief was made by a Joint Congressional Committee. It disclosed that *since* the war the United States had contributed between $19,-000,000,000 and $20,000,000,000 to other peoples, and the Marshall Plan still lay ahead for possibly as much again. In spite of Russian gibes and opposition, representatives of sixteen Western European nations met at Paris, July 12, to develop a plan for cooperating in their own relief and in working out the necessary machinery for carrying out the plan. Russia objected as far as she was able, but this time she had no veto power. Molotov claimed that the plan was aimed at destroying the independence of sovereign nations and wished the money to be given to each or any nation, individually, for such purposes as it might choose, including political ones. The Paris Conference of the Big Four, to which we shall refer later, had just ended disastrously and the split between East and West was plainer than ever, but while speaking of American aid in its various forms and amounts we shall conclude by recording the meeting of the sixteen nations who welcomed the Marshall Plan.

With reference to Russia's claim that the plan would destroy independence of action among the nations which accepted it, it is illuminating to note that she quite brazenly denied independence of action to her satellites. For example, although Russia was twice asked to attend the Conference but refused, all her vassal states were also invited. The Moscow radio announced that Finland, Rumania and Poland had rejected the invitation, yet all three nations denied this. Almost immediately, however, they *did* decline. Hungary accepted and, later, sent "regrets." Czechoslovakia accepted officially on a Monday. On Wednesday its Communist Premier and its Foreign Minister, Jan Masaryk, flew to Moscow, were talked to by Stalin in the Kremlin and, the next day, a Czech official communiqué declined the already accepted invitation with the comment that participation in the Conference by Czechoslovakia "could be interpreted as an act directed against its friendship with the Soviet Union and our other allies." In view of the evident desire of at least five of the satellite nations to participate in the discussions and share in the benefits of the American plan, it may be asked who was interfering with their sovereignty and freedom of action?

We have still to consider three other international con-

THE "RED" HERRING
From a cartoon by Marcus in *The New York Times*.

ferences which carry American history of 1947 to France, Brazil and Britain.

The Paris Conference was called during the first week of July, with invitations to practically every European country, except Franco's Spain, to consider some form of coördinated self-help as a preliminary to the Marshall

Plan. The United States was purposely not represented because its turn would come if Europe decided favorably. After five short sessions that conference ended in complete failure. The Foreign Ministers of Britain, France and Italy laid down principles which would lead the Old World out of its post-war morass and re-establish an economic basis for recovery and for a continuance of the peaceful development of European life and culture. The Eastern European nations, now under control of Russia, would normally exchange their goods with the West, but the iron curtain fell, and on July 13, in one hour, against the eloquent pleas of Bevin, Bidault and Sforza, Molotov divided the world into two parts. Including, to look ahead to February 1948, the coup d'état of that month in Czechoslovakia, the Soviet Dictators, who called themselves the "People's Government," had added to the Soviet control 650,000 square miles of land and roughly 110,000,000 people formerly outside Russia. The countries overrun and annexed were Czechoslovakia, Esthonia, Latvia, Lithuania, Yugoslavia, Albania, Poland, Bulgaria, Rumania and Hungary. The split was complete but for the sixteen nations, which met in Paris in July and, on September 22, signed an agreement in the free desire to use the Marshall Plan. With the help of the United States, which I have just detailed, they showed that European civilization and hopes were not all dead.

While the sixteen Western European nations were holding their fateful meetings in Paris, another conference was being held in the New World with the same aim of protecting life, as we have known and enjoyed it, from destruction by primeval forces.

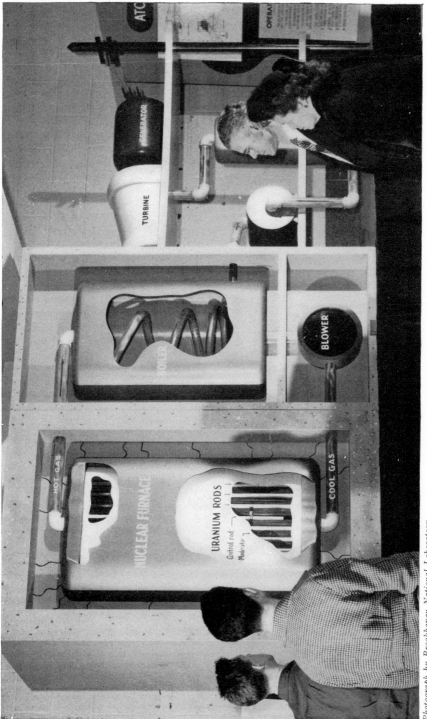

Photograph by Brookhaven National Laboratory

A MODEL ATOMIC FURNACE

This atomic furnace is similar to the one being built at Oak Ridge. When the uranium atoms in the furnace split, intense heat is given off. Rods of uranium become red hot and heat gas that is pumped over the rods. The gas flows from the furnace around coils through which ordinary water is flowing and boils the water to make steam. The steam flows to a turbine, which turns over a generator that produces electricity.

Photograph by Acme Newspictures

TRUMAN PLACING A WREATH ON MONUMENT IN MEXICO CITY

President Harry S. Truman, accompanied by U. S. Ambassador Walter Thurston, walks up the steps of the Monument of Mexican Independence towards the huge wreath which he placed at the foot of the monument during his good-will visit to Mexico City.

This meeting had been provided for in the Act of Chapultepec (see previous chapter). Its official title was "the Inter-American Conference on the Maintenance of Peace and Security," but it is generally referred to as "the Rio Conference," because it was held at Petropolis, a small town near Rio de Janeiro, Brazil, and the beautiful city of Rio is much better known than its small suburban neighbor, Petropolis. The official title of the Conference would conceivably have accommodated almost any topic which a constructive or obstructive delegate might have wished to have placed on the agenda, but the main object had happily always been understood and was firmly adhered to. That object was to draw up a formal treaty or agreement for union in American hemispheric defense. Truman, as already noted, had on his Mexican trip made a most happy impression on our proud South American neighbors, and when on September 1 he arrived at Rio by plane from Washington to take part in the closing sessions of the most friendly and important Conference ever held among the American nations, he was given a great ovation by a crowd of Brazilians estimated at 1,000,000. The following day, September 2, a pact was signed by representatives of nineteen American nations, including, of course, the United States, to protect one another mutually in case any one of them were attacked.

On December 8, the United States Senate ratified the Treaty by a vote of 72–1, the sole dissenter being Senator Millikin (Rep.) of Colorado. The treaty took into consideration the Charter of the United Nations, and the contracting parties agreed, in accordance with the terms of the Charter, not to resort to the threat or use of force among themselves and also to consider an armed attack against one American state as an attack against all, and then immediately to employ the best means of repelling such an attack, though no state was to be forced to use arms without its consent.

Meanwhile, in our quest for American history during 1947, we have to make one more trip to the Old World before settling down to record domestic politics and other home affairs.

On November 25, there was a meeting of the Foreign Ministers of the Big Four in London. Throughout the preceding months, relations between Communist Russia, Western Europe and the Americas had been steadily worsening, not only because of the almost obscene attacks, especially on the United States, by Russians or representatives of her puppet states in the U.N., but also on account of increasingly outrageous statements from the Kremlin and by so-called Russian statesmen. The main objects, supposedly, of the Conference were to resolve the problems which were preventing the long over-due peace treaties, especially those with Germany and Austria, and thus the restoration of peace and of some sort of political and economic order to Europe.

The long-drawn-out overture, so to say, had not been promising. It had been becoming more and more obvious that Russia, for its own purposes, did not wish peace or prosperity in the world at large. That is not the environment in which world revolution flourishes. The crescendo of vilification had been rising steadily until it finally called forth from our long-suffering Secretary of State,

George Marshall, such remarks, in his now famous speech at Chicago on November 18 (less than a week before his leaving for London), as: "The clarity of the record and of our intentions, however, has not prevented Soviet officials and Communist groups elsewhere from waging with increasing venom a calculated campaign of vilification and distortion of American motives in foreign affairs. These opponents of recovery charge the United States with imperialist design, aggressive purposes, and finally with a desire to provoke a third world war. I wish to state emphatically that there is no truth whatsoever in these charges, and I add that those who make them are fully aware of this fact."

The same thing went on in London. By the middle of December, it was obvious that the Conference would get nowhere. In demanding enormous reparations from Germany, Russia, without admitting the vast additions to her own population, resources and territory, acquired by stealing from others, made fantastic statements about the huge sums which the other powers had made out of the war. Marshall made an angry reply, not only denying Molotov's statements but stating that Molotov himself knew that they were not true. Bevin, Foreign Minister of the British Labor Government, and Bidault, Foreign Minister of France, were equally furious.

Three weeks after it had begun, the Conference "adjourned indefinitely." It was more than the temporary winding up of a meeting. It was the break-up of the brittle war alliance, the splitting of East and West, evidence that the three Western nations can confer, compromise and agree but that Russia does not suggest but

267

only demands and makes those demands in lying and insulting terms. There was no use going on. Several small items remained to be swept into the dust-pan. Vishinsky had declared that Russia was so strong militarily that no other power could stand against her. Russia cut the nominal value of her war bonds (to which she had forced her citizens to subscribe) by two thirds, and the value of the ruble (the standard coin) by 90 per cent. The Government paper, *Iszvestia,* speaking of the belief in certain countries that Czechoslovakia could be a "bridge between East and West," commented that "they forget that in a vital struggle there can be no middle position." In less than two months we were to learn what had so obviously been meant by that. And now we may return from our journeyings, to see what 1947 has been like within the United States itself.

If, in 1947, international affairs loomed larger in proportion to our domestic ones, it was because never before in our history had we been so involved with the entire world and, also, because, for reasons we shall at once relate, in home politics it was a year of "slack water." It was not a Presidential election year nor even an "off" election year. The year 1944 had been a resounding Presidential one politically, with a President, for the first time in our history, nominated and elected for a fourth term. We must go back to that for a moment, to understand the Truman term.

The long tradition handed down to us from the days of Washington and of Jefferson, both of whom inveighed against even a third term, was, it is now fairly evident, broken in the case of Franklin Roosevelt because the party leaders and the electorate believed he was the only man who, from his knowledge as Commander-in-Chief and his personal international ties with other world leaders throughout the greatest struggle in which we had ever been engaged, could carry on to a successful conclusion. The war and the possible peace appeared to be all that mattered. It was not a fourth term for the New Deal, as the dumping of Wallace for the Vice-Presidency, and the by-election of 1946 clearly showed. It was the war, and the experience and connections of the man who had thus far seen it through, which made possible this complete break with American tradition and even with our theory of constitutional government. It had never been envisioned, for example, that any Chief Executive, by serving for sixteen or more years, would be the appointer of practically the entire judiciary branch of the government, including the whole of the Supreme Court.

It came about, nevertheless, but when, in April 1945, the President suddenly died and the war with Japan, Germany and the other Axis Powers ended a few months later, Roosevelt's successor, Truman, was left dangling. The war, to conduct which the nation had elected Roosevelt, was over. The peace was indeed still to be made but, after one attempt at Potsdam, Truman gave up the Roosevelt rôle with respect to that. His experience as Vice-President, merely a presiding officer of the Senate and not a member of the Cabinet, had left him unprepared for it. He had not been elected to carry on the policies of the New Deal. Like the man in the old story of "Japhet in Search of a Father," where was he to turn? The public had been sympathetic toward him in his sudden elevation to an extraordinarily difficult position. He himself appeared willing to try to work with a Congress controlled by the opposite party. The year seemed to promise as well as could be expected.

That promise, however, was none too good. Truman's personal popularity and prestige were nothing like what Roosevelt's had been. Let us look at the beginning of 1947. The Presidential election was due in 1948. It was unfortunate, but in our American political system that fact is bound to have its deflecting influences. A national election, after sixteen years of one-party, almost one-man, rule acted for many like a bar of iron held near a magnetic compass. When Roosevelt had been elected for his fourth term, Congress had been safely Democratic:

The Senate		The House	
Democrats	56	Democrats	241
Republicans	39	Republicans	192

The set-up of the 80th Congress was quite different:

The Senate		The House	
Democrats	45	Democrats	187
Republicans	51	Republicans	245

The war in Europe was twenty months behind us; that in the Pacific, sixteen. The Presidential election was only twenty-two ahead. There was, due to the accident of death, a Democratic President in the White House; a Supreme Court of whom eight of the nine had been appointed by one Democrat by reason of the accident of unprecedented tenure of office; a Congress, after sixteen years in the wilderness, overwhelmingly of the opposite party. The entire situation was explosive and, to say the least, difficult for all. That it worked out even as well as it did is a high tribute to the American way of life.

The new Congress was quickly organized and, in general, with a minimum of disharmony. In the Senate, Senator Vandenberg of Michigan was elected President *pro tempore,* and became also chairman of the immensely important Committee on Foreign Relations. In the House, Representative Martin of Massachusetts was named Speaker. In these cases, as in most others, there was full harmony, and in those in which there was some bitterness it could be ascribed to the already advancing shadows of the presidential election of the coming year. Before beginning to recount political events in their chronological order, we may skip for a moment to the summer. At that time, an event occurred which materially changed the possible positions of Vandenberg and Martin in political history.

As had happened a number of times before, the death of a President and the succession of the Vice-President had left the Senate without its presiding officer and the office of President without an elected successor. Since 1886 it had been legally provided that, if both the President and the Vice-President should die, or be otherwise unable to serve, the line should run down the list of members of the Cabinet in the chronological order in which their departments had originally been established —that is, from State, Treasury, and so on, down. There had been many flaws in this arrangement. For example, a Secretary of State, who might have held office for a day only, might become President in place of some other Secretary who had been a Cabinet member for many years. Moreover, Cabinet members are appointees of the President and are not elected by the people. Truman had brought up the question a number of times and the bill he suggested was passed by the Senate on June 27, 1947. It provided that, regardless of party, the first in order of succession to a deceased President and Vice-President should be the Speaker of the House of Representatives, next the elected President-pro-tem of the Senate, and then on down the list of Cabinet officers.

This plan had many advantages. It would not only make the first successor to the two Presidents, in case both should die, a man who had been elected by the people but, as Representatives are elected every two years and Senators only every six, the succession of the Speaker of the House would bring the possible President, at the time of his accession, still nearer to the people.

It must be credited to Truman that he stuck to his idea in spite of the fact that the election had brought it about that both of his possible successors were Republicans. That, however, under certain circumstances, might well be a great advantage, and Truman in this case was working on a high constitutional and not on a merely political plane. He and his predecessor had both been able to do this on occasion, and with far better results than those achieved by the narrow partisanship of Wilson. Before the war, the appointment by Roosevelt of Stimson and Knox, both Republicans, as Secretaries respectively of War and the Navy, had undoubtedly greatly helped the war effort when it came. So also, under Truman, the constant use of the Republican and Democratic Senators, Connally and Vandenberg, undoubtedly helped to form a consistent and dependable bi-partisan foreign policy. On July 10, the House passed the Succession Bill by a vote of 365 to 11. Passed by the Senate, and with the signature of the President assured, an important step had been taken in our constitutional development and stability. The remainder of our domestic political chronicle was, for the most part, of a more ordinary sort.

At the opening of the 80th Congress the personnel and political complexion of that body had largely altered and there were many new faces in other parts of Washington, due to actual or immediately impending resignations, such as that of Bernard Baruch and his able aides, who had been dealing with the atomic bomb situation; Eugene Meyer and Harold Smith as President and Vice-President of the International Bank; former Ambassador Winant as American member of the U.N. Economic and Social Council; Dean Acheson as Under Secretary of State; Admiral Leahy as Chief-of-Staff to the President; and others.

Moreover, due partly to the political set-up and partly to recent legislation, the nature of the President's Message to Congress at the opening of the year had also changed. In fact, for the first time, there now had to be three Messages. The first was the one which had always been known as "the President's Message," and which has been sent or, rarely, read in person, to Congress by the President ever since the days of George Washington. The Constitution provides that the President "from time to time shall give to the Congress information of the State of the Union, and recommend . . . such measures as he shall judge necessary and expedient." Purely as a matter of custom, every President, annually, immediately after Congress convenes, has sent an elaborate message and this is considered "the state of the Union" message, although during the course of a year there may be many more special messages. Now, however, two more are specifically required—the Annual Economic Report called for by the Employment Act of 1946, and a Message on the Budget also required by special Act.

Truman had already declared that hostilities in the Second World War had ceased and, with them, many of his own special powers. A few days later, on January 6, he appeared personally before Congress to deliver the first of his required three Messages.

Certain facts and figures would be contained in the other messages that were to follow. For a Democratic Executive speaking, for the first time in sixteen years, to a Republican-controlled legislature the tone and attitude were more important than precise recommendations as to what he might "judge necessary and expedient." Although somewhat vague regarding practical details, the Message seemed more evenly balanced in its reference to the need for capital and labor to work together to make the free-enterprise system function than had been some of the later New Deal pronouncements. Truman asked that industry reduce prices wherever possible; that labor refrain from unjustified wage boosts; that everything be done to bring about a high production of peacetime goods; that some reforms be made in labor practices; and he was conciliatory in his attitude, as a Democratic Executive, to his Republican Legislature. A honeymoon seemed a possibility.

On January 8 came the second of the Messages, the first of the Reports required by the Act of 1946—the Report on Economic Conditions. Under that Act, a permanent Council of Economic Advisers had been created to assist the President, and a Joint Committee of the two Houses of Congress to consider it. The theory had been that not only would the President have a continuing body of experts but that Congress would have a guide for the growing number of committees created for the steadily expanding functions of big government. To what extent the multifarious forms of private enterprise in a nation of some 145,000,000 people, spread over 3,000,000 square miles at home, and in more or less responsible contact with almost every corner of the globe, can be wisely guided by a small group of so-called experts, and by Congressional committees, remains to be seen. So far, all that we can say is that the reports, forecasts, and actions of these have been somewhat confused. Some experts have been afraid of inflation, some of deflation, some predicted a near boom and some a bust, some even foresaw that, some months hence, 8,000,000 would be unemployed when, actually, we came to have 60,000,000 gainfully employed, the record number on the country's pay-roll. In any case, the Report was made.

The next of the three Presidential Messages now required, by statute or by custom, at the beginning of a Session was that on the Budget. This, although the President insisted it was "realistic," was also somewhat confusing. He estimated the expense of government for the ensuing fiscal year at $37,500,000,000, with receipts of $37,700,000,000, which would permit a "surplus" of

$200,000,000. With figures so vast and unpredictable on either side of the ledger, the small "surplus" hardly appeared "realistic." We say "unpredictable" because, only a year before, the President, in consultation with his advisers, had said that the expenditures of the Government during the second year after the war would run to only $35.1 billions and now, in the third year, he asked for between $2 and $2.5 billions more. Moreover, in October 1946 he had stated that the budget would, according to his figures, be balanced by June 30, 1947, whereas there promises to be a deficit of well over 2.3 billions and, if the Government figures had not underestimated income by $8.7 billions, the deficit would have been over $11 billions! Yet to get a "surplus" now of only $200,-000,000 he estimated that business during 1947–48 would be much better, despite many estimates to the contrary. He also asked for "a prompt expansion of the Social Security system" and a much larger contribution by the Federal Government to the State Governments, for education.

Apart from the specific increases asked for, he had stated that the cost of government could not be reduced, although in the third year after World War II they were still at about 38 per cent of their wartime peak, whereas in the third year after World War I they had been reduced to 19 per cent. Of course, the comparison is not quite fair, for the world came back to normal—or seemed to do so for a while—more rapidly after the first than after the second war. This does not explain it all, however. When, in February, the Report of the Joint Committee on Reduction of Non-essential Federal Expenditures, of which the Democratic Senator Byrd of Virginia was Chairman, was made public it showed that, outside of the Office of Emergency Management, which dealt with war problems, the departments and agencies of government were much more numerous at the beginning of 1947 than they had been even at the peak of war activity in 1944. The Senator stated that the investigation showed clearly that there had been "little reduction in the tremendous war-expansion of the Government" and that, on the contrary, with the exception of the Army and Navy and the war agencies, the growth of government "was constantly increasing." In thinking of bureaucracies one is reminded of the rise and fall of huge animals, such as dinosaurs and others, during geologic periods. Their bodies increase enormously in bulk and food needs until they are out of all proportion to the size of their skulls and brains, and then . . .

Of the proposed budget, well over $11 billions, or about one-third, was allotted to the armed forces and, including that, about 75 per cent to items connected with war or arising from past wars. We may speak here, therefore, of the greatest change ever made in the military organization of the United States. Congress, which had got off to a somewhat slow start, partly by reason of its political realignment, did pass a number of important laws before recessing at the end of July. There had always been, as in all countries, much jealousy between the Army and the Navy, each of which had a Secretary of Cabinet rank. War has changed in its character, and it had become evident that power in the air was as important as power on land and sea. Everywhere this added new complications as regards organization and prestige.

Finally, while Congress was anxious to adjourn and the President to fly to his dying mother, who was ninety-four years of age, a bill was passed and the President held up his flight to sign that bill in his plane, an incident symbolic of the new age which had so complicated both war and peace.

The bill provided for the unification of all our armed forces under a single military establishment with a single head, the Secretary of Defense, who was to be a member of the Cabinet. Under him there were three departments —the Army, the Navy and the Air Force, each headed by a Secretary with sub-Cabinet rank. The Secretary of Defense appointed was James V. Forrestal, former Secretary of the Navy, a very able man, popular with all the services and who, it had been said, gave up during the war a salary of $180,000 in private business to serve as an adviser to the President at $10,000. It is interesting to note, in passing, that the Government had grown steadily in strength and activities since the days of George Washington and that this was the first time that the number of members in the President's Cabinet had been reduced rather than increased.

Besides the reforming of our military organization, we may mention briefly some of the other more important legislation passed during the First Session of the 80th Congress.

The Taft-Hartley Labor Act, amending in many important respects the National Labor Relations (Wagner) Act, was passed by both Houses in June, vetoed by the President and passed again over his veto the same month by a vote of 68–25 in the Senate and 331–83 in the House. Long and complicated as it is, it helped to redress the balance of management and public interest against the excess powers given to unions and autocratic labor leaders in earlier measures, but it by no means deserved the name which the latter at once gave it, terming it the "Slave Labor Law." It is impossible to discuss clause by clause so controversial a measure, but we may note one clause which is important and has already been invoked by Truman. This clause provides that, in case of an industry-wide strike or lock-out which imperils the national health or safety, the President may appoint a Board of Enquiry and direct the Attorney General to petition for an injunction to last for 60–75 days, during which time a secret vote shall be taken of all the employees of the employers involved in the stoppage.

In May, a Portal-to-Portal Act was passed and approved modifying the liabilities and punishments under certain obscure prior Acts which had involved, by a Court decision, both the Government and private employers in potential damages of some five billions of dollars. The earlier Acts had threatened, for a while, to play havoc with the whole economic structure.

Two bills for reduction of taxes were passed by large majorities in both Houses, but both were vetoed by the President and could not muster the two-thirds vote necessary to over-ride the vetoes, although the second one did so, in the House of Representatives, by a vote of 299–108.

The honeymoon was over. Truman had given the impression that he would work with Congress, in spite of the difference in parties, but the 80th Congress was hampered by the constant threat or use of the veto, even when both Congress and public opinion seemed over-whelmingly in favor of a measure. In the case of the Labor Bill, both the President and organized labor—or its leaders—had used every means to influence both Congress and the public, but without effect. The President, nevertheless, vetoed in scathing terms not only that bill but both tax relief bills. In the case of the Taft-Hartley Bill, the tremendous vote in the Senate over-riding the veto could be compared with the stinging rebuke suffered by Franklin Roosevelt in connection with his Court-packing plan.

Historically, the development of the veto power of the President has been interesting. Before the Revolution, Acts passed by the colonial popular Assemblies were in many cases subject to a double veto by outside powers —the Royally appointed Governor of the Colony and the Privy Council in London. The statesmen who drew up our Constitution and administered it for the first generation or so feared an over-strong Executive as against the popular will. The power of the veto was put in the Constitution but it was understood to be for limited purposes only. Throughout the one or two terms of each of all the first sixteen Presidents none of the first six used the veto at all and by all the remaining ten it was used, inclusively, fifty-seven times. The Government had three distinct branches—the Executive, almost exclusively occupied with the enforcement of laws; the Legislature, to make the laws and to appropriate money; and the Judiciary, to pass on constitutional and other legal questions.

Andrew Jackson, who vetoed twelve bills, may be said

to have been the first President to set up his own judgment as regards the wisdom or advisability of a measure passed by the elected representatives of the people. It is not uncommon to find, in any country, that putting in the seat of power a man who claims to stand for the common man has had similar results. As compared with the first sixteen Presidents, who vetoed in all only fifty-seven Acts of Congress, the sixteen who followed Lincoln have vetoed over 1785! The tripartite nature of our government, with its presumed "checks and balances," was threatened most by Franklin Roosevelt, who tried to become a sort of Legislature in himself by vetoing more than 630 Acts of Congress and by his effort to make the Supreme Court an adjunct of the Executive. He *did,* in fact, name eight of the nine Justices, and if he had lived out the balance of the sixteen years for which he had been elected he would almost certainly have named them all. Both Congress and the nation—at least in considerable part—had become uneasy, and the latter, having voiced their wishes in the change of Congress in 1946, the increasing number and tone of Truman's vetoes, even of finance bills, began a split between him and a considerable number of even his own Democratic followers.

About a month after Congress had recessed, the President made his mid-year review of the Budget. It showed that there had again been rather amazing miscalculations by the fiscal authorities and advisers. Not only had the Budget for the fiscal year shown a surplus for the first time in seventeen years but the amount of this surplus and the miscalculations in advance were startling. Owing to misjudgment, the expenditures as estimated in January had decreased by $700,000,000 and the income had increased above the January estimate by $4 billions, leaving a surplus for the whole fiscal year of $4.7 billions. The President, having vetoed the two tax bills passed by the Legislature, which by old English and American tradition is supposed to hold the purse strings, somewhat blandly stated in his Message that the unexpected [and miscalculated] windfall of well on to five billions, including "the present cash balance, will be devoted to retirement of the public debt."

There were other troubles. Administration advice and practice had fluctuated, as I have said, between the fear of inflation and the fear of depression, "boom or bust." Prices were to be kept down, yet wage rises had been encouraged. The shortages in goods for peacetime domestic consumption and the increasing need of exports for European aid placed an added strain on the economy and turned up the thermostat on price rises. On October 1, the Council of Economic Advisers is said to have made a secret report to the President predicting a depression on account of rapidly rising prices and falling purchasing power, though we have noted the huge unexpected surplus and the two vetoes of tax relief. Money for Europe was also fast running out. For these, and for other reasons, there had been many demands that the President call a special session of Congress immediately but he had refused, for many weeks, while in Brazil and after his return. Finally, on October 23, there was an unusually long Cabinet meeting lasting more than two and a half hours, then other meetings and, later in the day, Truman called a special session of Congress for November 17, seven weeks ahead of the scheduled return to Washington of the 80th Congress. The reasons given were "the alarming and continuing increase in prices . . . and the need for emergency foreign aid."

After Congress convened, they received first the Marshall Plan. Secretary Marshall was three whole days on the witness stand explaining it. Then, five different volumes were boiled down to a little over 1150 pages, for members of Congress to study. In brief, there was to be without delay stop-gap aid to certain nations amounting to $597,000,000. The long-range program, which was to cover four years and extend to the sixteen nations already mentioned as signing the agreement in Paris, plus Western Germany, would get somewhere between $16 and $20 billions. That posted Congress as to European aid. The President, in his 4500-word address, talked of prices at home, which he said had risen 23 per cent since mid-1946 and were still rising. He asked for restoration to him of almost all the economic controls of the past war years, which Congress, under his leadership, had been abandoning since V-J Day two years before.

On December 19, the President again addressed the Congress, stating that to keep Europe from going Communist we must adopt the Marshall plan, or, as it has come to be known, the European Recovery Plan—E.R.P. He asked for $17,000,000,000 to cover four years, of which $6,800,000,000 would be needed during the first fifteen months. The continuation of the story will fall in the following months of 1948.

In the field of labor, the year following 1946, which

had topped all records for strikes and for lost work and production, was again a very disturbed one. Without detailing all examples, we may point to a few unusually interesting cases. As noted in the section on labor in the previous chapter, Lewis and his union, the United Mine Workers, had been fined respectively $10,000 and $3,500,-000 in December 1946. In fact, some of his leading labor leader colleagues had blamed Lewis for bringing about the Taft-Hartley Act and a changed attitude in Congress by his coal strikes and other actions during the war. On March 6, 1947, the Supreme Court, 7–2, upheld the decision of the lower Court, and a majority confirmed the $10,000 fine against Lewis personally but reduced the fine against the Union to $700,000, provided that it would rescind its notice to the Government (then in control of the mines) of cancellation of contract. Lewis yielded at last and signed the order. Later in the year, however, there were more mine strikes, and in one of these Lewis appeared to have gained a victory in the matter of wages and other benefits.

Nevertheless, the feuds went on among the big Unions and big leaders. Lewis, after getting out of the C.I.O., had rejoined the A.F.L. and been made a Vice-President—one of thirteen. Among other clauses in the Taft-Hartley Bill, was one which refused to labor unions the right to bring their cases before the N.L.R.B. unless their officers signed an affidavit that they were not members of the Communist Party and did not believe in the overthrow of the Government by force. If the general officers of the A.F.L. did not sign, the effect would be to bar all their sub-unions from access to the N.L.R.B. All the officers signed except Lewis, who claimed that the demand was insulting. He was dropped from office but remained head of the U.M.W., after expressing his opinion of the A.F.L.

There were many strikes and, especially from the end of April on, the "pattern" was set for a second general rise in wages and consequently in costs. The strikes in coal, steel, motors and other industries followed the usual form, and the details need not concern us year after year.

A strike of school teachers, on the scale of that in the city of Buffalo in February, was something new, as were the several strikes, with picketings and the usual trimmings, of "white collar" employees in banks and stock exchanges both in New York and elsewhere. There was a big strike among that highly paid and usually public-spirited and intelligent group, the telephone operators. There were even strikes in hospitals. On the whole, it may be said for 1947 that, although there was far less violence or bloodshed than in some of the great strikes of the past, such as the Pullman or Homestead, there was a disturbing factor in that there seemed to be developing a more cold-blooded disregard of the rights, necessities, health and even lives of large sections of the public of all ages who had nothing whatever to do with the causes or settlement of the strikes. It is not to be wondered at, if labor in vital trades is "getting that way," that the public, caught helpless, is becoming increasingly insistent that government take a hand, and that Congress is reacting to the public sentiment. It is unfortunate but natural. The pendulum always swings too far, either way.

Among the provisions of the Taft-Hartley Act is one

which requires labor unions to make accounting of their finances and internal affairs in detail to the Labor Department and, if fully complied with, this may yield interesting information on the salaries of the leaders. In August, when Daniel Tobin, the old president of the International Brotherhood of Teamsters (A.F.L.), startled his followers by refusing an increase in pay, a few figures were published in some of the daily newspapers. Tobin had been president for forty-one years, was well off, his children grown up and in good jobs, and his own salary was $30,000 a year. Harrison, of the clerks' union, was said to have a still larger salary, and Caesar Petrillo received $45,000 a year from his union. The salaries of certain others would make interesting reading. Justices of the Supreme Court now get $25,000 a year; members of the Cabinet $15,000 each; the President of the United States $75,000, and the Vice-President $15,000.

Of the unusual events of the year we need mention only a few. First the weather, of which Charles Dudley Warner once said that "everybody talks about it but nobody does anything about it." The winter of 1946 had been a record one for severity all over Europe, but in 1947 they had a mild winter in the Old World and the record passed to the United States, where rains, floods, hurricanes, tornadoes and snow wreaked their havoc on us. In the East of the country, the winter of 1947–48 was the worst in more than a generation. New York City had the most expensive succession of snow storms in its history; the storm that began on the day after Christmas cost $6,000,-000 to clear up the streets. In November, one of the most disastrous fires in the history of the eastern section of the

Photograph by Press Association, Inc.

TIMES SQUARE AFTER THE CHRISTMAS SNOW STORM

A lone pedestrian braves the drifts in Times Square, New York, on the morning of December 27th following the blizzard of the day before.

THE AUTOMATIC DOUGLAS C–54 SKYMASTER WHICH CROSSED THE ATLANTIC WITHOUT A PILOT

The automatic flight was made by self-controlled pre-set mechanisms. The plane carried the emergency crew shown at right, though no human hand touched the controls on the entire flight.

Official U. S. Air Forces Photographs

country swept the forests of Maine and was pronounced a national emergency. It caused also the almost complete wiping out of the old and fashionable resort of Bar Harbor, with the destruction of perhaps $25,000,000 worth of houses and invaluable treasures within them.

There were also a notable number of airplane catastrophes, with a long list of casualties, but in September a remarkable feat was performed which may have a great effect on the use of planes both in peace and in war. An American Douglas C–54 Skymaster crossed the Atlantic from America to England, and made a perfect landing at an indicated field, without a pilot. There were fourteen persons on board, but as observers only. Not a human being during the entire trip touched any of the controls. The machine was equipped with what is called a "mechanical brain," which responded to the least impulse sent to it by radio from shore. It was evident that the contrivance would almost insure safe landings, even under conditions of "zero visibility." It was also evident that if, without human aid on board, we could send a plane across the ocean carrying fourteen people, we could also send such a plane, without people, but loaded with an atom bomb.

This extremely difficult and nerve-wracking year had included this new air development, talk of a "germ war," steadily rising tension with Russia, and the labor and political complications of a pre-Presidential-election year. Perhaps partly due to the increased strain, the year took also an unusual toll of the lives of prominent Americans, two of them unhappily by suicide—Herbert L. Satterlee, aged eighty-three, a distinguished New Yorker, son-in-law of the late J. P. Morgan; and John G. Winant, fifty-eight, former Ambassador to Great Britain. Both tragedies pointed to the strain under which men were living.

Among the other deaths, we may mention that of former Mayor Fiorello La Guardia, three times mayor of New York City and one of the ablest and most notable Americans in public life. We have already spoken of the death of Mrs. Truman, the President's mother, and have also to record that of Mrs. T. J. Preston, widow of former President Grover Cleveland, and one of the best-loved First Ladies the nation has had. There were too many deaths of outstanding individuals to permit us to go into biographical details and we merely cite some of them as indicating the passing of an era: the widow of Thomas A. Edison; Henry Ford, who did so much to transform American industrial life; Nicholas Murray Butler, President of Columbia University and a national and international figure for three generations; Senator Bilbo from Mississippi, long a stormy petrel in our political life and whose re-election was being contested at the beginning of the 80th Congress; Willa Cather, a distinguished novelist; Mrs. Carrie Chapman Catt, in her eighty-ninth year, long a leader in the Woman's Movement; Andrew Volstead, father of the Prohibition Act; and many others, noted in business life, politics, and in the arts and sciences, who if young could ill be lost to our culture and whose passing, in old age, seemed to set the seal on the transition from one type of life and thought to another.

The next chapter promises to be an exciting one, with turmoil at home and abroad—far-reaching decisions and vast responsibilities.

CHAPTER VII

THE RECORD OF 1948

THE year 1948 was one of unusual interest and of marked change in trends, both national and international. Internationally, the chief factor was the continued refusal of Russia to join with the West in re-establishing a real peace, and in consequence the continuance of the "cold war" between the greatest two powers in the world, the Soviet Union and the United States. We have spoken, in earlier post-war chapters, of the political vacuums left by the disappearance of Germany as the strongest state in the middle of Europe and by the partial liquidation of the British Empire. Although, during 1948, there were crises in China, Korea, and elsewhere, which concerned us in our new and not wholly welcome position as the strongest of all nations, we were in the main to concern ourselves with the rebuilding of Europe as offering, in our opinion, the best prospect of establishing once more a world of peace, civilization and progress.

Nationally, it was a presidential year, with all that that means in the various phases of our life. Moreover, the election, as Arthur Krock wrote—and he is, in my opinion, the ablest and most historically minded of all news-paper correspondents in Washington—was unique. For these reasons we shall reverse the order of the previous chapter and, after discussing world matters, concentrate at greater length on domestic affairs. Owing to our vast power and prestige, we are now obliged to discuss global affairs; but to talk over, later, that typical American event, a presidential election, will give us a sense of getting home again.

Turning, therefore, to international matters first, we shall speak of the United Nations. Much important work was accomplished at Lake Success during the earlier part of the year, but when the third regular session was opened in Paris, on September 21, it was faced by what our Secretary of State Marshall called "an unusually critical world situation." As early as March 28, the Pope, in his Easter address to a vast throng in St. Peter's Square, had warned that the world was facing a year of great danger, in which events which might prove "definitive or irreparable" for religion and society would occur. The all-important election in Italy was, at that time, only three weeks off. President Truman had just asked Congress for both an economic and a military program to check Russian "internal and external aggression." War clouds hung over all the earth.

Russia had persistently used the United Nations as a sounding-board for its propaganda which, shamelessly, bore little relation to facts. The debates were among the most remarkable in any public assembly, as when the Russian, Vishinsky, asserted that the report of the Special Committee on the Balkans was merely a "pile of garbage." Throughout the year, the United States and Britain were constantly accused by the Kremlin, its controlled newspapers and representatives, of almost every crime. But we shall have to treat of the East-West conflict as a matter by itself, and are here concerned only with the U.N.

Its Paris session opened under sinister circumstances. A few days before the members met, Count Bernadotte and his aide had been assassinated in Jerusalem, apparently by members of the notorious Stern gang, which boasted of the murder. The Palestine situation became more complex than ever. Russia had just tried a clever trick in Korea, but, as we cannot in one short chapter write the history of the United Nations as well as that of the United States, for even one year, it will make for clarity if we discuss, one by one, the various international problems of the U.N. as they concerned us. We must, however, summarize U.N. accomplishments.

In the first place, in spite of Russia's obstructionism, the U.N. survived as a world force. That, in itself, was a great step forward. Even Russia, with often insulting language, felt obliged, for some reason, to be represented there, if only to block progress and cast votes. (On October 25, Vishinsky, in a Council vote of 9–2 in a clear-cut decision between East and West, cast the 28th veto of the Soviet Union, joined as usual only by the Ukraine.) During the life of the U.N., while more and more nations, large and small, had been clamoring to join it, Russia and her satellites had steadily been losing in influence. The almost inevitable veto might block and delay, but the lying propaganda and the vituperations were losing their effect, much as a drug for pain which is overused. The Korean resolution, carried against Russia and her five satellites by a vote of 48–6, was an example.

During the Paris session of the representatives of 58 nations, 600 meetings were held and 17,000,000 words spoken, in various languages. The East-West issue emerged clearly, and two very important measures were passed. One was the Declaration of Human Rights for all human beings everywhere, and the other was the Genocide Convention. On reading the Declaration, you may say "just more words," yet words have often been winged. As the *Herald-Tribune* said, in an editorial, think of Magna Carta, the English and American Bills of Rights and other documents which have changed our histories and our lives. When the U.N. Bill of Rights is put into a treaty between the genuinely democratic nations, which is the next step, the fundamental difference between them and present or future dictatorships terming themselves democracies will be increasingly difficult to cover up by bad language or vetoes. The Genocide Convention also promises to be of marked influence in international law and in warning future

Hitlers, and other dictators, what may lie in store for them. The U.N. has not been operating in the expected time of normal peace; even so, it has not done badly.

Before passing from the U.N. to our relations with certain individual nations and with certain sore spots in the world, we must note what has been referred to as the most generous action ever taken by any people in history. In the preceding chapter we spoke of a speech made at Harvard, on June 5, 1947, by Secretary of State Marshall, outlining his ideas for helping to put Europe on its feet again according to what came to be popularly known as the "Marshall Plan" and, later, more officially, as the European Recovery Program (E.R.P.). After much discussion, here and abroad, the matter came to a head in Congress, in January 1948.

Appearing before the Senate Committee, Mr. Marshall took personal lead in getting the measure through Congress. The opposition came mainly from a few remaining isolationists, who dubbed the plan "operation rat hole," and from the supporters of Henry Wallace, who feared it would lead to war with Russia. It did not, though Russia opposed it from the start, apparently on the ground that it would help to bring peace and prosperity to Europe and thus interfere with her plans for world revolution and Communism. Marshall himself had said at Harvard that "our policy is not directed against any country or doctrine but against hunger, poverty, desperation and chaos." He had added that we must not interfere with the sovereignty of any country; that we must count on enough of them helping us to help them to help themselves.

Great Britain and France immediately sent out invitations to all European nations, including the Soviets, to join in a meeting to discuss the proposal. Sixteen joined in the Paris Conference, although Moscow and eight of its controlled countries declined, two of them apparently under orders and against their own desires. The nations attending the Conference through the year up until September were Britain, France, Austria, Belgium, Denmark, Greece, Eire (Ireland), Iceland, Italy, Luxembourg, Norway, Holland, Portugal, Sweden, Switzerland and Turkey. Meanwhile, the United States had set its shoulder to the wheel and, on January 2, signed bilateral agreements with France, Italy and Austria, granting them "interim emergency aid" to the extent of $522,000,000. Before Congress, Marshall had asked for an "all or nothing" adoption of his plan; as late as April 1, Senator Taft and some others thought nothing could be done until July 1. However, by April 3, the Bill had passed Congress and had been signed by the President, although the entire four years' needs were not voted at once. Congress, to start the ball rolling, did vote over $6,000,000,000. Later, in September, the Paris Conference, at its final session, asked for a total of $21,-780,000,000 of loans and credits from 1948 to 1952. I know of no country emerging from a great and costly war that has ever voted nearly $22,000,000,000 and perhaps much more, most of which its citizens never expected to get back again. The act, however, was not one of thoughtless generosity but, we hope, of enlightened statesmanship. We have at last learned that we cannot, under modern conditions, live and prosper to ourselves alone.

Congress was slow in appropriating the money, then moved quickly when Russia, in one of its customary coups, took over Czechoslovakia. Meanwhile, two points had been gained. The work of handling the help to Europe had been put under one head, Paul G. Hoffman, a Republican, and former president of the Studebaker Company. The appointee was to hold Cabinet rank but under control of the State Department. At last reports, at the beginning of 1949, it was going well for such a vast and unprecedentedly complex undertaking. Besides what was requested, under the Marshall Plan, from our government (which means of course all of us individually), the 16 nations attending the Paris Conference asked for additional credits of over $3,000,000,000 from the International Bank for Reconstruction and Development, and from private investors. The reason for such huge amounts was also clearly stated. The official report went on to say that "The scale of destruction and disruption of European economic life was far greater than that which Europe had experienced in the First World War. Industrial production in Belgium, France and the

Netherlands was reduced to 30 to 40 per cent of pre-war and in Italy to only 20 per cent; production of bread grains fell to only two-thirds of pre-war; 300,000 freight cars had been destroyed but a total of 2,800,000 were damaged." The participating nations also pledged themselves to a "wide range of actual and potential mutual help," though adding that the task was so great it would take at least four years. They needed not only rehabilitation but a period of security in which to work out their difficult, long-term problems. The later discussions of some sort of a United States of Europe, and of an Atlantic union for mutual defense, appear to have sprung from the Paris discussions.

As we have noted, Russia and her satellites would have nothing to do with these plans; and those of the Kremlin, as far as an outside observer can determine, seem to be directed toward a further demoralization of the old European system and civilization. As we have also noted, the whole year was taken up with vituperative threats and rumblings of war in an atomic age. The "cold war," and ideas of revolution and further conquest, instead of peace and rehabilitation, had followed apparent victory. Some of the abortive efforts to get together in meetings, at various diplomatic levels, may be mentioned, although we cannot enter into all the details of the "garbage," to paraphrase Vishinsky, of the twelve months. We shall touch first on a few of the high spots with regard to Russia.

In December of the previous year, 1947, the meeting, in London, of the Ministers of the Big Four had broken down, and, on the 31st, Molotov declared in Moscow that the United States had been mainly responsible for the failure because it had blocked discussions of the peace terms for Germany. This was as fantastic as many other statements made by the Russians throughout the meetings of the U.N. and at conferences, but may, in the opinion of the Communists, have served their purposes of propaganda, domestic and foreign. At the Conference, Marshall had already referred to Molotov's accusations as "insults and abuse," and the meeting broke up when the Russians demanded a $10,000,000,000 indemnity from Germany and Four-Power control of the rich Ruhr.

What came next was the publication by the American State Department of a volume of 362 pages containing the cream of about 2,000,000 documents, from the German Foreign Office, captured, in April 1945, by our Ninth Division in lonely châteaux in the Harz Mountains. Fortunately, the keeper of the archives had disobeyed orders to destroy them, and they have been studied ever since by American, French and British scholars. Extracts from the correspondence and agreements were printed in *Newsweek,* issue of February 2, 1948. Stalin, Molotov, Hitler, von Ribbentrop and other leaders all had a hand in the witches' broth. Among other things, they show that it was the Soviets, not the Nazis, who asked for the non-aggression Pact which led Germany to invade Poland, and that Moscow had asked for a secret division of Europe into Nazi and Russian spheres, as well as much else. We had had the documents but Marshall had kept them secret to facilitate negotiation in London, and when all hope of success came to an end, with the consent of France and Britain, he ordered immediate publication. Moscow registered rage, and from then on has included all three leading Western nations in her vituperative slander.

As there seemed no hope of making a real peace treaty to fill the vacuum left by the disappearance of Germany, the three started, under great difficulties, to build up some form of government in western Germany. This again infuriated the Russian Bear. It is impossible to write definitive history, if there ever is such a thing, based on the contemporaneously recorded events of the moment. Especially in the past, it has usually taken many decades, or even centuries, for original documents to be released or come to light. I recall, when working on research in the Manuscript Division of the Library of Congress, looking with envy at two piles of cases, one of Theodore Roosevelt papers and the other of Taft papers, neither to be open to the public for, thirty-five years, I think it was. How could a historian write of that celebrated feud until he had read those papers? Time, like distance, however, seems to be shortening; not only generals' and statesmen's memoirs but official documents appear with hitherto unheard-of promptness.

Judging by the Russian-German papers published as above, and by the actions of the Russians since, it would appear that Russia had had an eye on Germany, whose disruption would serve the purpose of enabling her to absorb such parts of it as she needed, using the same methods she had used in Poland and in the Balkan countries she had coveted. She had fought the Marshall Plan for bringing peace and prosperity, and did not want a settled government in western Germany. The "cold war," as the East-West situation had come to be called, had been intensified, and one of its most spectacular episodes was initiated on April 1, when the blockade of Berlin began. On that day, the Russian general in that city announced many restrictions on rail and road traffic with the western zones, controlled, under the Potsdam agreement, by Britain, France and the United States respectively. A few of these unlawful restrictions were accepted, though not all. The Russians were evidently willing to sacrifice the Berlin civilian population. Our General Clay replied that he could supply the 10,000 Americans in the city by air, and the British joined us by putting thirty-two planes in all into the service of carrying food. The celebrated "airlift," or "Operation Vittles," began. It expanded amazingly and, by November 1, the United States alone had 600 crews in the work, with planes arriving at three Berlin airfields, one every three minutes. The Germans, as well as the Americans and others, received the needed food and fuel at the rate of 3000 tons each twenty-four hours. The Berlin agreement of June 5, 1945, had been signed by the four Allies, stipulating that Berlin should be occupied and administered by all four jointly, through their military representatives. Russia, who had obviously broken the agreement, claimed that her Allies had done so, but they held firm. There were many war scares. Among other incidents, on April 5, a Russian pilot in a fighting plane dived on a British passenger plane, killing not only himself but 14 on the passenger plane including, besides British, two Americans. The matter dragged along its diplomatic course, and there were other incidents, in the air and on the ground. There were Communist demonstrations against the German-elected municipal government, the squabble over the currency of the four sectors of the city, and other moves that seemed headed for trouble.

On September 17, after meetings with Stalin and Molotov in Moscow—wholly fruitless—our State Department published a White Paper entitled, "The Berlin Crisis: a Report on the Moscow Discussions, 1948." At one meeting it had been agreed that the four military governors in Berlin should proceed, according to a Moscow "directive," to lift the blockade and to do certain other things of a hopeful character. The Russian General Sokolovsky ignored the directive and the fat was in the fire again. In October, the Berlin crisis was placed by a vote of 9–2 on the agenda of the Security Council of the United Nations, the dissenters being, as usual, Russia and the Ukraine. Without going into further details, by the end of 1948 the Berlin imbroglio was as unsettled as ever, although "Operation Vittles" was astounding both the Berliners and Russia. In the middle of November, however, Russia refused to lift the blockade and the Western powers declined another conference until she should do so. Another stalemate!

In the meantime, the American-Soviet drama had taken, in New York, a dramatic turn, which reminded one of Hollywood and klieg lights. The propaganda war of reckless lying had been waged by Russia since V–J–Day in 1945, but in August 1948 it met with a mad disaster. The lie machine had claimed that a Russian widow of fifty-two, by name Kasenkina, a schoolteacher who had taught chemistry to the children of Russians here on official missions, and another Russian teacher, Ivanovitch Samarin, had been "kidnapped" by Americans. Moscow broadcast it wildly and made official protests to Washington. It proved the worst boomerang in the history of the "cold war." As the facts gradually emerged from the shadows of mystery they proved to be that Mrs. Kasenkina, in terror at being forced back to Russia, had taken refuge on the farm of Miss Alexandra Tolstoy, the sixty-four-year-old American-naturalized daughter of the celebrated Russian novelist. From there, Kasenkina was snatched away by Jacob Lomakin, Soviet Consul in New York City, and the Vice-Consul Chepurnykh. She was kept incommunicado in the Consulate on 61st Street and the Consul answered all inquiries to the effect that she was well and not a prisoner. A writ was served on Lomakin, who later denied having accepted the paper. In Washington, Secretary Marshall said that, while he would not invade Soviet rights, any individual who complied with our laws would be assured of freedom and government protection. The Soviet Ambassador held a press conference to denounce the American Government as abetting abduction and a criminal conspiracy. In Moscow, Foreign Secretary Molotov called in the American Ambassador at midnight to accuse our government of conniving with a "gangster organization." The Ambassador replied that if the Samarins "wished to return to the Soviet Union, their travel would be facilitated." Meanwhile, Samarin had said that he would be returning to his death and, with his wife, had escaped to a hide-away in New Jersey—a man hunted on free American soil by a foreign nation. Mrs. Kasenkina preferred death in America to life in her own Russia, and, at 4:30 P.M., on August 12, she jumped out of a window in the room of the Soviet Consulate, falling several floors to the concrete-paved court. She would have suffered instant death had not some telephone wires broken her fall. She was, however, very seriously injured. In spite of her protests, employees of the Consulate tried to drag her into the building. New York police were happily quick in scaling the high iron

ing a moment at the front door, we must mention Korea, for Russia and ourselves face each other there. A glance at a map will show the great strategic importance of this Asiatic peninsula with a coast line 6000 miles long, dividing the Yellow Sea of China from the Japanese Sea. During its 900 years of history, it has been the scene of many contests and conquests, and was the chief cause of the Russo-Japanese War of 1904–05. The Japanese called it the "dagger aimed at their hearts" by Russia and, as a result of the war, obtained control of it. After Japan's defeat in World War II, Korean independence was restored but with a temporary provisional government (1946) of ten members, five from the United States and five from the Soviet Union. Elections were to be held, local popular governments were to be formed and the foreigners were to withdraw. On May 1, 1948, a puppet government was set up in Northern Korea, which claimed jurisdiction over both North and South, and some 700,000 local troops, it is said, were trained. Southern Korea, however, refused to be drawn under this Communist cloak and, a week later, elections were held there and a government formed under observation on the spot by a special committee of the United Nations. Russia would not accept this and demanded that the United States withdraw her troops if Russia did. The trouble was that if we did so the Northern puppet government, with its trained army, could overrun the South, and we should have abandoned our trust. We have gone rather into detail regarding this apparently minor matter taking place so far away, because it shows in some degree what our new world position has entailed and the essential difficulty of dealing with the Kremlin. Korea is not only rich in minerals; but in its relation to Manchuria and facing China and Japan, as it does, it cannot be neglected.

One of the most unselfish and steadily pursued of the foreign policies of our government has been that with regard to China, one phase of which was initiated by John Hay and known as the "Open Door" (1899–1900). By the end of 1948, however, it looked as though the Chinese Nationalist government, headed by Chiang Kai-shek, would have to yield to the Communists and, owing to their propaganda, Americans had come to be hated by large numbers instead of being considered, as of old, China's best friends. Some of our last grant of $400,-000,000 remained at China's disposal but we had refused the billion which Madame Chiang had come to Washington to procure. China, with its huge resources and a population of some 462,000,000, remained for us, at the year's end, an unsolved problem. So did Indonesia, with regard to which we had sent a rather sharp note to the Netherlands, also an old friend. South Africa was seething with native unrest, and the government headed by the great statesman, Jan Smuts, had been defeated. Something was happening all over the world.

At Bogota, Colombia, an important Conference began

on March 30 (adjourning May 2), with delegates from 21 republics in North and South America. It adopted an Organization of American States, superseding the old Pan-American Union of 1890, although the earlier organization was retained as a central organ and secretariat. Among much other business accomplished, perhaps the two most important items were approval of a treaty of hemispheric economic co-operation and a resolution, sponsored by the United States, for united resistance to the threat of international Communism. This brings us to an interesting point.

Moscow had apparently decided to break up the Conference. Our C.I.A. (Central Intelligence Agency) had known of this and reports had been made out to be sent to Washington but some minor State Department official in Bogota had, with the approval of our Ambassador there, suppressed the dispatches so as not to "alarm the delegates unduly." In any case, an important assassination occurred April 9, followed by a revolution lasting five days. (*Newsweek,* April 26, p. 23.) Bogota was hardly a place for quiet negotiation, but Secretary Marshall, lacking some of the suppressed documents regarding what was being planned, had insisted on going on, and then had insisted on staying. The Conference began and ended in Bogota, and probably fortunately, as showing that the United States was not to be intimidated by such "Commie" tactics.

The later European compact, already mentioned, the

North Atlantic Pact, which was in the making at the close of the year, the Italian election, the failure of the general strike in France, and many other straws in the wind all pointed to a gradual decrease, during the year, in the power of the Russian *Politburo,* although it is still too early to take out our pipe and put on our slippers. Czechoslovakia had been swallowed, but Italy and France seemed to be getting safe, and Yugoslavia had, under Marshall Tito, openly rebelled, not against Communism, however, but against Russian domination.

Meanwhile, in Havana, in March, there had been another meeting, with representatives from fifty-three nations, from all over the world. It was a corollary of the Geneva Trade Conference of April 1947 and designed to continue the rehabilitation of world trade, which the two World Wars, and subsequent economic restrictions, had so severely disrupted. Besides signing a "Charter of the International Trade Organization," known as the I.T.O., 123 trade agreements between individual states were signed, to simplify and otherwise facilitate trade.

There were, however, always reminders, great or small, of the flux in which the downfall of the old system, paralleling the downfall of the Roman Empire, had left the world. On our side of the Atlantic, an ocean which has ceased to be a sundering sea to become merely a highway, two such reminders occurred that deserve mention. At the very beginning of the year, an international quarrel developed over, of all places, Antarctica.

Nobody knows to whom its barren wastes belong, yet it may prove valuable—because of its hidden resources, strategic importance in war or peace, or, with the world and its transport changing so fast, in almost any way. Claims to at least sections of it, based on all sorts of alleged factors, have been made by Britain, Australia, New Zealand, Norway, France, South Africa, Argentina, Chile and, of course, the United States. Suddenly, Chile and Argentina decided to make their claims very vocal indeed. Chile dispatched a warship and sent along its President to unfurl a flag and make speeches. Britain sent a warship to what she had always claimed were *her* Falkland Islands. At the end of the year, these almost *opera bouffe,* but nevertheless dangerous, performances were still unfinished business. In December we had another headache. We had just signed with the South American nations the International Treaty of Reciprocal Assistance, of which Article 3 reads: "The High Contracting Parties agree that an armed attack against an American state shall be considered as an attack against all the American states, and, consequently, each one of the said Contracting Parties undertakes to assist in meeting the attack." Costa Rica suddenly claimed that she had been invaded by armed troops from Nicaragua. Hurried meetings were called by the Council of American States but on New Year's Day this too was still unfinished business.

We shall touch on only one more of the sore spots which involved the United States abroad, leaving Greece and certain others in much the same condition as we found them in the preceding chapter. In that chapter, we spoke at length of the complex Palestine question. It was too complex to be solved, at least in 1948. With regard to no other country or race has our foreign policy been more shifting or less understandable to the general public, unless it be with regard to China. Truman had insisted on the partition scheme and urged it on the U.N., then suddenly discarded it. The U.N. sent Count Bernadotte of the royal family of Sweden to the Holy Land to effect some sort of compromise; we have already mentioned his assassination by a band of Hebrew terrorists. His assistant took over; but neither individual nations, the United Nations, the mediators or anyone else proved able to bring about a solution. Conferences went on, war went on, between Hebrews, Arabs and Egyptians. Boundaries, religion, history, previous possession, and many other factors, precluded a peaceful settlement. The United States was not alone in its undecided and vacillating policy. Great Britain's Foreign Minister, Bevin, was as uncertain as was Truman. Britain, however, had had far more experience in dealing with problems of the Near and Far East, though perhaps the Laborites had not. At the end of the year nothing had been settled except that before, or soon after, the New Year, many of the leading nations, including the United States, Britain, and others, had given either diplomatic recognition, or promise of such recognition, to the somewhat ill-defined new nation of Israel. The prospects of some final settlement seemed brighter early in 1949. What may happen in that year is still hidden and belongs in the next chapter. We may now stop our globe-trotting and return to the domestic scene with its more familiar landscape of economic and political affairs.

Although they are closely intertwined, we shall start with the former. Economically, the year 1948 was a very prosperous one, in spite of Truman's warning to Congress, on January 14, that a severe recession might be coming, and his recommendation that grants in aid be given to the States to help support perhaps 4,000,000 unemployed. This message belongs later in the political section of the year and we shall note here only that, instead of 4,000,000 unemployed, employment had, by summer, risen to an all-time high of about 61,500,000. There *was* inflation during the year, but, instead of there developing any need for a return to rationing and other wartime restrictions, business made a rather amazing approach to peacetime quantity of production. Rising prices came from other causes, such as the amount of money in circulation, high wages and other high costs, including unprecedented taxes due to war and to governmental extravagance.

Strikes continued, but with a marked difference. In 1946, they had resulted in a loss of 116,000,000 manpower days; in 1947, of 34,600,000 of them; and in 1948, of, apparently, still less, although the final accurate figures are not yet computed. These, of course, retarded the production of goods long desired during the war and brought about a consequent rise in prices due to the discrepancy between the amount of goods and the amount of money in circulation. The high cost of living affected most seriously those living on fixed incomes and the white-collar workers on salaries which always move upward more slowly than do wages.

The position of the wage-earner was a matter of dispute, and it was the much-debated relation of wage income to the cost of living which was to deflect the strike movement and tactics throughout the year and probably for some years to come. We shall mention a few strikes or threats of strike which illustrate the point.

In January, Walter Reuther, one of the ablest labor leaders, and more broad-minded than many, led his United Automobile Workers in their third round of wage demands from General Motors. They made their demand on the claim, based on very questionable statistics, that living costs had gone up much faster than had wages. This was not borne out by the figures prepared by the U. S. Government through the National Conference Board and based on data collected by the Bureau of Labor Statistics. Who were more likely to be correct—Reuther and his union or the highly paid government bureaus of supposed experts? This had been, more or less, the standard pattern for strikes since the war. Later in the year, General Motors headed off another threatened strike by giving a small increase but tied up with a clause relating future wages to the Cost-of-Living index as reported by the Bureau of Labor Statistics. The cost of living for all had shown a marked tendency to level off and even to decline. As regards this new form of bargaining it will be interesting to see what labor unions will do when the cost of living goes down.

Meanwhile, however, there had been another coal strike, which gives us one more lead for the future. John L. Lewis claimed he had not ordered a strike but that 360,000 men had decided, at the same moment, to take a vacation. On March 23, President Truman was obliged to invoke the Taft-Hartley Act, something the Administration had to do, several times, during the spring, but for us here the interesting point about the strike is the fact that 360,000 out of 400,000 soft-coal miners had taken a walk, reducing the nation's vital coal production for industry and transport by 80 per cent, not for an increase in wages but for pensions of $100 a month for all miners who had reached sixty-two and were otherwise eligible under the pension plan. This was one of those "fringe" demands which were coming to be more frequent as the old gag about wages *vs.* cost of living was losing the argument and, consequently, its effect.

The President, as has been said, had to invoke the Taft-Hartley Act, which, during his campaign, he continued to damn, and, in order to avert the breakdown of transportation through the threatened action of three recalcitrant Railway operating unions, he had to turn to an old law passed for the war emergency, and seize the railroads. These points should be borne in mind, as they will play a part in the story of 1949. There were many other strikes, such as those in the industrial plants of Ford and Chrysler, strikes of dock workers, maritime workers and others, which need not be described in detail. The main two points, I think, are the shift in emphasis from the wage increase to those matters included in the "fringe" (and no one can tell where the latter may go and what they may add to costs, but Lewis has led the way and the other labor leaders must follow), and the happy fact that the Communist influence in Labor groups, especially in the C.I.O., has markedly waned.

We now turn to what we may call the more purely political events of the year and, toward the close, to what was perhaps the most extraordinary presidential election in our history. In the previous chapter, we noted that under new laws the President, beginning with 1947, had to deliver three messages to the Congress, when it convened, instead of one. The second Session of the 80th Congress, which was to loom large in the campaign of this election year, convened with brief ceremony on January 6. The next day, it received the first of the President's three messages, that on the State of the Union. In it the President, who had been steadily opposed to any reduction in taxes, advocated a $40 cost-of-living credit, and an additional $40 for each dependent of a taxpayer. He also advocated that the $3,200,000,000 loss in revenue which would ensue should be made up by increased taxes on corporations. "Corporation" is a wealthy word which sounds as if it could be soaked without hurting anything human, but any one who knows anything about the American economy knows that a great corporation—and it is the great ones which pay the great taxes—is a cross-section of American human life, owned by tens or hundreds of thousands of stockholders, often women with small holdings and means, such as is the case with the huge American Telephone and Telegraph Company; and affording employment in like numbers of thousands.

Both Congress and the people knew this and Truman's rather naïve system of taxation or non-taxation did not get across. He also pleaded for the passage of his equally unacceptable anti-inflation measure but at the same time urged an increase in minimum wages from 40 to 75 cents an hour. The "honeymoon" had long been over, and the start of the new Session was not auspicious.

On January 12, the President presented his second required Message, that on the Budget. He indicated that the necessary outlay for the coming fiscal year would have to be about $39,700,000,000, the largest peacetime Budget in our history, and this with the war three years past. He added that about 79 per cent of what he asked for represented the cost of the last war, its aftermath and prevention of another war. He did admit that some tax relief should be given to those suffering hardships—but who was not? He also thought that the national income would leave a surplus of about $7,500,000,000, which should be used to pay off a small part of the government debt. Nothing was said about reduction in government expenses as a contributing factor to that very desirable end. The required Message on the Budget had been made obligatory, with the thought that it would give both Congress and the people a view of what was in prospect and what would be needed, but the very wide difference, as noted in the preceding chapter, between the figures presented in former estimates and the realities, made this new Budget Message fall somewhat flat.

Finally, on the 14th came the President's Economic Report, as required to be rendered to Congress. He continued to urge the $40 credit to taxpayers, an amount which meant nothing to those above the small wage-earner brackets, and a 75 per cent corporation excess-profits tax, whatever that might be. He also urged again his whole anti-inflation program lest otherwise we might have a recession and could not be sure that it might not be "severe, and recovery slow and painful." It was an election year and the President was not beginning well. His "honeymoon" with Congress had long been over and his public popularity seemed to be declining. His three Messages already mentioned had contained practically nothing new or interesting, and were unmistakably political. When Truman delivered his Message on the

State of the Union, the Republican Whip of the House is said to have commented later that it suddenly occurred to him that for the first time he "was participating in a Democratic Convention." To quote a few words from *Newsweek*: "Some Congressmen scowled. Some twiddled their thumbs. Others squirmed in their seats, suppressed yawns, or fell fast asleep. What the 80th Congress thought [of the Annual Address on the State of the Union] was all too obvious. Its mood, on both sides of the aisle, ranged from frowning annoyance to soporific boredom." What the President thought of the 80th Congress was also to become "all too obvious" later in the campaign! At the moment, as the correspondent of the Baltimore *Sun* was reported to have remarked, "To get Harry out of here they'll have to chop a hole in the ice."

We emphasize the first few days of Truman's new year partly in order to bring out in strong relief the most amazing story of his triumph now to come, which was to set him apart in history as the darkest of dark horses who ever won a presidential race, though he himself, almost alone of the whole nation, refused to consider that he was such. But before we continue with the various campaign incidents, we shall go on with the business of Congress.

The work of Congressmen, Senators and Representatives alike, has become, like that of a President, almost too heavy to be borne. For example, during the approximate six months of the second Session of the 80th

Truman's campaign had already begun in the first week of the year. At that time, the most conspicuous candidates were Truman, Henry A. Wallace and Senator Taft, with the shadow of General Eisenhower looming over both parties. Except for his "inherited" position as President, Truman would probably not have been considered. His record in solving or understanding government finance or other problems connected with the change from war to peace had not been impressive. A simple, genial soul, who liked people, he had none of the abilities or qualities which led such vast numbers of voters almost to worship, or else to hate, Franklin Roosevelt. Few, if any, hated Truman. They just did not think much of him, one way or the other, and were waiting for another President, be he Republican or Democrat, as the election might go. The war was over, and there was now no question, as there had been with the ill Roosevelt, of swapping horses while crossing a stream. The world, however, had not settled down to peace, everything was in turmoil, and there *was* a question as to whether Truman was strong enough to steer the ship. He had tried to play Roosevelt in world affairs, going to Potsdam to meet Stalin, but he soon gave up that role. He was indeed in the White House, though that, as history has shown, does not count for much. Of the six Vice-Presidents who, in the past, had succeeded to the Presidency because of a President's death, only two had been later elected to the office, or even been nominated by their party, and both had been Republicans: Theodore Roosevelt and Calvin Coolidge.

The Democratic Party leaders did not like Truman's candidacy at all. They did not think he had the slightest chance of leading the party to victory, yet it would be difficult, when he had been President for almost four years as successor to, and choice of, Franklin D., to push him out without seeming to stultify their own record as Democrats in office for sixteen years. Everyone knows, but we shall record later; what so amazingly happened.

There was another odd point. Roosevelt had not only made himself President for four successive terms, he had virtually chosen two Vice-Presidents and another President, besides a Supreme Court, practically all of whose members were his own appointees. Of Wallace we shall have more to say in a moment. When, after he had been Vice-President for four years, Roosevelt dropped him, and insisted on Truman instead, the public felt that Roosevelt had appointed his own successor. The Presidency, even under the best of circumstances, and for the usual eight years, is killing work. Roosevelt not only had the physical handicap which he had so heroically overcome, but had served twelve years during the greatest war in history, and the colossal strain was beginning to show. Pictures of him, from the one taken at Yalta to the one taken in a Pullman car in California during his last campaign, indicated to many of us that he could not complete another term and that Truman would become

President by inheritance, as he did very soon. Whether this was obvious to the two men perhaps no outsider will ever know but it must have been so to the discarded Wallace who, if he had not been discarded, would have been President, instead of Truman, for at least the nearly four years of Roosevelt's unfinished term. We now turn to the candidacy of Wallace.

As far as I can judge from contemporary comment and personal observation, Wallace had been even less generally popular with party leaders than had Truman. I recall, for example, listening in on the radio to the Democratic Convention when Roosevelt, with Wallace as his running mate, was nominated for the third time. Others who also listened in confirm my very clear recollection of the boos and hisses which greeted the nomination of the Vice-Presidential candidate. He had, during the previous twenty-five years, been a Harding-Coolidge Republican and an Al Smith Democrat, and had jumped like a sand-flea from one issue to another, finally becoming a New Dealer. Thanks to Roosevelt, he was nominated and elected, with the rest of the Democratic ticket.

Why Roosevelt did not want him a second time, I do not know. It may have been because of an inkling that whoever got the Vice-Presidential nomination in 1944 would be President before 1948. He did appoint him Secretary of Commerce, however, a post from which he was removed by Truman, as explained in an earlier chapter. Wallace had always claimed to remain true to

Roosevelt. Apparently, it had rankled that Truman, through no fault of his own, not only spent four years in the White House, with all the immense power and prestige of office which Wallace thought should have been inherited by himself, but had also fired him out of the Cabinet and from his job as Secretary of Commerce. All that may, or may not, explain a great deal, as an old mountain woman once said when told that her name was the same as that of the English royal family.

In December of 1947, a group of Leftists, who, with a good deal of conceit, call themselves the Progressive Citizens of America, had urged Wallace to start a new political party, and, on the Monday night before the New Year, he broadcast from Chicago, on a nation-wide hook-up, saying, "I shall run as an independent candidate for President of the United States, in 1948." He damned both the old parties, especially with regard to their policy as it related to Russia. As yet, he had no organized party, no platform or running mate. Comment was lively, running from the huge headlines and shrieks of joy of the Communist paper, *The Daily Worker,* which spoke of Wallace's candidacy as "historic," to that of the New York State Democratic Chairman who merely remarked that "Henry has read himself into oblivion."

During this century, somebody has tried to start a third party about once every twelve years and in only one case has it vitally affected a national election—I refer, of course, to Theodore Roosevelt and his Progressive Party. Despite his great prestige and enormous popularity, he could not succeed in getting himself re-elected but only in defeating Republican Taft and electing Democratic Wilson. Wallace had no chance of being elected in 1948. His following was made up of the rag-tag and bobtail of extreme Left-wing radicals with emphasis on the Communists. He was partly motivated perhaps by his peeve against the Party which had honored him for thirteen years as Cabinet Member and Vice-President. It has been suggested that he knew he could not be elected but was looking forward to 1952. This seems to have been the case as regards the Communists, both here and in the Kremlin, who supported him. Their idea was, it has been suggested, that the best way to defeat the Marshall Plan, Universal Military Training and the Democratic Party in general would be to run Wallace, and, if the Republicans put up an isolationist or an ultra-Conservative, this would hasten their downfall also, so that in 1952 the field would be fairly clear for a "New Messiah" campaign by Wallace, who had clearly shown he would follow the Party line.

For just a little while, it looked as though this long-term scheme, if there had been any such, might bear some fruit. However, all went askew.

Governor Dewey of New York had not yet "thrown in his hat" but, though not popular with a considerable number of the G.O.P. leaders, he was generally thought of as the most likely nominee of his Party. Senator Taft, son of former President Taft, and head of the Party in the Senate, had been angling for the nomination openly and for some time. By many it was thought that Wallace's Third Party might destroy the nominal chance that Truman might have and make the election of any Republican certain. Following the argument further, Republican leaders could say: "If the bird is already in the hand, why bother about hunting with Dewey, who has already been defeated once? Why not nominate Taft? He is not too popular nationally but he is safe, conservative, a member of the 'Old Guard' and dependable."

Fortunately, it did not work out as the Kremlin, badly informed and with its usual ignorance of other countries, had planned, though, amazing as it may seem to us, the Kremlin seemed to remain certain to the end that Wallace would be elected and become its man here even without waiting for 1952. We shall have to skim events for the next six months, politically, until the race really starts. Many things happened, however, to alter the list of chief characters and their chances.

Toward the middle of January, General Eisenhower, in an extremely dignified and statesmanlike letter, which an editorial in the *Herald-Tribune* said would remain "a classic statement of the duties and obligations which fall upon military leaders in a free country," and which was an appreciation of the division between military and civilian service, which, the same editorial said, "only the rarest of soldiers could possess," refused the Republican nomination. It was meant to be final, and was so taken by most, although the refusal had later to be twice repeated. Senator Vandenberg also again declined to be considered. On the 16th of January, in Albany, a few days before the meeting of the Republican National Committee, Dewey announced that he was available. On February 23, young Senator Glen H. Taylor of Idaho, who had campaigned as the "singing cowboy," left the Democratic Party to become the Vice-Presidential running mate for Wallace, thereby adding another bizarre touch to Wallace's caravan of fellow travellers and others. From the standpoint of the presidential campaign, until the Conventions of all three parties in the summer, we need dwell on only a few points.

After Wallace had announced his intention to run, there was much discussion within the two old parties regarding from which party Wallace might capture the more votes. It was not thought he would make much of a showing with the farmers, and labor was very widely split over him. His movement had been openly called a "Red Front," by the A. F. of L. Still, one never could tell. How far Left the people had gone would be an interesting question to have the answer to, in November. At this point, we are speaking of February, when he gave the Democrats a jolt.

There was a Congressional election to be held in the Bronx on the 17th, and Wallace backed for this office one

Leo Isacson, the extremely Left-wing, if not Communistic, candidate of the American Labor Party. The victory was overwhelming. As one local Democratic leader, quoting General Stilwell's famous remark, said: "We got the Hell beat out of us." That settled the fact that Wallace would from then on stick in the campaign. The Democrats were despondent, the Republicans jubilant. The vote cast had been light, but the shrewdest politicians of both parties realized that the result could not all be blamed on the small vote. On the Pacific coast, former Governor Stassen (another Republican aspirant) said that his party would have to "present a progressive, humanitarian program in keeping with the early traditions of the party under Abraham Lincoln." On the other side, Bowles advised Truman to "get back to the principles of the New Deal and outline a second new deal." This local election was a turning-point and, in the light of a greater election a few months off, very interesting.

From that time on, Wallace turned steadily to Russia and Communism, although he has said he himself is not and never was a Communist. He even started a correspondence with Stalin over Palestine and seemed, in his foreign policy, uniformly pro-Russian and anti-American. We need not go into the details of one primary or another, of one State campaign or another, which eliminated, or greatly reduced, the chances of certain temporary candidates, such as General MacArthur. They were probably of some influence in shaping the course of events at the Conventions but it would take too much space to discuss them at length. The campaign may be said to have gotten its real start with Truman's 8500-mile trip over the country, beginning in June.

The trip was remarkable in many ways. Truman started it with a beaming face just when his political fortunes and future appeared, to almost all the politicians, to be at their extreme nadir. Many things, some of which we have mentioned, had steadily been reducing his popularity, while, owing to his insistence on his civil-rights program, the South had broken out into open revolt the middle of May. On the 10th, under powerful Southern leadership, 1000 "Dixiecrats," as they called themselves, representing ten States of the old Confederacy, held a mass meeting to secede formally from the President and to hold their own Rump Convention, should the Democratic one nominate Truman. In other words, in 1948 a large body of Southerners were willing to bolt Truman and their party just as in 1860 their ancestors had bolted Stephen Douglas. There was indeed much of the 1860's in the air.

Franklin Roosevelt's party, that of the New Deal, had always been a good deal of a hodge-podge, although not quite so much so as that which Wallace was trying to weld into form. Roosevelt, however, had had a personality and a popularity far transcending those of either Wallace or Truman, *and* he had counted on the "Solid South" as a back-log.

Nevertheless, Truman, to the amazement, and often to the despair, of the old-timers in the political game, remained supremely confident. On June 3, with the Congress he had so damned still in session and the international situation in a crisis, the President started his trip, in a sixteen-car Presidential Special, Truman himself settling down in the "Ferdinand Magellan," the private car with armored sides which the Association of American Railroads had built especially for Franklin Roosevelt. Truman had tried to maintain that his long swing around the circle was wholly non-political in character, but, after a day or so of speaking, that faded pretense had to be discarded, unless perhaps in the disbursing office of the Treasury. He had, however, changed his tactics, and gave up his long speeches read from prepared manuscript, which, like Coolidge's, were very dull, and, except for large meetings in cities such as Los Angeles, he gave offhand folksy chats. Even so, the audiences did not seem enthusiastic and those who were sure Truman could not possibly be elected did not change their minds. Meanwhile, and right up to the November election, the vast majority of the best political writers in leading newspapers and magazines, as well as all the poll reports, were equally certain that Truman could not win. I have never known such almost complete unanimity of expert opinion against any candidate. We must now get on to the three nominating Conventions.

The Convention of the Republican Party came first

and was held in Philadelphia from June 21 to 25. On the first day, there were seven serious contenders, with the usual fringe of "favorite sons" in the wings. It looked like Dewey, however, and the next day the supporters of Senator Taft and Governor Stassen tried to start a last ditch "stop Dewey" drive, but neither of the two just mentioned would step aside in favor of the other. On the fourth day, on the third ballot, Dewey was nominated unanimously. It was the first time in its ninety-two years of history that the Party had renominated a candidate who had previously been defeated. (Dewey lost to Roosevelt in 1944.) Governor Warren of California was nominated for Vice-President.

The Democratic Convention was held in Philadelphia, in the same hall, from July 12 to 15. Truman remained confident as ever, but the Party was alarmed lest he get the nomination, which, in their view, would mean certain defeat in the election. Some still hoped to draft Supreme Court Justice Douglas or General Eisenhower. The latter had already expressed himself positively, not only in the letter already mentioned but in another letter to the publisher of the Manchester (N. H.) *Evening Leader,* in which he wrote: "I am not available for and could not accept nomination to high political office. . . . My decision to remove myself completely from the political scene is definite and positive. . . . I could not accept the [G.O.P. presidential] nomination even under the remote circumstances that it were tendered me."

In his January letter, to which he referred in the one just quoted, he had said, *inter alia,* "It is my conviction that the necessary and wise subordination of the military to civil power will be best sustained, and our people will have greater confidence that it is so sustained, when life-long professional soldiers in the absence of some obvious and overriding reason abstain from seeking high political office."

In spite of these letters and other public pronouncements, some jittery Democrats, who apparently could not believe the straightforward statements of an honest man, still wanted to preserve the Party from defeat as they foresaw it by forcing Eisenhower to run, among them James and Elliott Roosevelt and Senator Pepper of Florida. Pepper telegraphed Eisenhower to draft him and received a wire in return again declining the nomination and calling attention to his earlier letters and statements. The heat was then turned on Justice Douglas. In reply, he said, on July 9, "I am not a candidate, have never been a candidate, and don't plan to be a candidate." The refusals of Eisenhower and Douglas left James Roosevelt and others of the "stop-Truman" group out on a limb and some of them, including the politically minded son of the late President, swung down like monkeys from that limb to the band-wagon of Harry Truman.

For three days, however, the Democratic Party had been threatened with destruction and not merely with defeat in one election. There were incipient booms for a dozen or so minor Senators and others, such as Pepper of Florida, while, on the other hand, the Dixiecrats had threatened to bolt if Truman were nominated with a Civil Rights plank in the platform.

Nevertheless, Truman rode the pandemonium of the three days and was finally nominated on the first ballot, after an inspiring speech by Senator Barkley of Kentucky. Before this, however, the adoption of a strong Civil Rights plank by a vote of 651½ to 582½ led not only to the walking out of the Convention of the entire Mississippi delegation of 22 but, likewise, of 13 of the Alabamians, and to the unexpected nomination by the remaining Dixiecrats of Senator Richard B. Russell of Georgia against Truman. The latter was an easy winner, with 947½ votes (he had needed only 618) against Russell's 263. Senator Barkley, whose keynote speech had restored some hope to the shattered nerves of the Party, was nominated for the Vice-Presidency, unanimously, by acclamation.

A week later, the so-called Progressive Party of Wallace held its first national Convention. It was not important in itself but interesting in indicating, with other minor Party conventions, some of the trends of thought in the electorate. It adopted the name that Theodore Roosevelt gave to his third party in his Bull Moose campaign. There were 3240 delegates, who nominated Wallace for President and the "Singing Cowboy," Glen H. Taylor, for Vice-President. Both refused to repudiate

Communist support. Rexford Guy Tugwell headed the platform committee, and Vito Marcantonio and Leo Isacson, both of the American Labor Party in New York, were mainly influential in drafting the Party's program. The campaign slogan chosen was the somewhat misleading one, "Wallace or War."

The platform called, among other things, for negotiations to find areas of agreement with Russia, destruction of all atom bombs, repeal of the draft law, scrapping of the Truman Doctrine and of the Marshall European Recovery Plan, restoration to Communists of all their constitutional rights, abolishing the Committee on Un-American Activities and the loyalty requirements as of the present, together with such other matters as repeal of the Taft-Hartley Act, a minimum wage of $1 an hour, government control and lowering the cost of food, clothing and housing.

At the Convention of the Communist Party, held in New York from August 2 to 6, the ticket of the Progressive Party was adopted and virtually the same platform, including an offer of friendship with Soviet Russia. Wallace, in his acceptance speech, had gone the same way, claiming that the tension between the United States and Russia was due to American policy and that we should get out of Berlin.

Of the other minor Party conventions it is not necessary to do more than mention their names: The Socialist Labor Party, The Socialist Party, The Prohibition Party.

There was one more—the seceding Dixiecrats, who held their Convention in Birmingham, Alabama, on July 17, after their defeat in Philadelphia. Their hope was not that they could, on their separate ticket, elect a President but that they might take enough electoral votes to prevent either Truman or Dewey from receiving the required number, in which case the election would be thrown into the House of Representatives, where the South held the balance of power. Among the signs in the hall were such strongly worded ones as "To Hell with Truman." Even if the Dixiecrats were uncertain about being able to send the election to the House, they did feel, as they laid their plans, that they could at least defeat Truman.

Then came the weeks before election. The President made another campaigning trip, a shorter one, and Dewey did so also. The hullabaloo of Conventions and speech-making was coming to an end. From a political standpoint, it had been an interesting and, in many ways, a dramatic summer. On the other hand, as "the shouting and the tumult" died, there was, or seemed to be, no drama, nor excitement left. Never, since the first election, that of Washington, had the people, regardless of their own personal preferences, been so absolutely certain who would be the next President. All the small parties, including Wallace's, could be dismissed without a thought. Of the candidates of the two great parties, Truman did not stand a chance. Many of his own party had not wanted him. The panic and dismay had been all too evident. The "bosses" of the big cities, Hague in Jersey City, those in Chicago and elsewhere, had shown themselves cold to Truman; the Solid South, backlog of the Democratic Party, had not only been alienated by his Civil Rights program but had put up a candidate of its own. During the week before election, it was taken completely for granted that it would be Dewey—so completely, in fact, that, in spite of my professional interest, I, like innumerable others, did not even take the trouble to sit up as usual so as to get the late returns over the radio, and did not learn, until I took up my morning paper the next day, that Truman and Barkley were elected. I shall not repeat what I said at the time but only what Barkley was reported to have said when the news was brought to him: "Well, I'll be doggoned!" I have long been an observer of, and commentator on, the American scene and have never before known such absolute consternation over a political event. I have known such an event to produce anger, fright or what-not. This was plain consternation, mixed with a lot of jocosity because so many of us, and particularly the specialists in politics and public opinion, had been so wholly wrong.

We shall give the figures below, but may pause to ask why we had all been so positive and just how it all came about. There have been many post-mortem, as it were, explanations, and many of them do not, perhaps, belong in this brief review. Yet certain aspects of them *are* important historically. Of course, there were the usual ways

333

of approaching Truman's candidacy. I have already mentioned some of these, such as the fact that of the six Vice-Presidents who had become President by the death of the President only two had, later, been elected, which made Truman's chance only one in three. This was, of course, by no means decisive. Then there were all the other adverse factors I have already mentioned. The party which Franklin Roosevelt had held together had been made up of a most heterogeneous lot of elements. He was not only personally popular, he had always kept the Solid South and the city bosses of the big Northern cities. These were opposed to Truman, who, besides, was certainly not of the caliber of a Roosevelt. In addition to these and other points already mentioned, there is one that should give us pause.

We Americans like short-cuts and are given to getting our supposed knowledge from headlines and polls. During this campaign, almost every daily and weekly pumped into us the notion that Dewey was so far in the lead there was practically no election coming—that Dewey, from the moment of his nomination, was already in. To be sure, Truman's unprecedented "non-political" trip of 8500 miles of speech-making was far more vigorous and effective than such speeches as Dewey delivered. Nevertheless it had seemed obvious that every card was stacked against Truman; all the polls, headed by the trusted Gallup, had been for many months so unanimously certain Dewey had an unbreakable lead that the campaign seemed as dull as a horse-race with only one horse. The next morning, a stunned America, somnolent the day before, woke up.

As finally corrected, the count showed that 49,363,798 ballots had been cast and that 683,382 failed to indicate any choice for the Presidency. Of the total votes which did so indicate, Truman received 24,104,386; Dewey 21,969,312; Thurman (States Rights) 1,169,312; Wallace, 1,157,100; and the rest were scattered in small numbers among the minor Parties. Truman got 49.5 per cent of the total and Dewey 45.1 per cent.

Although Truman's popular vote, large as it unexpectedly turned out to be, was less than any vote cast for Franklin Roosevelt, the election indicated certain interesting things. Truman, on his long trip, had not only travelled in Roosevelt's former private car, but had tried, at the suggestion of his advisers, to live himself into a new "New Deal." He had promised, if somewhat obliquely, all sorts of things to all sorts of groups, which pledges might turn up later to plague him. Roosevelt's influence still carried weight, and the beliefs he had tried to inculcate in people as to what they should expect from government. In the two years since the previous Congressional election, there had been another swing to the Left but not toward Communism or Socialism. The complete flop made by Wallace must have been a great blow to the Kremlin. The election also showed the vagaries of our electoral system. The popular votes have been given above; in the Electoral College, the votes were: Truman, 304; Dewey, 189; and Thurman 36; no other candidate any. Truman's luck was to win some States by very slim margins yet enough to give him the entire vote of such States in the Electoral College.

The election was, of course, the chief event in our domestic history for 1948. We may mention a few minor ones which are still of some interest. On December 26, 1947, a snowstorm began in the East which, between dawn and midnight, buried New York City and vicinity under a fall of 25.8 inches, almost 5 inches more than fell in the great blizzard of March 1888. Continued falls, with no thaw, played havoc all through New York and New England and made the winter a memorable one.

Population showed notable gains and California became the third in population of the forty-eight States. The political center of gravity was shifting. Another change of a different sort took place in Kansas when that center of Prohibition voted wet during the summer. Also, in August, the American Indians were finally given the full privileges of American citizenship. To end on the unfortunately usual funereal note, the following leading Americans died during the year: Thomas W. Lamont, banker, diplomat and philanthropist; Lewis B. Schwellenbach, Secretary of Labor; General of the Armies John J. Pershing; Wilbur L. Cross, educator and for several terms Governor of Connecticut; and Mrs. Theodore Roosevelt, the widow of the President.

INDEX

INDEX

Argentine, 31, 81, 174

Arizona, battleship sunk at Pearl Harbor, 2

Arkansas, battleship used in atomic bomb test, 207

Armed Forces, 24, 25, 34, 37, 60, 61, 86, 138, 150; *also see* World War II

Army Appropriation, passed, 57

Army Nurses, at Bataan, 8

Arnold, General H. H., 66, 67; in command of all American Air Forces, 92

Assam, Americans fly supplies to China from, 88

Atlantic Charter, accepted by United Nations, 6, 7

Atlantic City, New Jersey, International Conference at, 77

"Atlantic Wall," Hitler's boasted wall crashed, 140, 141

Atomic Bomb, opened new era, 146; first bomb in history successfully exploded by United States, 155; dropped on Japanese cities, 159; a new weapon, 161, 162, 163, 185; tested at Bikini, 205, 206, 207, 208; problem of control, 260

Attlee, Clement, 171, 177

Attu, in Aleutian group, 86

Australia, 134, 158, 308; feared invasion by Japanese, 9; attacked by Japanese, 17; American forces in, 74; Reverse Lend Lease, 203

Austria, 294

Automobiles, new cars disappear from American life, 10; retail sales prohibited, 10

Automobile Workers Union, C.I.O. strike lasted 113 days, 216

Avery, Sewell L., Chairman of Montgomery Ward & Co., 112, 113, 114, 115

Axis Powers, 7, 37; surrender in Africa, 92; collapse of, 146, 147, 164, 194, 209; *also see* World War II

Bache, Jules S., financier, death of, 131

Balkans, vote wtih Soviet in United Nations, 198; report on Balkans attacked by Vishinsky, 291; Russian tactics in, 299

Bar Harbor, resort in Maine almost destroyed by fire, 287

Barkley, Alben, resigns as Majority Leader, 104; nominated for Vice President, 330; elected, 333

Baruch, Bernard, Report on reconversion, 127, 128; Report on atomic control, 208, 273

Baruch-Conant Report, 43

Bataan, Americans forced to retreat, 8; "foxholes" of, 9; epic will live, 32; "March of Death," 135

Battle of Bismarck Sea, 87, 133

Battle of the Bulge, 142, 149, 150

Battle of Coral Sea, 30

Battle of Indian Ocean, 18

Battle of Java Sea, 17

Battle of Midway, 30

Battle of Solomons, 32; *also see* World War II

Battle of Tarawa, 87

Battle of Tunisia, 91, 92, 93

Bavaria, overrun by Allies, 151

Belgium, 7, 294, 295, 296; Reverse Lend Lease, 203

Bell Telephone System, strike, 212

Berlin, almost destroyed, 88; falls to Russians, 150, 151, 152; end of Hitler, 153; *also see* Germany

Berlin Agreement, The, 300

Berlin Blockade, British join Americans in carrying food by air, 299; Russians refuse to lift blockade, 300, 301

"Berlin Crisis," The, White Paper published by State Department, 300, 301

Bernadotte, Count, assassinated in Jerusalem, 291

Bevin, Ernest, British Foreign Secretary, 172; at Moscow, 244, 245; London Conference, 267; Palestine question, 309

Bidault, Georges, Foreign Minister of France, 244, 245, 267

Biddle, Anthony D., U. S. Attorney General: Montgomery Ward Case, 115

"Big Business," 106

"Big Four," 78, 81, 204, 205, 240, 241; at Moscow, 244; at Paris, 261; at Potsdam, 269; at London, 266, 267, 297

"Big Three," Alliances, 147, 148, 173; Grand Alliance, 165; at Yalta, 166, 167; at Potsdam, 168, 170; Truman and Attlee in place of Roosevelt and Churchill, 171; *also see* Conferences

Bikini, atomic bomb tested at, 205, 206

Bilateral Agreements, "interim emergency aid," 294

Bilbo, Senator, stormy petrel from Mississippi, death of, 288

"Bill of Rights," new one proposed, 75, 100

Black, Justice Hugo L., row with Justice Jackson, 226

Black Markets, 65

Bogotá Conference, 305, 306

Bon Peninsula, enemy retreats to, 92

Borneo, 16; Australians in Northwest, 158

Brazil, 15, 83; accepts Atlantic Charter, 7; declared war against Axis, 31

Brest, 141

338

INDEX

Declaration of Human Rights, 292

de Gaulle, General Charles, 26, 35

Delano, Frederic A., 75, 76

Democratic Party, 43, 64, 117, 121, 129, 320, 321, 322, 323, 324, 325; Flynn incident, 53; Convention at Chicago, 1944, 119; Convention at Philadelphia, 1948, 328, 329; Civil Rights plank of, 330, 331

Denmark, 294

de Valera, Eamon, Prime Minister of Eire, 6; refused to ask recall of Axis representatives, 137

Dewey, Thomas E., 76, 322, 323, 324; elected Governor of New York, 43; nominated for President in 1944, 118, 119; nominated for President in 1948, 328; defeated, 333, 334, 335

Dickey, J. Sloan, President of Dartmouth College, 187

"Dixie-crats," bolt from Democratic Party, 326, 330; Convention at Alabama, 332; nominate Senator Russell, 332

Doenitz, Admiral Karl, becomes Fuehrer in Germany, 151, 152

Dominican Republic, accepts Atlantic Charter, 7

"Doodlebugs," 137

Doolittle, General James H., leads raid on Tokio, 19, 134

Douglas, Justice William O., declined to be candidate for President, 328, 329

Draft, The, 39

Dubinsky, David, Union leader, 121

Dumbarton Oaks, Conference at, 142, 143; Four Point Plan, 144

Economic Conference, 124, 125

Eden, Anthony, British Foreign Secretary, 85

Edge, Walter E., 64

Edison, Mrs. Thomas A., wife of inventor, death of, 288

Egypt, 30, 36, 309

Eire, claims infringement of neutrality, 6; refuses to ask recall of Axis representatives, 137

Eisenhower, General Dwight E., in North Africa, 34; problems with Vichy Government, 35, 36; becomes Supreme Commander in North Africa, 90, 91, 92; sets date of Invasion of Normandy, 141, 142; Supreme Commander of British and American Forces, 166; declined to be candidate for President, 323, 324, 328, 329

Elections, Congressional in 1942, 41; Republican majority, 43, 44; Republican success in 1943, 62, 63; "Pressure Politics,"

101, 103; President Roosevelt candidate for fourth term, 117; the Soldier vote, 118, 119, 120; power of Unions, 121; President Roosevelt re-elected, 122; "Minority" vote, 123; reverse trend in 1946, 229, 232; the political system, 269, 270; 1948 a Presidential year, 289, 290; President Truman's campaign for election, 318, 319, 320, 321, 322, 323, 324, 325; "Dixie-crats," bolt from Democratic Party, 326, 327; candidates for President, 328, 329, 330, 331, 332; President Truman elected, 333, 334, 335, 336

Electoral College, 43, 122, 258, 335, 336

El Salvador, accepts Atlantic Charter, 7

Employment, 68, 179, 180, 275; of women, 28; rise in, 310

Enemy Aliens, 37, 38, 39

England, *see* British Government

Engle, A. J., survey of wages in war plants, 70

Esthonia, annexed by Soviet, 264

European Recovery Plan, *see* Marshall Plan

Evening Leader, 328

Executive, The, 102, 103, 104, 114, 115

Export-Import Bank, 201

"Fact Finding," on wages, 212, 213, 214, 216, 217

Far East, 32, 33, 47; surrender of Singapore, 16; turmoil in, 196; rebellion in, 197

Farley, James A., could not approve fourth term for President Roosevelt, 117; resigns as Chairman, 117; declined to be candidate for President, 119

Farmers, 41, 42, 102, 186

"Ferdinand Magellan," private railroad car of President Truman, 327

Fifteenth Army, made up of many nationalities, 148

Fifth Column, at home, 37

Filipinos, treated with brutality by Japs, 135; remained loyal to United States, 135

Finland, 143, 172, 262

"Five Point Plan," 99

Flying Fortresses, 88

Flynn, Edward J., paving block incident, 53, 54

Ford, Henry, American industrialist, death of, 288

Ford Motor Plant, 217

Foreign Affairs, 187

Foreign Ministers, *see* Council of Foreign Ministers

Foremen's Association of America, 107, 108

Forest Fire, in Maine, 287

341

INDEX

Forrestal, James, Secretary of Navy, 132, 182; Secretary of Defense, 278
Forty Hour Week, 25, 40
Four Power Conference, 143, 297; *also see* Conferences
France, 197, 203, 295, 296; Free French, 25; Laval confers with Axis, 26; Vichy Government surrendered Indo-China, 27; Government in Africa, 35; French ships in American ports seized by U. S., 35; French Fleet, scuttled by its officers, 36, 135; Paris liberated, 141; Vichy Government in flight, 141; declines to sponsor invitations to join United Nations, 173; Dumbarton Oaks Conference not joined in by, 143, 173; signs fifty-year alliance with Britain, 244; signs bilateral agreement with United States, 294; general strike fails in, 307, 308
Frankfurter, Felix, Supreme Court Justice, 129
Freight Embargo, in 1946, 220
French Indo-China, rebellion in, 197
Fuel Administration, 65, 66

Gallup Poll, in 1948 Presidential election, 334
General Assembly of United Nations, *see* United Nations
General Motors, 10, 182, 211, 216; costly strike, 217, 311
Genocide Convention, 292
Germany, 29, 31, 289; Nazis in Paris, 26; German saboteurs captured in United States, 38, 39; key points bombed by Allies, 88; surrender of Forces in Africa, 90, 91, 92; unconditional surrender at Milan, 136, 148; von Rundstedt's counterattack, 149; war on two fronts, 150; Rhine crossed by Allies, 151; Admiral Doenitz becomes Fuehrer, 151; "Holy Soil" split in two, 151, 152; Berlin falls to Russians, 152; unconditional surrender of, 152; suicide of Nazi leaders, 153; Hitler believed dead, 153; Goering's hoard of loot found, 154; ten top Nazis hanged at Nürnberg, 194; almost had atomic bomb, 208; Russia demands large indemnity from, 297; Russia demands Four-Power control of Ruhr, 297; secret documents captured by Americans, 297; difficulties of Western Powers in, 298; Russian blockade of Berlin, 299; Americans and British supply food by air to, 299; Berlin crisis, 300; Russians refuse to lift blockade, 301
Gibson, Charles Dana, artist, death of, 131
Gilbert Islands, 87, 133

Giraud, General, French commander aided Allies in Africa, 35
Glass, Senator Carter, death of, 232
Global War, 29, 49, 81, 83, 97, 145, 147, 154; *also see* World War II
Goebbels, Joseph, notorious Nazi, 153
Goering, Hermann, 154; a suicide, 194
Goldsborough, Justice T. Allan, issued order restraining Lewis, 218, 219, 220
Government, *see* United States
Granite City Steel Company, C.I.O. strike lasted 150 days, 217
Great Britain, *see* British Government
Greece, 198, 203, 245, 246, 247, 257, 294; accepts Atlantic Charter, 7
Green, William L., A. F. of L. leader, 60; feud with John L. Lewis, 116
Grew, Joseph, Under Secretary of State, 125
Guadalcanal, epic will live, 32, 33; *also see* World War II
Guam, unprepared for attack, 7
Guatemala, accepts Atlantic Charter, 7

Haiti, accepts Atlantic Charter, 7
Halsey, Admiral William F., commander of Fleet in Pacific, 33, 132
Hamburg, German city destroyed, 152
Hancock-Baruch Report, 127
Hancock, John M., 127
Hannegan, Robert E., 120; Postmaster General, 182
Harper's, 138
Harriman, Averell, new Secretary of Commerce, 228
Haskell, Lieutenant General William, 64
Havana, meeting of nations at, 307
Hawaii, attack on Pearl Harbor, 1; Secretary Knox flies to, 2; Short and Kimmel, Army and Navy commanders at, 3; Knox and Roberts reports on disaster at, 2, 3, 4; U. S. forces distributed in, 7 (*also see* Pearl Harbor); sugar supply lost to United States, 12; President Roosevelt visits, 134
Hebrews, war with Arabs in Palestine, 309
Henri-Hay, M. Gaston, Vichy Government representative, 35
Herald-Tribune, 246, 292
Heydrich, Richard, "The Hangman," notorious Nazi, 26
High Cost of Living, 69, 70, 212, 283, 310, 311
Hillman, Sidney, chief figure in P.A.C., 116, 117; called before Congressional Committee, 120, 121
Himmler, Heinrich, chief of Nazi Gestapo, a suicide, 153

INDEX

AMERICA's place as a world leader today is due mainly to two circumstances, one planned by man, the other not. By great good fortune America is blessed with rich natural resources, and because of the foresight of her founding fathers, her government is such that these resources may be utilized for the benefit of all. For America encourages, and sometimes insists, that her citizens use their various abilities to increase or at least conserve these resources and ingeniously to implement them whenever possible. For it is only thus that America's rich natural heritage can be increasingly enjoyed by all.

The final pages of each volume of this edition of James Truslow Adams' *History of the United States* are devoted to picturing the theme of the volume. And on the following pages are depicted many typical scenes, showing why this country is great and rich and enjoys the highest standard of living any country has ever known.

AMERICA THE BEAUTIFUL

Courtesy of The International Harvester Company

This photograph would seem to be an almost perfect illustration of the first stanza of the song "America the Beautiful." Truly the spacious skies, majestic Mt. Nebo (11,871 ft.) and neighboring peaks in Santaquin National Forest form a beautiful backdrop for the modern harvest scene here depicted. A combined harvester-thresher is shown operating in a field of barley, located in the fertile Elberta Valley of Utah, some 70 miles south of Salt Lake City.

CONTOUR STRIP CROPPING

Courtesy of Soil Conservation Service—U. S. Department of Agriculture

This photograph shows both contour and strip cropping as practiced on a Wisconsin farm.

It has long been known that hillsides may safely be farmed by fitting the crop pattern to the slope of the land, for by running his cultivator across the slope on the contour, the farmer creates a whole series of dams lying across the path of the escaping rain water. Strip cropping, which is the practice of alternating bands of cultivated and non-cultivated crops on the contour, further increases water conservation and decreases soil erosion. Here we see alternating crops of corn, grain and alfalfa. In addition strips of close-growing, erosion-resisting crops, such as hay, may be planted above and below cultivated strips further to check the flow of water over long slopes. This method of farming also offers a convenient means of crop rotation.

A MECHANICAL COTTON PICKER

Courtesy of The International Harvester Company

Pictured here is one type of machine recently developed which bids fair to revolutionize the economy of the South. Although not in general use at present, the mechanical cotton picker is certain to attain widespread popularity among cotton farmers, for it equals the work of from 40 to 50 average field hands in the harvesting process.

CALIFORNIA CITRUS GROVE

By courtesy of the California Fruit Growers Exchange

Spanish adventurers brought the lemon to America and supposedly it was introduced into California at the same time
as the orange—though its commercial development was much
slower. Approximately 95 per cent of all lemons grown in America are produced in California. Although oranges are grown as
far north in California as the latitude of New York City, lemons
require a somewhat warmer climate and the majority of the
plantings are in southern California. Because of the protection
from cold northern winds afforded the interior valleys by the
high mountain ranges, because of other favorable climatic factors, and because both orange and lemon trees are evergreen,
California can ship fresh citrus fruits to market every day of
the year.

FRUIT PRESERVATION

Photograph by Moulin Studios, courtesy of National Canners Association

America is probably the best fed and healthiest nation in the world. One of the main reasons for this happy condition is the fact that our canning and preserving industries have reached such a high state of efficiency. The great volume of total American production of canned and preserved foods comes from canneries located in the rural areas. The proximity of the cannery to the source of raw produce is one of the principal attributes of this industry, for fresh produce is canned while still in its freshest state, thus preserving the most nutritious elements of the produce. In 1947 the average person in the United States consumed 19.5 pounds of canned fruit alone. This photograph shows one stage in the processing of peaches; in this instance the container is a glass jar. It is interesting to note the sanitary precautions taken here such as the use of hair nets, rubber gloves and aprons and clean uniforms.

REFORESTATION OPERATIONS

By courtesy of the United States Forest Service

America has only recently awakened to the fact that our timber reserves have dwindled dangerously, not only because of indiscriminate lumbering operations and carelessly started forest fires but also because there has not been a comprehensive reforestation program to replace losses.

The United States Forest Service is now working tirelessly to remedy this situation. This photograph shows a planting crew climbing the trail up Lookout Mountain located in the Columbia National Forest in Washington. Each member of the crew carries a planting mattock and bag of tree seedlings. The snags and fallen logs are all that remain of a once beautiful stand of virgin timber which was burned over in the Yacolt fire of 1902.

"PAUL BUNYAN" TOOTHPICKS

From a photograph copyright by Asabel Curtis

These massive timbers were hewn from Douglass fir trees. In addition to its other uses Douglass fir is the principal wood from which plywood is fabricated. Leading lumber companies are now cooperating with the United States Forest Service in a program of conservation in order that such sources of timber shall not be irretrievably lost. As an example of how seriously our government is thinking about the problem, the Supreme Court in a recent decision ruled that lumbermen who cut down forests are bound to replant them.

GLASS BLOWER AT WORK

Courtesy of Du Pont Company.·Lofman-Pix Photograph

An example of an art abetting a science. Glass blowers supply chemists with all types of special laboratory apparatus essential to exploring the chemical world. This complicated piece of equipment is a part for a high-vacuum still to be used in chemical research at the experimental station of E. I. du Pont de Nemours and Company.

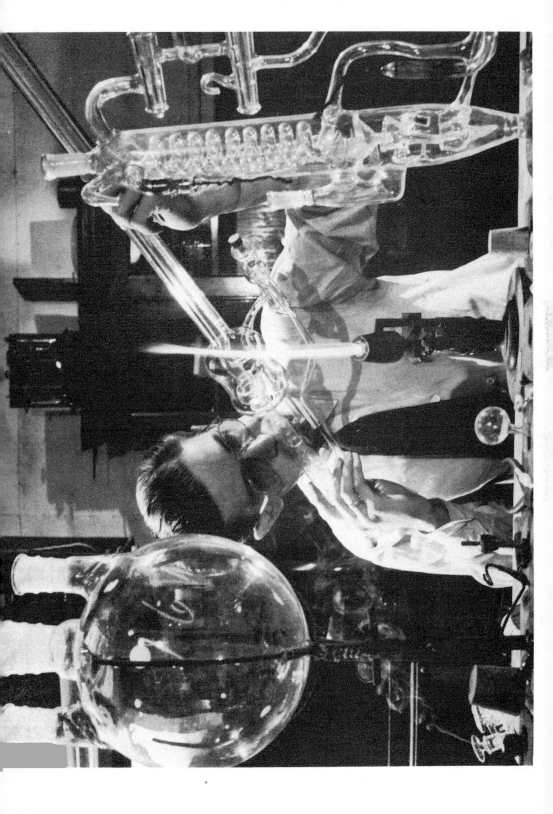

SUBMERGED LAND WELLS, ELWOOD FIELD, CALIFORNIA

From a photograph copyright by Spence Air Photos, Los Angeles

The continental shelf covers an underwater area of roughly 10 million square miles, about one tenth of which is contiguous to the coastlines of the United States and Alaska. Because of the geological character of the shelf it is believed that beneath it may be the greatest petroleum resources yet to be found anywhere. In 1945 President Truman decided to proclaim federal ownership of those lands off our own coast, and several states, primarily Louisiana, Texas and California, are fighting for State rather than Federal ownership. Although costs of drilling offshore wells are roughly three times those of comparable land operations, still the tremendous reserves (estimated roughly at 500 times the world's current consumption as of 1947) will make them increasingly valuable as our land reserves are depleted. In this picture the wells are directly offshore but in Louisiana some platforms are as far as 27 miles offshore in water up to 55 feet deep.

WORLD'S LARGEST OIL REFINERY

Courtesy of the Standard Oil Company (New Jersey). Photograph by Corsini

The Humble Oil and Refining Company's refinery at Baytown, Texas was commissioned in 1920 and now has a capacity to produce over 250,000 barrels of oil a day. It also has facilities for storing more than 21,000,000 barrels of crude oil and products and is operated 24 hours a day by some 6,000 workers.

NATURAL GAS PIPELINE

Courtesy of Consolidated Edison Company of New York, Inc.

A section of the 30-inch Texas-New York pipe line under construction in Mississippi. It will stretch some 1,840 miles and will bring natural gas from the fields of Texas and Louisiana to New York City. There it will be reformed and mixed with manufactured gas and will replace considerable quantities of oil now used for enriching the present type of manufactured gas. Four hundred and seventy thousand tons of welded steel plate will be required to fabricate the pipe used. The project was begun in May, 1949, and construction is expected to be completed so that natural gas can be delivered to New York City in the winter of 1950–51.

LONG–DISTANCE DIAL TELEPHONE
EQUIPMENT

Courtesy of The American Telephone & Telegraph Company

Automatic switching equipment in telephone toll offices permits operators to put through calls to distant telephones directly without the aid of other operators en route. This method of Operator toll dialing will increase immeasurably the speed and efficiency of long-distance phone calls. This system is being planned to give service to all parts of the United States and Canada.

NEW COLOR–CONVERTIBLE PRESS

Courtesy of The Christian Science Monitor, Boston, Massachusetts

This is a view of the new Hoe presses which are being installed for *The Christian Science Monitor*. They will make it possible to print 40-page papers at the rate of 120,000 an hour. To the right of the massive substructure may be seen the small railway tracks along which the 1,500-pound rolls of newsprint are brought to be fed to the giant presses.

FORD'S ROUGE PLANT

The Ford Motor Company's Rouge plant is the world's largest industrial city. Grouped into a single unit covering 1,196 acres are blast furnaces, coke ovens, docks, assembly lines, machine and repair shops. Here are railroad and bus systems, the world's largest production foundry, a paper mill and a glass plant, power house and laboratories. In the immediate foreground is the Rotunda building, exhibit building for Ford products, and facing it is the Administration Building.

SIGHT-SEEING TRAIN

The new Burlington Vista Dome Zephyr recently put into operation along the upper Mississippi. The eight-car diesel-engined train has five glass-domed sections for sight-seeing purposes. These trains do not ordinarily exceed 100 miles per hour, although speeds up to 122 miles per hour have been recorded. This stainless steel train averages from 75 to 90 miles per hour and makes the trip between Chicago and St. Paul, a distance of 427 miles, in 6 hours and 15 minutes including stops.

FLYING BOX-CAR

Courtesy of Fairchild Aircraft, Hagerstown, Maryland

This is a photograph of the model C-119 plane now being produced for the armed forces which will be the standard troop carrier transport plane of the Air Force. Access to the interior for bulky equipment is gained through clam-shell doors which open the entire rear of the square-cornered cargo hold. The plane is powered by two 2,650 hp. Pratt & Whitney radial air-cooled engines and has a cargo capacity of 2,700 cubic feet.

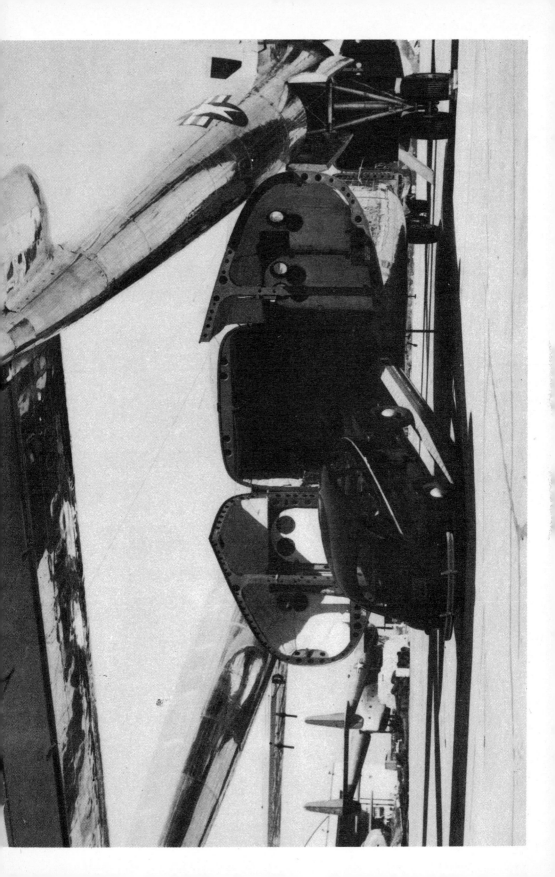